PARTICULAR SAINTS

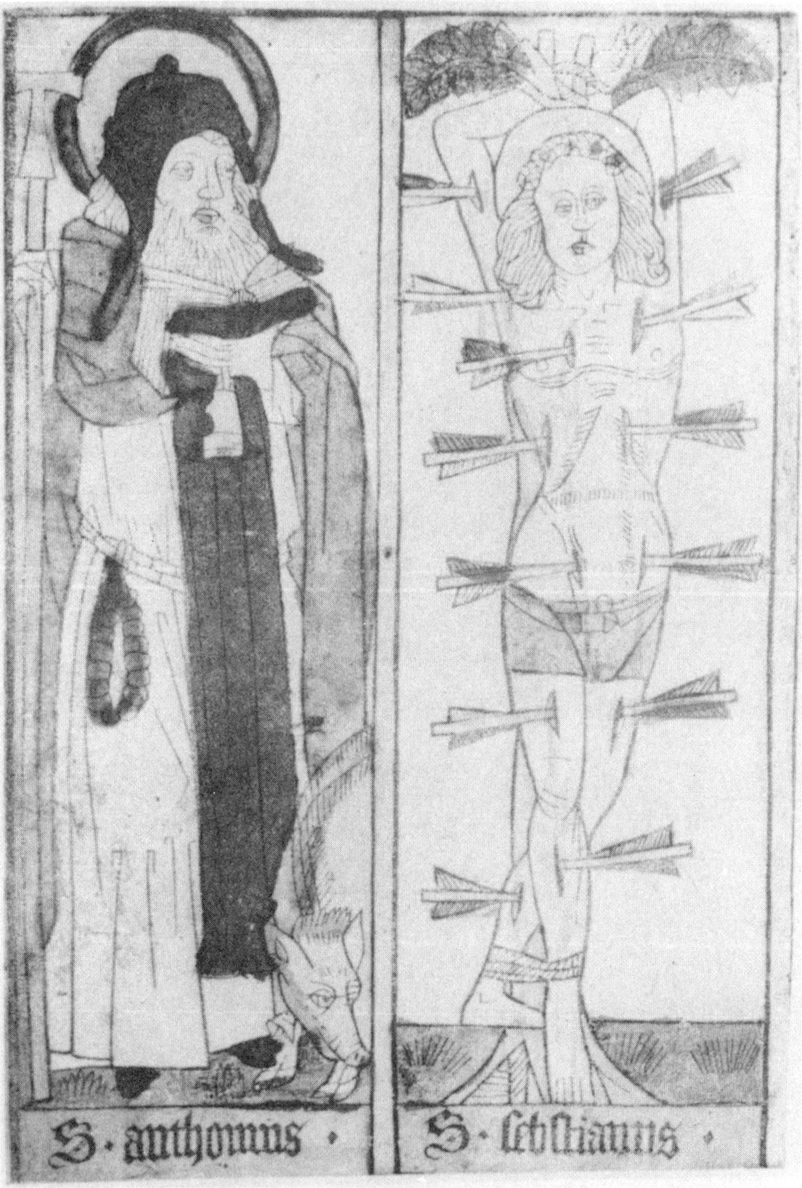

Anonymous (German), *St. Anthony and St. Sebastian*, before 1500.
By permission of Abaris Books.

PARTICULAR SAINTS

Shakespeare's Four Antonios, Their Contexts, and Their Plays

Cynthia Lewis

DELAWARE

Newark: University of Delaware Press
London: Associated University Presses

Associated University Presses
440 Forsgate Drive
Cranbury, NJ 08512

Associated University Presses
16 Barter Street
London WC1A 2AH, England

Associated University Presses
P.O. Box 338, Port Credit
Mississauga, Ontario
Canada L5G 4L8

The paper used in this publication meets the requirements of the American National Standard for Permanence of Paper for Printed Library Materials Z39.48–1984.

Library of Congress Cataloging-in-Publication Data

Lewis, Cynthia, 1951-
Particular saints : Shakespeare's four Antonios, their contexts, and their plays / Cynthia Lewis..
p. cm.
Includes bibliographical references and index.
ISBN 0–87413–630–X (pbk. : alk. paper)
1. Shakespeare, William, 1564–1616—Characters—Antonio. 2. Anthony, of Egypt, Saint, ca. 250–355 or 6—Influence. 3. Christianity and literature—England—History—16th century. 4. Christianity and literature—England—History—17th century. 5. Shakespeare, William, 1564–1616. Antony and Cleopatra. 6. Shakespeare, William, 1564–1616. Merchant of Venice. 7. Shakespeare, William, 1564–1616. Twelfth night. 8. Shakespeare, William, 1564–1616. Tempest. 9. Christian saints in literature. 10. Anthony (Name) I. Title.
PR2993.A58L48 1997
822.3'3—dc21 96–38090
CIP

PRINTED IN THE UNITED STATES OF AMERICA

For my parents, Dick and Gwenn Lewis

"Hang there like fruit, my soul,
Till the tree die."

"Aren't you afraid you will be damned?"

"I believe I already am, but not by the Holy Spirit," said Delaura without alarm. "I have always believed He attributes more importance to love than to faith."

Abrenuncio could not hide the wonder caused in him by this man so recently freed from the shackles of reason.

—Gabriel García Márquez, *Of Love and Other Demons*

Contents

Acknowledgments

The most important contributors to this book have been my students at Davidson College for the last twelve years. Patiently, they have allowed me to try out new ideas with them; avidly, they have responded to and challenged those ideas; shrewdly, they have offered and sparked better ones than I could devise alone. Proverbial praise for interactive teaching at small liberal arts colleges, however commonplace, does not deceive: nothing keeps me as honest and alert in my professional life as my engagement with the honest and alert undergraduates at Davidson. Extensive work on this project has yielded several talented and good-natured student research assistants: Alison Chapman, A. J. (Andrew Justin) Morgan, Leila Salisbury, Keri Slater, Ann Hatfield, and Kathryn Robinson Kross. To them I express special gratitude. I also wish to thank colleagues at Davidson—in particular, Randy Ingram, who read and commented generously upon the entire manuscript, and Trent Foley, Gail M. Gibson, and Nina Serebrennikov, who have assisted me liberally in studying church history, medieval literature and culture, and Renaissance art. My late colleague, Steven Lonsdale, graciously helped me translate Latin. Thanks are also due to the accommodating staff and to many good friends at the Folger Shakespeare Library—Werner Gundersheimer, Peter Blayney, and Georgianna Ziegler especially.

For permission to reproduce a slightly revised article as chapter 1 of this book, I gratefully acknowledge Northwestern University Press, which originally published "'Wise Men, Folly-fall'n': Characters Named Antonio in English Renaissance Drama" in *Renaissance Drama* n.s. 20 (1989): 197–236. Two other chapters of the book, although now radically transformed, began as seeds published earlier in three articles: "Antonio and Alienation in *The Merchant of Venice*," *South Atlantic Review* 48 (1983): 19–30; "Viola, Antonio, and Epiphany in *Twelth Night*," *Essays in Literature* 13 (1986): 187–99; and "Viola's 'Do not embrace me' as Icon," *Notes and Queries* 233 (1988): 473–74 (used here by permission of Oxford University Press).

PARTICULAR SAINTS

Introduction:
Particular Saints: Shakespeare's Four Antonios and Their Contexts

think'st thou thy oaths,
Though they would swear down each particular saint,
Were testimonies against his worth and credit
That's seal'd in approbation?

—*Measure for Measure*

So Duke Vincentio purports to defend the fallen Angelo from charges of abusing his public office. The lines' literal meaning—that Angelo is even more irreproachable than a saint—provides the ironic core of a play in which the human spirit resists absolute ideals, and the human body, however pure the soul's intentions, refuses to abstain from the pleasures of the flesh. Hence Claudio's rejection of the disguised duke's Stoic recommendation of death in 3.1, Isabella's venture into the complex world outside the convent, and the duke's own arrival at an "apt remission" toward his stern views about sexuality (5.1.498). Hence also Angelo's appearance as a "particular saint" himself, though in a sense unintended by the duke: Angelo's naive asceticism leaves him exceedingly vulnerable to temptation and thus a saint of the most compromised sort.

Shakespeare's four principal characters named either Antonio or Antony—the ones in *The Merchant of Venice*, *Twelfth Night*, *Antony and Cleopatra*, and *The Tempest*—are also peculiarly problematic saints.[1] They are "particular" in two other senses as well. First, they cohere as a group, sharing common characteristics not only among themselves but also with a plenitude of other characters by the same name scattered throughout English Renaissance drama. Second, each Antonio, while representing a tradition tapped by Shakespeare and his contemporaries, is also distinctive—not merely a type but a unique treatment of the type.

The ground that these characters have in common, as well as the individual properties of each, is the subject of this study.

The main tie among all Antonios is their origin. Chapter 1 delineates how they ultimately derive from the rich medieval hagiography and iconography of Saint Anthony of Egypt, as they made their precarious way through the transforming fires of the English Reformation. Thus they earn their title "particular *saints*." So, too, characters named Sebastian, who often befriend Antonios on the Renaissance stage, find their heritage in the lore of Saint Sebastian. These two saints came to share patronage in the medieval period over a sophisticated system of hospitals throughout Europe that cared for patients with skin diseases. Thus, their histories comingled, eventually becoming codependent. The final result—secular, Renaissance stage Antonios and Sebastians—serves as a forceful reminder: the Renaissance drama that we in the late twentieth century take for granted as categorically secular has deep and tangled roots in the Christian past, both distant and near. Unearthing that complex—a kind of sacred archaeology—recovers lost links between the religious and the nonreligious, the spiritual and the worldly, that reflect sixteenth- and seventeenth-century practice. The period of Renaissance and Reformation in England saw more and easier exchange between the sacred and the secular than does our culture, which tends to view such overlapping as, perhaps, violating firm boundaries.

The evolution of Renaissance stage Antonios and Sebastians from their medieval ancestry was well known in the period, as chapter 1 demonstrates. To understand it today is to help restore the individual plays in which these characters figure prominently. It is a process that reopens the plays in question, both submitting them to fresh considerations and returning them to familiar territory, though remapped in view of new discoveries. Such is the process undertaken in chapters 2 through 5, where each Antonio is, in turn, relocated within the play at hand. In the discussions of all four Antonios and their respective plays, the knowledge of how Renaissance stage Antonios came into existence, as offered in chapter 1, is held central and used to refocus the plays' overarching concerns and questions. Each chapter therefore revolves around a specific Antonio and yet circulates widely to illuminate the moral problems he faces, as well as those he elicits, within the drama.

Several of those problems recur in plays that feature Antonios. Most of all, their saintly background, which accounts in many cases for their attempts at selfless, charitable conduct, puts them at odds with their worldlier societies and their own worldlier desires. Antonios, in other words, stir up all manner of questions about love, both divine and human. Although that love is rarely explicitly Christian, the example of Christ's self-sacrifice is nearly always implied as its model. Antonios arrive at this juncture, as elaborated in chapter 1, by virtue of Saint Anthony's own spiritual tribulations and temptations of the flesh, as well as his eventual inclusion in the earlier Renaissance tradition of wise folly, made popular by Christian humanists like Thomas More and Desiderius Erasmus. Renaissance Antonios, many of them wise fools themselves and yet subject to their own temptations, often raise the large and general question of how body and soul do, can, or should merge. It is a question that assumes many forms across the canon and that surfaces in numerous other conflicts in these four plays—conflicts, for example, between others' needs and one's own desires, between the ideal and the practical, between the sacred and the mundane. But it is a question that, from play to play, can almost always be rephrased as another: What is the meaning to the practical life of those spiritual truths that would appear self-evident? Or another: How does divinity stand to shape our daily ends?

Two other issues continually arise in these plays, which, together with the one just mentioned, are intimately connected. All four of the plays that include a major Antonio are preoccupied by the subjects of theatricality and control. As to the former, the problem remains constant from play to play: it is that of distinguishing real from illusory love. The real thing is, quite simply, unconditional—grace. But, like the characters' identities, it can be either pretended or thoroughly masked with literal or figurative disguise. Finding it out is a consistent challenge for characters and audiences alike. So is revealing it. The problem of control in these plays is often that of relinquishing enough restraint (and sometimes self-restraint) so as to foster unconditional love. Not only Antonios—especially the merchant of Venice and Mark Antony—but also key figures like Portia, Viola, Enobarbus, and Prospero, struggle to express love while trying to preserve control, often through a form of theatrical manipulation. As they struggle, they train attention on the subject of ultimate control over human lives: where does it lie, if not in human hands, and how, then, does it interact with human will? Such inquiries, insofar as they address the relationship between Providence (or even fate) and human choice, reformulate the larger question posed above: Where and how do the supernatural and the natural converge in our experience?

Of course, such sweeping issues are articulated in various ways throughout the works of Shakespeare and his contemporaries, as exemplified by the opening reference to *Measure for Measure*. Characters named Antonio, however, provide the plays in which they appear with a distinct focus and orientation, owing to their descent from their saintly precursor. By the late sixteenth century, the names Antonio and Sebastian alone must have provided a literary-theatrical shorthand to an audience that, upon hearing them, would recall a host of possibilities for and expectations of these characters.[2] Most significantly, the audience would have instinctively associated Antonios with extravagant love and with the difficulty of expressing such love as human beings in the human sphere, which is bound by constraints. Their willingness to offer love freely is not guaranteed but may be subject to their extreme selectivity, to their peculiarities of character, or to troubles beyond their power to allay. Somehow or other, Renaissance stage Antonios are, much like Angelo, saints in only a limited, particular, fashion. Puzzling through the ethical complications associated with each of Shakespeare's four Antonios leads inescapably to scrutinizing the plays' most intricate cruces—like those of the trial scene in *The Merchant of Venice*, of the prison scene in *Twelfth Night*, and of Cleopatra's suicide—all of which pose notoriously difficult problems of tone, often setting audiences on edge.

For all their shared traits, the particular handling of the stage Antonio in any one play cannot be predicted on the basis of other examples; each Antonio presents a new opportunity, a different specific angle on the broad concerns that the name generally invokes. Consider, for instance, the case of *The Tempest*, where Antonio would seem to define greed, thus eroding the conventional associations of the type. Yet, as I shall argue in chapter 5, Prospero's brother can be read as a stark inversion of the type that, paradoxically, preserves the type; by passively receiving unearned grace rather than imparting it, as do most Antonios, this Antonio still participates in charitable concerns. In a similar example, the Antonios in *The Merchant of Venice* and *Twelfth Night* have much in common, as several critics have already noticed (see especially chap. 3). Yet they diverge markedly where the nature of their love is in question, the earlier Antonio being given to pretense. *Antony and Cleopatra* yields yet another distinct example, since this Antonio was not imported into a story but was already a given in the historical narrative. Yet, because Plutarch's Antony was himself a fool for love of sorts, his story lent itself naturally to the treatment of Renaissance stage Antonios. Here, then, Shakespeare cultivated the correspondences that Erasmus had sown before him between Mark Antony and the tradition that had grown up around Saint Anthony (see chaps. 1 and 4).

Indeed, with each version of Antonio, Shakespeare seems to have recapitulated some themes while pursuing variations on others. In other words, what is clearly a method of characterization avails itself of countless inconsistencies, so that discussing all four Antonios as a group can present difficulties. For example, in three of four instances—all but the final Antonio in *The Tempest*—the characters' sexual identities would seem to be at issue or in flux. Similarly, in two plays, the characters are so prominent as to be referred to in the titles—*The Merchant of Venice* and *Antony and Cleopatra.* In *Twelfth Night* and *The Tempest*, by contrast, the Antonios behave more consistently as foils, relegated to the margins of the plays by critics, if only apparently by the plays themselves.

Unavoidably, in this study, chapters 3 and 5, which concern these two Antonios, tend to reflect this marginalization, perhaps even appearing at first to conspire in it. But even when these chapters do not focus directly on the particular Antonio or Sebastian in question, they investigate the moral issues that cluster around characters by these names in plays and passages where they appear. The mere presence of an Antonio, even in a relatively minor role, ensures that certain questions are at hand, questions concerning self-love and charity, this world and the next. These questions wend their way into portrayals of other characters, both leading and supporting, within the plays—for example, Portia and Gratiano, Viola and Feste, Cleopatra and Enobarbus, Prospero and Caliban. In each chapter, then, I aim to entertain the whole play, to describe the contexts unique to each Antonio and Sebastian—contexts both cultural and dramatic. Antonios from different plays may thus prove distant cousins, each evolving distinctly from the same historical tradition, but they are nevertheless related. I hope to illustrate their relatedness from chapter to chapter without forcing comparisons between them that would distort the works themselves.

The Antonio in *Twelfth Night*, in fact, exemplifies just how central an apparently marginal character can be, while also showing how the retrieval of historical knowledge about this character type can specifically reinform our understanding of a play. Almost without exception, critics have taken Viola, Sebastian, or both as the moral center of *Twelfth Night*, perhaps following Barbara K. Lewalski's assertion in 1965 that the twins together represent the "dual nature of Christ as human and divine."[3] More recently, and echoing intervening critical works, Maurice Hunt has argued that Sebastian "is, after all, the epiphanic character suggested by the play's title."[4] But these assumptions are challenged by historical information linking not only Saint Sebastian but, more pervasively, Saint Anthony, with Christ (see chap. 1). As chapter 3 explains, such a connection, filtered through time, positions Antonio as the more Christlike and epiphanic of the two characters, a premise that is amply supported by textual evidence as well. Furthermore, appreciating how Antonio figures as a Christlike wise fool in *Twelfth Night* leads to a reexamination of the subplot, especially of Feste's role within it as a second and contrasting model of wise folly. Repeatedly, awareness of how the Renaissance stage Antonio evolved promotes a reevaluation of critical commonplaces or contributes a new slant on current critical debates.

The panorama of Renaissance stage Antonios and Sebastians, including Shakespeare's, also suggests in its very variety how the type may have become obscured to more modern audiences: it is anything but fixed. On the contrary, it was so manipulated by Shakespeare and his contemporaries to have been rendered quite malleable and hence, perhaps, difficult for later generations to recognize. Even so, I have placed great faith here in the scholarly tools of cultural history—church history and art history most prominently but also history of the theater and of literature—to excavate correlations among numerous examples of the Antonio type. Committed to the premise that Elizabethan drama is largely self-conscious, I think Renaissance playwrights deliberately exploited a reservoir of dramatic situations and theatrical conventions, some of which scholars can fully or partly mine, both within and outside the text.[5] Where those conventions are distilled from several sources across a culture, as no doubt many are, an interartistic or interdisciplinary approach is likely appropriate. At the same time, however, sifting through historical evidence, however concrete, is an inexact science, subject to guesswork and error. Exactly how or how much Shakespeare and his contemporaries influenced or were influenced by cultural and theatrical conventions may remain open to question. Still, in many instances—as, I would argue, that of Renaissance stage Antonios—a preponderance of evidence can point toward reasonable conclusions.

Testing the reasonableness of various conclusions often involves, for me, an additional orientation toward performance. I rely frequently on my experience with Shakespeare's plays in performance to assist my judgment about meaning. Since 1983, for example, I have taught five classes that have undertaken full-scale productions of Shakespearean plays with the express goal of re-creating an Elizabethan production as faithfully as possible. More particularly, my class in 1986 mounted a production of *Twelfth Night* that completely altered my thinking about the prison scene (4.2). Of almost equal significance for me was a two-day workshop on staging Shakespeare that I attended at the Folger Shakespeare Library in March 1993. Teachers gathered from across the country to tackle problems of staging *Antony and Cleopatra*, which was performed for us several times by the Shenandoah Shakespeare Express. During that spring, seeing all or parts of that production four times helped me come to terms with how Shakespeare's Antony fit into this survey of Shakespeare's four Antonios.

I have suggested that Shakespeare's continual experimentation with Renaissance stage Antonios reflects his abiding fascination with implications to the practical life of spiritual truths and divine forces. I have further remarked that Shakespeare's presentation of this relationship shifted from play to play, displaying radically different forms and changing emphases. Finally, I would add that the progression of these shifts asserts, over time, an increasing confidence that those truths belong in the world, even if discovering how and where becomes an ever more difficult prospect. In *The Merchant of Venice*, the claims of this world appear to bedevil the characters' every effort, however earnest and authentic, to practice idealism of any sort. Relative to that vision, *The Tempest* sees this world and the other as somehow inseparable, sometimes compatible. To put this idea another way, although all four plays acknowledge the unavoidable demands that the practical, secular world of commerce and politics lays upon humanity, they come increasingly to express the conviction that Browning invests in his Italian Renaissance artist: "This world's no blot for us, / Nor blank; it means intensely, and means good." In other words, that human life is played out in this world is to be neither mourned nor resisted but accepted, if not embraced, and explored, if not celebrated. Like Fra Lippo Lippi, a poetic creation whose "meat and drink" is to search out that meaning, Shakespeare's four Antonios, the legacy of an earlier monk, thread their way through an ever thickening fabric in which the values of this life and the next are ever more closely interwoven.

1

"Wise men, folly-fall'n": Characters Named *Antonio* in English Renaissance Drama

Renouncing this world as a "stage" of limited worth and risking his entire fortune to support his friend Bassanio, the Antonio in *The Merchant of Venice* sacrifices his earthly security for love of another man (1.1.78). He thus appears foolish, yet no more so perhaps than the sea captain Antonio in *Twelfth Night*. Despite the threat he faces of being arrested, he so "adores" Sebastian that the "danger" of following him into town "shall seem sport"; he also inexplicably turns over his whole "purse" to the youth (3.3.38, 2.1.47–48). Such irrational behavior brought on by intense love emerges in yet another Shakespearean Antonio—the one who in *Antony and Cleopatra* surrenders possession and position, one third of the world, all for love. Add to this list a sizable number of other Antonios from plays by Shakespeare's exact or near contemporaries, and a pattern comes to light: a majority of characters by this name become fools for love. Examples include the Antonio in Webster's *The Duchess of Malfi* and that in *The Changeling*. Middleton and Rowley's character literally transforms himself into a fool through disguise, as does Marston's in *Antonio's Revenge*. And, although Marston's Antonio may be said to play the fool more for the sake of revenge than for the love of Mellida, that character also proves the rule by giving himself completely to a cause.

Some English Renaissance Antonios behave differently from these examples. The degree to which any one of them acts on the principle of foolish self-sacrifice depends in part on the size of his dramatic role. For example, the Antonios in *Merchant* and *Twelfth Night* have far more in common with each other than does either with the Antonio in *Much Ado about Nothing*; his role is even less central to his play than is the sea captain's to *Twelfth Night.*[1] Yet even the Antonio in *Much Ado* feels extraordinary sympathy—so much so that he defends the wronged Leonato in a near scuffle with Claudio and Don Pedro (5.1), much as the Antonio in *Twelfth Night* substitutes himself for Viola/Cesario (3.4.312–14). Evidently, the very name *Antonio* suggested to audiences of high English Renaissance drama a willingness to compromise one's own well-being for a person or principle seen as more important—or higher—than the self.

As noble as this selflessness may initially seem, however, it is rarely above mockery or reproach. Most Renaissance stage Antonios are complex, and they are treated with a mixture of respect and irony. Webster's Antonio, for instance, can appear ridiculously shortsighted even as he earns respect for loving the duchess above all else. Audiences may find themselves embarrassed by his naiveté, and he even says of himself: "How I do play the fool with mine own danger."[2] But Shakespeare's merchant of Venice is more troubling because his conduct borders on false martyrdom. He hypocritically resigns himself to a gruesome death for Bassanio's sake, while in a letter he cloyingly begs his friend to come witness his sacrifice (3.3.26–36, 3.2.315–22). Such pride in his own virtue stains his motives with a selfishness that contradicts his apparent charity. He shares with a majority of stage Antonios a tendency to love "not wisely but too well," thus raising in the audience's mind questions about the possibility and the advisability of shunning life's practical considerations in pursuit of ideal love. Moreover, the moral ambiguity of his peculiar characterization presents the problem of altruism in its darkest aspect: this foolish lover slips inadvertently into self-admiration, approaching pride despite his good intentions.

Shakespeare's final Antonio, who vies with Prospero for dominance in *The Tempest*, is not merely a dark figure. Indeed, he suggests a black parody of Shakespeare's earlier fools-for-love in that he reverses the normal character type. Far from the irrationally generous Antonio in, say, *Twelfth Night*, this Machiavellian schemer exudes cold calculation and limitless egoism; he does not even pretend to be good. Yet, as *The Tempest* unfolds, we learn that Antonio acts every bit as foolishly, blindly, and obsessively for hatred as his earlier counterparts behave for love, and his extreme spite is just as out-of-step with the world as can be the boundless love of other Antonios. Ultimately, Prospero unveils the folly of Antonio's viciousness even as the magician comes to terms with his own potentially mad vengeance (5.1).

Different as these loving and loathing Antonios may appear at first, one is virtually a mirror image of the other, a variation on what must have been a familiar theme. These Antonios are versions of a single character type, stemming from a single historical source. Although at least one other critic, R. P. Corballis, has noticed the proliferation of Antonios on the English Renaissance stage, he does not explain why so many of these characters share what he calls a "simple, instinctive, irrational goodness verging on folly."[3] Corballis provides a comprehensive and surprisingly long list of characters named Antonio in sixteenth- and seventeenth-century drama. He also remarks on other traits that these figures tend to share besides their folly. First, the stage Antonio is often a "fool-who-is-no-fool"—that is, a wise fool (64). Second, his nature is usually fatherly, and he protects and advises a younger man (61–63). Third, some Antonios, such as the one in *The Changeling*, reveal a "sexual waywardness," which Corballis attributes to the popular Elizabethan association between lustiness and folly (65). In short, Corballis shows that the stage Antonio was a character type, fixed enough in the minds of Renaissance dramatists and audiences to have been recognized instantly as a convention. Playwrights are even known to have altered their source material to keep consistent with the tradition; John Fletcher, Corballis points out, changed the names of two characters from his source for *The Chances* so that the one called "Antonio" would be "better suited to the conventional associations of the name" (64).

Coincidentally, the basis for explaining the recurring traits of stage Antonios lies unobserved by Corballis in a quotation from *Women Beware Women* that he cites at the end of his essay: the virtue of a "true gentleman" and lover named Antonio is explicitly linked to the goodness of "St. Anthony."[4] Indeed, the study of stage Antonios repeatedly leads one to the rich European hagiography surrounding Saint Anthony of Egypt as it developed from the Middle Ages into the Renaissance and Reformation.[5] Reference to this hagiographic tradition—to both its literature and its art—can account for much about these characters named Antonio: in particular, why they so often manifest certain characteristics, why they nearly always reveal an ambiguity that arouses the audience's ambivalence toward them, and why high English Renaissance dramatists returned to this character over and again as a means of exploring specific moral issues. Shakespeare alone involved four of his plays in this tradition through major characters named Antonio and included in several other plays minor characters by the same name. Explanation of the medieval, Renaissance, and Reformation cultural conditions that helped fashion this character type is essential background to discussing each major Antonio in the context of his play, whether *The Merchant of Venice*, *Twelfth Night*, *Antony and Cleopatra*, or *The Tempest*.

I

Shakespeare and his fellow dramatists, as well as their audiences, all had numerous reasons for recognizing even the faintest dramatic allusion to the legends and the iconography that had accumulated around Saint Anthony of Egypt by the mid-sixteenth century. The life of this desert church father and founder of monasticism had been recounted by Athanasius in the fourth century, a source widely known in England from the time of Bede.[6] Saint Anthony, according to Athanasius, was born in 250 and lived for 105 years. When he was twenty, Christ called him to a solitary and ascetic life in the desert; Anthony accepted by giving his earthly possessions to the needy and by enduring the constant worldly temptations of the devil. His sole defense against his nemesis was a simple faith in Christ.[7] From the beginning of his hagiographic tradition, then, Saint Anthony is characterized as a type of Pauline wise fool by his scorn for this world, his self-sacrifice, and his piety, traits that other accounts of his life stress from the fifth century on.[8] Augustine favors Saint Anthony's simplicity above the learning of supposed sages; he cites Anthony's example in *The Confessions* as the major inspiration for his conversion.[9] And Robert Gregg, in his introduction to Athanasius's *Life of Anthony*, stresses continually the saint's deceptively foolish demeanor: although ridiculed by others for his lack of formal education and sophistication, Anthony always proved more knowledgeable than the philosophers who skeptically quizzed him on divinity.[10]

By 1100, Saint Anthony was also connected in Europe not only with simple wisdom but also with the healing of a disease called ergotism, popularly known as "Saint Anthony's fire." His guardianship over the victims of this horrifying malady may have derived from stories of his ability to revive the dead and even himself, after one of his physically exhausting bouts with devils.[11] Caused by a fungus that infests rye flour, ergotism affects the limbs, beginning with a severe, burning pain between the flesh and the bones, and then with discoloration of the skin, gangrene, and eventually loss of the infected extremity by amputation or by disintegration of the bones. Dozens of plagues had broken out in Europe, particularly France, from the eleventh to the fifteenth century, at which point the disease reached its height. Consequently, the early twelfth century saw the founding of a hospital, dedicated to Saint Anthony and run largely by lay brethren, that ministered to victims of "Saint Anthony's fire." The home for the Order of Hospitalers of Saint Anthony was the Benedictine monastery of Vienne, in east-central France. Although during subsequent centuries satellites sprang up throughout Europe, including England, few of them actually offered cures for the pestilence; most, instead, were hospices for travelers and efficient organizations for fund-raising on behalf of the mother institution in France. Hence, pilgrims flocked especially to Vienne in search of the miraculous *vin sacré*—a medicinal wine that had touched the bones of Saint Anthony, which had reputedly been moved from Egypt to the French hospital.[12]

Saint Anthony's election to the patronage of these hospitals thus added to his characterization an element of protectiveness that Corballis notes about Renaissance stage Antonios, side by side with their wisely foolish generosity.[13] It was also this office of healer in the saint's history that enlarged his iconography. Of the four most popular symbols attending Saint Anthony in medieval and Renaissance art—the Tau cross and staff, the book, the bell, and the pig—at least the latter two stem from the hospitalers' practices.[14] The lay brethren, who collected alms throughout Europe to support the head hospital in Vienne, would proclaim their entry into the towns they visited with "hallowed bells."[15] Accordingly, similar bells were hung on pigs owned by hospitals of Saint Anthony so as to distinguish the animals as privileged: no other pigs were permitted to roam the streets except those of Saint Anthony; feeding them was another form of charity to the order.[16]

Had these hospitals, their measures for soliciting charity, or the icons that grew from those measures disappeared in the late Middle Ages, then they would have held little interest for Elizabethan dramatists. But in fact they did not disappear. *Hôpitals des démembrés*, where limbs amputated from victims of ergotism were hung outside in the view of all the townspeople, existed in France as late as 1702.[17] That such an image haunted the imagination of northern Europeans is clear, for instance, from a woodcut, dated 1504, by Hans Weidetz: a disproportionately large Saint Anthony stands before his suffering votaries (one of whose hands is literally on fire), while the dismembered limbs of unlucky patients hang from a burning hospital in the background. If the saint's facial expression is transcendent, it also suggests an eerie powerlessness to stop the ravages of ergotism.[18] But more to the point, where the influence of Saint Anthony on English drama is concerned, the Antonite Hospital in London survived in one form or another until the Great Fire destroyed it in 1666.

Hans Weidetz, *St. Anthony*, 1504. By permission of Hacker Art Books.

Its situation on Threadneedle Street, moreover, placed it well within a mile of the Theatre, the Curtain, the Fortune, Blackfriars, and the Globe.

That proximity may well be significant in light of the hospital's sixteenth-century history. Although operations at Saint Anthony's in London became increasingly curbed as the Reformation proceeded, they were not altogether suspended until the later sixteenth century because the acts of Henry VIII and Edward VI for dissolving hospitals and monasteries did not apply to the Antonites. Before the Tudors ruled, the London hospital had won its financial independence from Vienne in 1387, after which it had enjoyed over a century of prosperity. According to Rose Graham, the famous Saint Anthony's School, established in the mid-fifteenth century, could claim a "great reputation in the first half of the sixteenth century" and such illustrious graduates as Sir Thomas More and John Whitgift.[19] Decline of both the hospital and the school, however, began late in the reign of Henry VIII and continued under Edward VI, who in 1550 allowed a twenty-one-year lease of Saint Anthony's church to Dutch and French Protestants. Although in 1554 Philip of Spain and Mary of England permitted the renewed collection of alms by lay brethren in the order, the Antonites by this time appear to have become irremediably poor. Elizabeth I again checked their source of revenue in 1562 and later sanctioned the leasing of the church to French Protestants.

Yet, despite these losses in funds, housing, and prestige, the Antonites maintained a high profile throughout most of the sixteenth century. Bell-ringing collectors visited outlying parishes until the beginnings of the Reformation.[20] John Stow recalls in his youth "the Anthonie pigs [in London] feeding on dunghills and whining after citizens, who gave them bread."[21] Stow also remembers the frays between the incomparable scholars of Saint Anthony's School and students of their rival Saint Paul's, "who would call them Anthonie pigs."[22] Furthermore, despite restrictions that Elizabeth placed on the Antonites' collections after 1562, they could still solicit funds for their "scolers" and for the support that the order had traditionally extended to twelve homeless men—"pur men who praye upon their knise tweys every day for the Quenes estate and the realme of Englande."[23] In other words, the order persisted in many of its academic and charitable practices until the close of the century. Before that time, it had long been a familiar part of life in London, as Stow recollects.

No wonder, then, if an early sixteenth-century writer like Thomas More, who had himself attended Saint Anthony's school, chose the likes of this prominent saint for a model of Christian humanist wise folly. Simply put, Saint Anthony had forfeited worldly delights in imitation of

Christ, but not without an ongoing and intense struggle. Thinkers like Erasmus and More understood earthly temptation, as had their predecessor Augustine. Indeed, I think it is largely through Christian humanist authors like More that the conception of Saint Anthony as a wise fool was developed and eventually bequeathed to later Renaissance playwrights.

More's connection with what Saint Anthony had come to represent by 1500 is especially strong. Richard Marius states that Anthony was a saint "dear to More"[24]—so dear that More identifies himself with the desert father in one of his last works, *A Dialogue of Comfort against Tribulation* (1534). Written in the Tower just before More's execution, this lengthy allegory presents the elderly Anthony as a thinly veiled More and the youth Vincent as an equally transparent disguise for More's daughter, Margaret Roper.[25] The immediate parallel between More and the saint is plain: both were repeatedly subjected to bodily torture—Anthony, by devils, and More, by Henry's imprisonment and threat of execution. In addition, both men were sorely tempted by fear of their physical pain to deny Christ's efficacy and to succumb to earthly power. Yet More's stance in the *Dialogue*, a work that prepares him spiritually for the physical torments to come, concurs precisely with Saint Anthony's—both men reject this world, rely on Christ alone for help, and seek comfort in meditating on the suffering Christ's incomprehensible sacrifice.[26]

Long before More adopted Anthony's name, however, he was introduced to teachings about the saint through direct experience. This exposure came in the four years that More spent as a young man with the Carthusians. As E. Margaret Thompson stresses, the "Carthusian purpose" evolves directly from the doctrine of desert fathers, most notably Saint Anthony: "[The Carthusian] sacrificed everything, almost his personality, on the altar of his love to Christ. . . . Carthusian asceticism was, moreover, avowedly founded on the severe austerity of the eremitic monks of Egypt."[27] Hence the brutal slaughter of Carthusian monks who refused, along with More, to recognize Henry VIII, a mere politician of this world, as "supreme head of the Church of England."[28]

The Carthusian asceticism that More encountered matched in spirit the popular lore about Anthony that, at the turn of the sixteenth century, already suggested the saint's wise folly. This hagiography, in turn, was made considerably richer and more complex than earlier medieval legends about the saint, largely because of his gradual association with two other figures—Saint Sebastian and Christ. Furthermore, the late medieval and then Renaissance pairing of Saints Anthony and Sebastian is of particular interest in connection with Elizabethan drama: the Renaissance stage Antonio frequently appears with a companion named Sebastian.[29]

Shakespeare clearly offers this couple twice—in *Twelfth Night* and in *The Tempest*; I would suggest a third, less obvious example, *The Merchant of Venice*. The Italian diminutive for the name Sebastian, and for the saint as well, is "Bastiano," a nickname barely different from the name of "Bassanio," Antonio's close friend.[30] The stage Sebastian who often accompanies a stage Antonio owes his characterization to the saints' combined hagiography. And the history of Saint Anthony's hospitals in late fifteenth-century Europe begins to explain how this hagiography made its way into the drama, partly by way of Northern humanists like More.

Because of Saint Anthony's association with the healing of pestilence, he came to be grouped with three other saints who were also invoked to protect their votaries against disease: Saint Roch, Saint Adrien, and most often Saint Sebastian.[31] Like Anthony, Sebastian is repeatedly linked in his hagiography with the theme of revival, resurrection: although riddled with the arrows of Roman soldiers because he refused to worship pagan gods, Sebastian miraculously survived his bodily torture, reappearing before his tormentor, the emperor Diocletian. When Sebastian failed to convert the emperor through his apparent return from the dead, Diocletian again abused him physically—this time, by having him stoned to death. Thus, Saint Sebastian probably earned his place among healers in part through his own defiance of death.[32] In any event, he began to share the patronage of some Antonite hospitals with Saint Anthony himself.[33] Numerous paintings and engravings of the late fifteenth and early sixteenth centuries attest to the two martyrs' cooperation in comforting the sick, but none so grand in scale and so moving as Grünewald's Isenheim Altarpiece. Now housed in the museum of Colmar, France, this multifaceted work was originally owned by the Antonite hospital in Isenheim. It focuses on parallels between Saint Anthony's trials and triumphs and those of both Christ and Saint Sebastian.

The united patronage of these two saints discloses much about the relationship between the Renaissance stage Antonio and stage Sebastian. First, the fatherly protectiveness of the one toward the other is predicted by the traditional ages of the two saints as they are usually represented in literature and art: Saint Anthony is almost always elderly, and Saint Sebastian, nearly without exception, is depicted in his youth.[34] This difference in their ages sets up their stage relationship as one of mentor and protégé. Second, the sexual "looseness" that Corballis notices about many stage Antonios may well involve the fact that eventually the Order of Antonite Hospitalers administered to victims not only of ergotism but also of the Black Death and, later, of syphilis.[35] By the time that sufferers of venereal disease fell under the order's care in the late fifteenth century, Saint Sebastian had become firmly allied with Saint Anthony. The identification between these saints and their sexually promiscuous wards may have been transformed, over several decades' time, into a link between sexual appetite and the saints themselves. Such a displacement is especially likely to have occurred to England from France—where, the English insisted, all syphilis originated. If this transformation in fact occurred, it suggests why so many Antonios are drawn to women, as Corballis points out; the homoerotic attraction that critics of *The Merchant of Venice* and of *Twelfth Night* have sensed between each play's Antonio and Sebastian may be yet another version of this sexual passion.[36]

A third and more important influence that the pairing of Saints Anthony and Sebastian surely had on the English drama entails the theme of wise folly that, as we have seen, attended Anthony from the origins of his hagiographic tradition. By More's time, popular lore about Saint Anthony already included references to wise folly, references that had extended to Saint Sebastian as well. One notable example, William Caxton's version of the *Legenda aurea* by Jacobus de Voragine, includes stories of both saints that emphasize their foolish wisdom. Caxton translated and expanded this late-thirteenth-century work in 1483 as *The Golden Legend*. That his English version went through at least nine editions between 1483 and 1527 testifies to its great popularity. Indeed, Richard Marius asserts More's thorough acquaintance with *The Golden Legend* and his general approval of such hagiography.[37] The work's popularity is exemplified by a legend that Caxton relates about Saint Anthony's defense of childlike play; the same tale recurs in several other lives of the saint from the fifteenth and sixteenth centuries.[38] In the legend a young bowman, passing through the woods, happens to see Anthony at play with his fellow monks. When the bowman looks on them disapprovingly, Saint Anthony asks him to shoot several arrows from his bow. Caxton continues:

> Thenne demanded hym saynt Anthony why he helde not hys bowe bente? And he answered that it shold be thenne ouer weak and feble, thenne said to hym saynt Anthonye, in lyke playe the monkes, for to be after more stronge to serue god.[39]

Anthony's clever retort might have come from pages written by either Erasmus or More and is characteristic of Christian humanist wise fools. His humility toward his weakness suits his customary disdain for this world and bears out the passage from Saint Paul on which the Christian humanist idea of wise folly is based: "Let no man deceive himselfe. If any man among you seeme to bee wise in this world, let him bee a foole, that hee may be wise. For the wisdome of this world is foolishnesse with God."[40] The bowman's pride shows too much attachment to the world; he is a fool indeed. But Anthony, acknowledging his own folly, appears wise. Anthony does not cynically withdraw from the world. Instead, he uses this life meekly—as through child's play—to strengthen his spirit. Finally, Anthony's contempt for the world is tempered by his awareness that, if properly approached, the world can serve him.[41]

Whereas this anecdote about Saint Anthony implies the theme of wise folly, Caxton's portrait of Saint Sebastian is explicit from beginning to end about the saint's foolish wisdom. As the narrative of Saint Sebastian's martyrdom progresses, he and the Romans he converts to Christianity are continually called "folyssh" by Romans who remain pagan. Just as persistently, Sebastian and his fellow believers seek to correct the pagans' "folyssh" view by distinguishing true folly from wise folly: the one mistakenly clings to "thys world which deceyueth"; the other recognizes that real power is "thamyte of themperour celestyall."[42]

As in Jacobus and Caxton's legend of Saint Anthony, in this narrative too Sebastian's repeated allusions to the wisdom of foolishness with God look forward to Northern humanist doctrine. Sebastian's invitation to martyrdom, for instance, could be spoken as easily by More's Anthony in *A Dialogue of Comfort*:

> It is folye to doubte more humayne puyssaunce than the puyssaunce dyuyne, they that ben cruel ayenst vs maye wel tormente our bodyes but they may not take from our herte Jhesu cryst.[43]

Saints Anthony and Sebastian thus participated alike in the late medieval literature of wise folly that Northern humanists inherited and elaborated. The connection of these saints with the theme of wise folly was no doubt furthered in medieval and Renaissance culture by the steadily increasing comparison of both saints, particularly Anthony, with Christ. Christ epitomized foolish wisdom to humanists like Erasmus, who in *Praise of Folly* equates Christ and the fool: the Savior assumed a human form, argues Folly, and, after all, humanity is universally foolish.[44] To imitate Christ, then, was to become a fool, and by the publication date of *Praise of Folly* (1511), Saint Anthony had collected about him an impressive number of parallels between himself and Christ—more, perhaps, than any other saint ever has. They include his disdain for worldly goods, his solitary temptation by the devil in the wilderness, his asceticism, his much admired simple wisdom, and his "resurrection" after he was apparently killed by tempting devils. Pictures of the life of

Saint Anthony that adorn the backs of stalls in Carlisle Cathedral even show him walking on water.[45] Robert Gregg summarizes this aspect of Anthony's hagiographic history: "Without losing his personal identity as a man named Anthony, the saint yet has changed undeniably . . . into, in some sense, a christ."[46]

Anthony's identification with Christ was not lost on Erasmus, who in *Praise of Folly* implicitly compares even the pagan Mark Antony's simplicity with the Savior's:

> It is quite intelligible that the Lord has a kindly feeling for fools, even the highest princes are suspicious of those who are too clever. Just as Julius Caesar distrusted Brutus and Cassius, but had no fear of Antony so Christ disliked men who boasted of their wisdom.[47]

Although Erasmus's Folly here draws an analogy between Christ and Caesar, she implies that Antony is the truly Christlike fool. The original audience of the *Encomium* clearly thought so. Evidence of this view appears in one of the eighty-two drawings that Hans Holbein the Younger playfully inserted in the margins of a first edition of Erasmus's book in Basle (1515). Holbein's illustration to the passage just quoted portrays "Julius Caesar using a friendly gesture toward Antony who wears the fool's cap."[48] That the triple association among Christ, foolishness, and men named Anthony was secure in Europe in the early sixteenth century seems certain.[49] Even the title of Shakespeare's source for *The Merchant of Venice* fits the paradigm: *Il Pecorone* means, literally, "big sheep," but figuratively "blockhead" or "dunce"; the entire work catalogs instances of extravagant romantic love, but the title's glance at "lamb" (*pecorino*) would also aptly describe Ser Giovanni's sacrificial Ansaldo, as well as the romancer Gianetto, and comes even closer to characterizing *The Merchant*'s Antonio, as Shakespeare may well have appreciated.

Moreover, this complex of religious and secular associations was most likely handed down to later sixteenth-century dramatists with the help of Christian humanists. The late sixteenth- or early seventeenth-century play called *Sir Thomas More* provides ample evidence that playwrights of the time, and by extension their audiences, firmly identified More with the concept of wise folly. This work, itself a kind of hagiographic tribute to its subject, presents a jovial, playful More whose very epithet is "merie."[50] He prudently resolves court cases (see, for example, scene 2) and successfully puts down Lincoln's insurrection (scene 6) without a moment's loss of the impishness that spurs him to play a practical joke on Erasmus (scene 8). He also pauses at one point to discourse on the inseparability of "witt" and "follie" when he encounters the player who is

Hans Holbein the Younger, "Julius Caesar using a friendly gesture toward Antony who wears the fool's cap. Brutus stands at the left," c. 1515.
By permission of Öeffentliche Kunstsammlung Basel, Kupferstichkabinett.

about to perform the role of Inclination, the vice in *The Marriage of Wit and Wisdom*:

> *Incl.*. . . . we haue no follie in our play.
>
> *Moore*. Then ther's no witt in't, Ile be sworne: ffollie waites on witt, as the shaddowe on the bodie, and where witt is ripest, there follie still is readiest.[51]

Insisting throughout the play on marrying to serious concerns the folly that bespeaks humility, More also clearly values the common people because they are "sillie," "like fooles."[52] He goes to his execution with like simple dignity, tempering the occasion's gloom with humor. Although never performed, *Sir Thomas More* nonetheless reflects a culture's perception of one of its founding heroes. That perception was probably given considerable shape from the books by More and Erasmus that were required reading in sixteenth- and seventeenth-century universities,[53] and it makes More himself the embodiment of Christian humanist wise folly. Thus, More, who once referred to himself as "Anthony" in a dialogue that enjoyed a wide readership, emerges as one source for the invention of the stage Antonio.[54]

Yet, this appealing notion of wise folly that became attached to More would seem at odds with the aforementioned ambiguity in tone that frequently attends stage Antonios. Indeed, the impression that Christian humanists made on English Renaissance dramatists cannot fully explain our frequent sense that these unusually generous characters are not wholly admired—or are even disparaged—by their authors. Thomas More, after all, is but one contributor in a complicated theatrical history. Though his visibility makes him an excellent example of one route in that history's course, he and his fellow humanists did not single-handedly bring the character type named Antonio onto the Elizabethan stage. Still, I believe the seeds of an ambivalence toward wisely foolish altruism can be found in the works of early Northern humanists. Here again, More serves as an illustration, especially in contrast with Erasmus.

Although it goes without saying that works like *Praise of Folly* and *Utopia* are structured on ambiguity and paradox, Erasmus's book is anything but equivocal on the virtue of Christlike wise folly. The *Encomium* is aimed primarily at advancing Christian charity born of humility and simple piety, and the process of achieving this ideal does not raise substantial ethical problems for Erasmus. It does, however, for More. As Richard Marius maintains, More remained skeptical toward the prospect of behaving selflessly without falling into the countertrap of taking pride in one's own goodness.[55] The Utopians are unwittingly caught in just this snare. Living on a fortified island, they remove themselves from the world outside in ostensible imitation of monks like Saint Anthony, and their communal way of life suggests Christian sharing and asceticism.[56] But, by proudly spurning the manners of other cultures, as when they low-mindedly criticize the lavishly dressed Anemolian ambassadors, they vitiate their supposed charity and humility.[57] These hypocrites detest war—or so they say—and yet "reioyse and auaunte themselves" when they "vaynquyshe . . . theire enemyes by crafte and deceyt" (112). In addition, they are unwilling to sacrifice the lives of their own people but find it fit to hire mercenaries, thus encouraging the subjection of others to the very war they presumably despise (118). So much for true community—as well as for true asceticism, since the Utopians encourage their adversaries to betray their public officials for huge sums of money (113–14). Even More's fool, who appears briefly in book 1 to goad monasteries into supporting the poor (27–28), seems to embody both the desirable wise folly of Christian love and the repulsive arrogance of self-righteousness.[58] In essence, More pinpoints the practical difficulty of striving for the spiritual purity that Saint Anthony pursued throughout his life: the search for perfection can quickly lead to presumption.

II

This same moral problem appears to have fascinated the Northern artists who portrayed Saint Anthony in the fifteenth and sixteenth centuries. Their works betray both a reverence for and an undermining of saintliness in general—a combination that parallels More's mixed tone toward the Utopians' quest for perfection. Countless Northern Renaissance images of Saints Anthony and Sebastian suggest how these artists helped to condition audiences to behold the saints from a complex perspective.

The Northern artistic representations of saints during the transition between the medieval and Renaissance periods center frequently on their humanity, rather than their sanctity. Few images seem totally to discount the sanctity; the matter is mainly one of emphasis. But it is an important emphasis indeed. First, it helps to explain how these saints could become translated into figures suitable for Renaissance secular drama and, at that, drama whose characters in the late sixteenth century were rapidly becoming more psychologically real, more recognizably "human." Second, the tension in these images between the saints' humanity and their saintliness can produce an ambiguity in tone that predicts the ambiguity about Renaissance stage Antonios in the later sixteenth century. Many artists chose to convey the saints' humanity by focusing on their vulnerabilities and their struggles with evil.

This attention to the chinks in saintly armor developed only in the North. Italy, for instance, offers innumerable paintings of Saint Sebastian—and nearly as many of Saint Anthony—from the turn of the sixteenth century, but none that I can find in which either figure suffers as a true human being. Even the most anguished of Saint Sebastians appears somehow transcendent, above the pain of physical torture. Sebastian, an especially popular subject in Italian Renaissance art because of his youthful, muscular body,[59] never loses his poise or visible strength, no matter how many arrows are shown to have pierced him.[60] Whereas Italian Renaissance paintings of Saint Sebastian portray him at the dramatic moment of his martyrdom, Italian paintings of Saint Anthony from the same period avoid all allusion to his weaker moments. These works show him not in furious battle with demons but in repose—for example, calmly attending on the Virgin in the company of other saints.[61] He displays even less humanity and more sanctity than does Saint Sebastian in similar paintings.

The austerity and self-possession with which Renaissance Italian artists endowed Anthony, however, can hardly be detected in many Northern Renaissance images. In these works we see far less a serene *saint* than a faltering *man* who has lost his self-control. This human Saint Anthony is not above us but like us—perhaps to our embarrassment for his loss of dignity, yet also to our satisfaction that we do not suffer alone. Many late fifteenth- and sixteenth-century Northern artists thus gravitate toward two particular incidents from the hagiography of Saint Anthony that lay open this vulnerability. One is his temptation—sometimes his physical abuse—by demons, an event that recurred throughout his life. The other is his meeting with Saint Paul of Thebes, the "Prince of the Hermits." According to legend that evolved from Saint Jerome's *Vita Pauli*, the aged Saint Anthony awoke one day, fully satisfied that he was the most ascetic of all the desert hermits. Suddenly, however, God informed him that the epitome of self-sacrifice was to be found in Paul, who also dwelt in the desert. Anthony immediately sought out his rival, who miraculously fed them both with bread dropped by a raven. But they ate only after having debated at length over who would break the loaf.[62]

That anecdote, as in the late fifteenth-century *Picture Book of the Life of St. Anthony*, came to concern Anthony's pride in his own virtue. It is an appealing treatment of a problem that, as we have observed, intrigued More. The problem, in fact, can be traced to the origins of the eremitic tradition; Geoffrey Harpham elaborates on the element of competition among early Christian ascetics:

> Athanasius addresses his manuscript to Syrian monks seeking to outdo Egyptian monks in feats of self-denial, and the text remarks that Anthony, from his position of sublime isolation, was enough of an athlete to respond to competition in virtue. . . . Behind the notions of athleticism and competition lies the assumption that denial is arduous and quantifiable. . . . The assurance that Anthony will be "famous everywhere" is the only encouragement that God offers Anthony [in Athanasius's *Life*].[63]

The same problem held fascination for English Renaissance dramatists, as attested by the several stage Antonios whose self-righteousness tends to subvert their apparent goodness. Examples that come to mind include Marston's obsessive revenger, whose cause may be valid but who nevertheless presumptuously takes justice into his own hands;[64] Shakespeare's Antony, who ostensibly dies for love of Cleopatra but whose wounded pride may motivate him to escape ignominy; and the ever troublesome Antonio in Shakespeare's *Merchant*, who ironically trumpets his moral excellence in the very act of demeaning Shylock and others (for example, 1.3). A panel from Grünewald's Isenheim Altarpiece represents well this attribute of many stage Antonios. Dedicated to the meeting between Saints Anthony and Paul in the desert, the painting contrasts the two men's attitudes toward the world. Relative to Saint Paul, who is dressed in a plain shift of brown reeds, Saint Anthony appears royal. The luxurious texture and color of his flowing robes calls attention to Anthony's false pride in an asceticism that in truth smacks of worldliness. But the artist does not condemn the saint, who freely accepts Paul's meager supper without the bickering to which other versions of the legend refer. The panel implies an ambiguity: that Anthony is capable of both arrogance and humility, both foolish and wise folly.[65]

Whereas the meeting between Saints Anthony and Paul invites artists to explore a subtle tension between Anthony's aspiration to perfection and his susceptibility to pride in his achievements, the subject of Anthony's temptation permits other artists to disclose more blatantly—and even chillingly—the saint's carnal weakness. By far the most intensely human Anthonys—and therefore the ones who most resemble ordinary members of an artist's audience—are those who struggle physically with evil demons. A group of works, including the left panel of Hieronymus Bosch's *Saint Anthony Triptych* (Museum of Lisbon) and Grünewald's *Temptation* (Isenheim Altarpiece), study the saint's moral fragility through emphasizing the devils' fearsome brutality and Anthony's lame

Matthias Grünewald, *St. Anthony and St. Paul*, from the *Isenheim Altarpiece*, 1515.
By permission of the Musée d'Unterlinden.

attempts to defend himself against them. These Anthonys are simultaneously the least awesome and the most sympathetic. Paradoxically, their loss of control in the fight against this world can make them appear both piteously inadequate—fools in suffering—and yet worthy of admiration—wise sufferers. If they are losing the battle, they have at least tried to contend with their demons.

Those demons, moreover, are decidedly *theirs*. In other words, the wicked creatures who prey upon the frail Saint Anthonys of Bosch, Grünewald, and others are a projection of Anthony's inner being; they are an innate part of him—not separate but inseparable from him. When he wrestles with them, he is essentially grappling with his own soul, with his own earthly desires and his proclivity to sin. This implication, in turn, fortifies the sense that Anthony is less a saint than a man: he, like us, is corruptible; he, too, has felt the seduction of the material world.

Perhaps the most gripping case in point is the *Temptation* by Lucas Cranach the Elder. And possibly the most telling comment to make about the woodcut is that, on first looking at it, one sees nothing in particular, no recognizable forms. As the devils attack Saint Anthony in midair, an energetic swirl of lines blurs the distinction between the saint and his fiendish assailants. They blend together so thoroughly that the one seems welded to the other. Where Anthony's anatomy ends and the demons' bodies begin cannot be perceived, so that the creatures extend from him physically and, by implication, spiritually. Closer scrutiny of the image helps the audience to identify a few discrete shapes, but in many places Cranach has deliberately confused the victim and his enemies, establishing their kinship. Anthony's right arm and right leg, for instance, cannot finally be discovered. The devils encircle him in a sphere of temptation—some of them embedding themselves in his cloak, others peering directly at us, drawing us into the action and forcing upon us the recognition of our own demons within. As battered as Anthony is, his face expresses stamina. He does not cry out in turmoil, although he has reason to. Obviously sensitive to pain, like the lowliest human being, he bears up under it—if not quite like a saint, then like the noblest of men. Ultimately, this Anthony focuses the tension between inner strength and weakness that is echoed in English Renaissance stage Antonios.[66]

Grünewald's Anthony, however, shrieks in horror at the demons who pin him to the ground in the *Temptation of Saint Anthony*, part of the Isenheim Altarpiece. Grünewald creates an even weaker Anthony than Cranach's by strengthening even more the connection between the tormented saint and his audience, the diseased pilgrims who traveled to Saint Anthony's hospital in search of relief and comfort. Therefore, he designs a complex of associations within the work, culminating in the

Lucas Cranach the Elder, *The Temptation of Saint Anthony*, 1506.
By permission of Abaris Books.

Matthias Grünewald, *The Temptation of St. Anthony*, from the *Isenheim Altarpiece*, 1515. By permission of the Musée d'Unterlinden.

identification between the victimized Anthony and the suffering viewer. Both are infected, whether physically or spiritually.

One of Grünewald's associations lies between Saint Anthony and the demons who plague him. Like Cranach, Grünewald refers to the inseparability of the two by intermingling them. Devils have crept inside Anthony's cloak as though they dwell within him. Some of them also wear clothes like his, revealing his affinity with them. Yet the inward nature of Anthony's evil is imparted chiefly through recapitulated images. Most prominent are the sticks and clubs with which the fiends beat the saint. These weapons echo the few worldly possessions that Anthony owns: his desert hut, which in the distance crumbles into sticks like those wielded by the demons, and his Tau staff, which he clutches in his right hand while a devil assaults his grasp. Such visual play suggests that Anthony's demons stem from him; they, like his few material possessions, symbolize his own attachment to the world, which now threatens his asceticism.

Furthermore, the image of his afflicted hand alludes to the raised arm of the lesion-covered figure in the lower-left corner—a victim of Saint Anthony's fire who has lost his left hand to the disease. That this sufferer in some ways resembles the demons—for instance, through his webbed feet—secures the triple connection among the saint, the devils, and the original audience of the painting: much as the demons prey on Anthony, so does illness eat away at human beings, disfiguring their fragile bodies into monstrosities. To be human, Grünewald implies, is to decay in both flesh and spirit.[67] Grünewald further links Anthony with the helpless invalid in the bottom-left corner by supplying more visual parallels between them. Both recline in anguish, although at different angles—the sick man draws the sick viewer into the painting by leaning toward the audience. In addition, while Anthony grips his staff, the other victim tugs the cover of the book that, in traditional iconography, Anthony usually holds or reads but that, here, he has evidently lost. Both victims, in effect, seem bereft of hope.

Yet Grünewald presents comfort in Christ, who stands on high. The staff He holds again echoes the demons' weapons and the crutch of Saint Anthony that now lies impotent. He comes to allay physical pain, and the fuller meaning of His presence seems manifest: neither Anthony nor the sick can heal themselves. No worldly remedy will suffice. Christ alone can cure these sufferers, one and all. Any mortal claims to healing are vain pretensions. If Anthony exerts power over the diseased, then, it is not that of restoration, for the pilgrims who came to him were destined to die or to live severely impaired. Rather, Grünewald's Anthony can commiserate and so urge like victims to endure because a better life awaits them after death.[68]

Other artists treat Anthony's humanity with less gravity than does Grünewald. One of Dürer's many Saint Anthonys, for example, sits quietly on a hill outside a city that partly resembles Nuremberg, and yet this peaceful soul is as recognizably human as is Grünewald's suffering Anthony. Dürer has taken pains in this small, exquisite engraving (approximately 4" x 6") to show that, while Anthony is rapt in the book he reads, he unconsciously curls his toes. That detail may be worth a hundred *Temptations* for characterizing Anthony as a mere man. Dürer's Anthony is lost in another world but not a world unfamiliar to anyone who has ever been absorbed in a good book. So intent on his reading that a passerby might startle him, he also seems accessible enough to welcome the company. Dürer has subtracted a good bit of saintliness from the saint but has omitted neither warmth nor attractiveness.

I have been trying to show in the discussion of these Northern artists the widespread familiarity in the earlier sixteenth century with the idea that saints—in particular Anthony—were not above human weakness. The exaltation of one human being by others is fraught with dangers that evidently concerned Northern thinkers like More and artists like Grünewald: the one exalted may be flirting with pride, and those exalting

Albrecht Dürer, *St. Anthony*, 1519. By permission of Abaris Books.

may be glorifying a man, not the God of man. Without altogether rejecting the saints themselves, Northern artists learned to avoid the worship of saints; they prevented misplaced devotion by portraying the saints as less saintly, less capable of being worshiped. Yet, in the process, some of them raised another problem, that of ambiguity in tone: a saint like Anthony, once shown in a human light, can appear all too human to inspire unqualified admiration. Portraits of Anthony that suggest his mixed goodness show him to be not only a sort of wise fool in his saintly forbearance and long suffering but also, in his susceptibility to earthly temptation, a fool in fact. In turn, English Renaissance dramatists, fascinated by the strain that the practical affairs of this world increasingly placed on ideal codes of behavior, would naturally have found interest in Saint Anthony. He had come to embody the struggle between wanting to live out high ideals gracefully and yet lacking the strength to do so. In English Renaissance drama, the stage Antonio is also caught between the idea of perfection and the reality of imperfection—imperfection of his own nature and of the world he inhabits. He is both wise fool and foolish fool.

III

This tension between the worldly and the otherworldly that surrounds Saint Anthony and his successor Antonio appears to have been a stock element of medieval saints' lives, which were, not surprisingly, much influenced by Athanasius's *Life of Antony*. Thomas Heffernan asserts in *Sacred Biography*:

> By the mid-fourth century, these austere ideals [like antifraternal, solitary, and ascetic practices] had formed a congeries of complex beliefs rooted in the church's theological and philosophical teaching and can be seen complete in Athanasius's *Vita Sancti Antonii*. These ideologies inform the crucial antinomian dialectic, exemplified throughout the breadth of medieval sacred biography, of the conflict between the *civitas Dei* and the *civitas hominis*.[69]

This long-standing problem—of reconciling one's godly calling with one's human nature—was passed down in northern Europe well into the sixteenth century. As we have seen, it is one explanation for the reappearance of such a tension in Renaissance stage Antonios. But it is only a partial explanation. What remains to be understood about the development of this ambiguously foolish stage Antonio lies in a sixteenth-century literary and theatrical history that has been rendered woefully obscure by the English Reformation. Still, some conjectures about how the stage Antonio came to be handled with mixed admiration may be hazarded in view of what is known about late fifteenth- and early sixteenth-century English drama. The history of the saint play is especially pertinent here. More particularly, the moral ambiguity of characters named Antonio is not confined exclusively to Elizabethan drama. Rather, this ambiguity seems a natural outgrowth of attitudes toward sainthood to be found in many earlier sources: Christian humanist writers and their later medieval predecessors, Northern Renaissance artists, and, as we shall see, early Tudor adaptors of the saint play.

Performed for the dual motive of devotion and fundraising, saint plays were still being presented in England as late as the 1530s and 1540s.[70] Although records of many plays have been passed down, only two—one about Mary Magdalene and one about Saint Paul—remain available (in the Digby Plays Manuscript). No English play or record of one about Saint Anthony exists, but one or more very well may have existed. Lynetta Muir catalogs an extant play, *St. Antoine de Viennès*, from early sixteenth-century Provençal and another lost play about "St. Antoine."[71] She also cites an extant French Saint Sebastian play, from the fifteenth century, which was performed four times in Maurienne between 1546 and 1567. In addition, Kathleen Falvey describes an extant Saint Anthony play in her article on saint plays in Perugia, a town whose drama was broadly influential in Italy.[72]

That saint plays were more vigorously stamped out during the English Reformation than were mystery plays owes largely to Reformation doctrine. The mysteries, coming straight from the Bible, were scripturally sound. But the former were rarely scriptural, and postbiblical saints were rejected along with the papacy that had canonized them.[73] Moreover, the prevalent reformers' view toward worshiping saints resembled the earlier Wycliffite and then Erasmian fear that saints would be confused with God. Any encouragement—by a play or an image—to worship the saint himself, rather than God *through* the saint, was forbidden. An audience (or congregation) must be reminded that saints' efficacy—or anyone's faith—originated with God alone.

In other words, saints were acceptable so long as they were not themselves the object of worship. Catholic tradition, though in some ways adamantly resisted, in other ways meandered into the Renaissance. Hence, Protestant playwrights simply borrowed the form of the saint play and supplied their own religious material to fill out the form. Peter Happé, in his useful article on "The Protestant Adaptation of the Saint Play," discusses at length the case of John Bale. This propagandist, approaching drama as a thoroughly Protestant adult with a Catholic background steeped in the likes of Saint Anthony's teachings,[74] somehow blended the two opposing religious traditions in his plays. His doctrine is every inch Reformed: in a lost play, he "attacks" the Catholic saint Thomas Becket and in an extant play offers a new kind of martyr—King John—who once fought off the Pope (217). Still, Bale's medium is nothing new; he simply appropriates the saint play to his own purposes. Similarly, according to Happé, Lewis Wager "reworked" the Digby *Mary Magdalene* (c. 1550): Mary can remain an acceptable dramatic subject because her justification is now shown to derive not from her own works but exclusively from God (226–35).

Such substitution in sixteenth-century Reformed drama was not limited, as in the preceding examples, to the replacement of a Catholic element with a Protestant element. Indeed, exploring another sort of substitution shows further how Saint Anthony developed into Antonio. As the Reformation progressed, the religious was increasingly replaced by the secular. Here again, the form of the drama remained constant but was simply transferred from the realm of *civitas Dei* to that of *civitas hominis*. One telling example, in fact, happens to concern Saint Anthony specifically.

Writing about the celebration in Henry VII's court of the marriage between Richard, duke of York, and Anne Mowbray in 1477, Gordon Kipling adds that Lord Rivers seized on the occasion to retire from knighthood. He donned the habit of Saint Anthony the hermit and entered the court in procession, during which he was housed in a "spectacular hermitage, its walls hung with black velvet and broken by translucent windows fashioned of the finest linen."[75] This iconography, already a mingling of the religious and the secular, made clear Rivers's intent to retire from the active life and withdraw into a life of contemplation, more befitting a knight of older years. Rivers established this iconography and ritual as a type to be repeated throughout the sixteenth century by knights meaning to retire. In 1590 the type was used for the last time at the Retirement Tilt of Sir Henry Lee. Employing the now familiar hermit-knight iconography to express his intent to retire, however, Lee transformed his hermitage into a "temple to Elizabeth" (126). Kipling elaborates: "[W]hereas the Yorkist knight had once withdrawn to embrace the contemplative life of St. Anthony, now Elizabeth's Hermit departs . . . to 'feed on prayers' and meditate upon his Vestal Virgin" (126). This moment in English history reaffirms that late sixteenth-century audiences instantly recognized Saint Anthony as one who rejects or withdraws from the world, as do so many Renaissance stage Antonios. But this example also discloses how easily Saint Anthony's devotion to God was supplanted by devotion to an earthly ruler. An audience that could follow such a symbolic transformation would no less readily associate Saint Anthony with a secular stage Antonio who devoted himself to a friend, a lover, or a cause.[76]

Lord Rivers's adaptation, however, does not brush up against the particular trait that continually marks the northern European Anthonys and Antonios—that is, the irony directed toward their pious retreat from the world. But other Renaissance metamorphoses from religious to secular tell more about that irony. John Wasson, while analyzing one such metamorphosis, indirectly illuminates the ambiguities that hover about the folly of Renaissance stage Antonios. Wasson argues that Elizabethan playwrights borrowed formal elements from the saint play, as Bale had done, but, unlike Bale, omitted the religious content of the drama. He suggests that the later Elizabethan attention to saint plays centers on two of their characteristics: their frequent thematic interest in conversion and their structural capacity to have added to them an infinite number of episodes, a feature congenial to an age that loved an intricate plot.[77] In offering examples of how he believes a late Elizabethan dramatist adapted these two ingredients, Wasson cites many Shakespearean plays and dwells particularly on *Henry V*. To Wasson, "This is a clear instance of a secular conversion play" in which the convertite performs "miracles" like the victory at Agincourt (249):

> Henry himself is depicted as a human but hardly an Everyman: he is historical, special, saintly, and capable of perceiving closely hidden treason or of inspiring courage in a desperate army. He is, in short, an exemplar for all kings to follow. (249)

Wasson, of course, is not alone in describing Shakespeare's tone toward Henry as worshipful. Then again, many critics of the play have detected no little irony in the portrayal of this Machiavellian king who sees to it that the English triumph, even if he must slaughter old men, mothers, and babies, as he threatens to do at Harfleur (3.3).[78] More to the point, the kind of ambiguity directed at Henry V is remarkably close to that aimed at most Renaissance stage Antonios: it arises from the incongruity between a saintly, even martyred, demeanor and less than saintly behavior, an incongruity that characterizes, for example, the Antonio in *The Merchant of Venice*. Henry is not truly pious and humble, the audience suspects, but in actuality proud of his conquests and very much a part of this world. He is perhaps less wisely foolish than truly foolish.

Furthermore, the irony surrounding Henry V seems very like that which Happé attributes to John Bale's treatment of Dissimulation in *King Johan*:

I do not doubte it   but I shall be a saynt;
Provyde a gyldar   myne image for to paynt.
I dye for the Churche   with Thomas of Canterberye.
Ye shall fast my vigyll   and upon my daye be merye.
No doubt but I shall   do myracles in a whyle,
And therfor lete me   be shryned in the north yle.

Surely Happé is right in calling Bale's tone here "satirical,"[79] and the crux of the satire is, once again, foolish pride and false pretensions to sainthood. Bale's Dissimulation is the antithesis of his King Johan, the real saint. He is also the forerunner of later "saint" types, like Henry V and numerous Antonios, whose creators departed from Bale by questioning whether sainthood is possible, in this life, under any circumstances.

Thus, the pull in Henry V's character between the claims of other-worldly piety and this-worldly acquisition looks backward, in some sense, at least as far as the early Tudor era. It also glances at early sixteenth-century portraits of saints in the North, like Grünewald's saintly and human Anthony. In addition, it is reflected in later Renaissance drama by the recurring saintly type called Antonio, who combines wise folly and sheer foolishness. *The Merchant of Venice*, *Twelfth Night*, *Antony and Cleopatra*, *The Tempest*—these plays and many more from the English Renaissance address the same general problem, largely through characters named Antonio. How can one refrain from compromising one's integrity in a corrupt world? Or, to rephrase the question slightly, how can one love completely—as a wise fool—when pure love is so easily subjected to selfish concerns, like pride, greed, and fear of rejection?

Shakespeare's *Merchant* explores the tension between "what were good to do," as Portia puts it, and what can actually be done through various conflicts—for example, that between the medieval church's idealistic injunction against usury and the real mercantilist practice of taking interest (1.2.12–13). Antonio the merchant mirrors this conflict. He attempts to avoid usury as well as emotional claims on Bassanio (1.3.61–62, 1.1.153–57). In reality, though, he turns to a usurer for love of his friend and then resorts to emotional blackmail when he believes he might die because of that love (see, for example, 3.2.315–22). His generosity has strings attached, as does Shylock's money. Antonio wants Bassanio's affection in return for his love and so refrains from objecting when Bassanio offers his wife in place of himself (4.1.282–87). Antonio's self-involvement—his foolish folly—works against his wisely foolish generosity. Yet, what is more unsettling about Shakespeare's merchant is that, even as he participates in the world, as through his venturing, he pretends otherwise, often appearing to pose as a martyr rather than confront the difficulties of an extrememly difficult world. Like Saint Anthony himself, this Antonio is tempted by the riches and manipulations of this life, but unlike so many of the Saint Anthonys represented in Renaissance art, he is also tempted to escape the world rather than contend with its demons.

Twelfth Night's Antonio complements *The Merchant*'s. Rather than avoid the harsh challenges of worldly engagement, as by dodging arrest in Illyria, Antonio the sea captain freely and genuinely imperils his own life and relinquishes his money for his friend Sebastian. A true martyr and fool for love, he thus rights the false martyrdom of his dramatic predecessor and also reveals, through contrast, the measure of self-love in other characters' actions and attitudes—Viola's, Feste's, and the revelers' in particular. While *Merchant* studies the folly of a man who would presume to wisdom in an imperfect world and society, *Twelfth Night* allows that wise folly can have its influence in a society whose enlightened vision leads to "willing love" (2.3.11). The world of *Twelfth Night*, though still far from perfect, is more hospitable than that of *Merchant* to idealism. As suggested by the prison scene, if a demon persists in this play, it is the "darkness" of "ignorance," the fond trust in one's own knowledge and control as supreme (4.2.43). Such folly is countered by the revelation of wise self-sacrifice in Antonio and, eventually, Viola.

Shakespeare's Mark Antony alludes to Saint Anthony not only by virtue of his sorely tempted flesh and foolish repudiation of this life. Like the saint, he even faces his temptation in Egypt. Through Antony's trials, *Antony and Cleopatra* interrogates the difference between wise and foolish folly; the relationship between the two is further explored through Cleopatra's final choices. On the edge of "universal peace"—both the pax Romana and the birth of Christ—the play's action would seem to portray any outright rejection of this world as ineffectual, an outlook as lame perhaps as Antony's bungled suicide (4.6.4). Cleopatra's death, on the other hand, reconciles the values of this world and the next, of wise and foolish folly. Her twin motives of humiliating Caesar and marrying Antony through taking her own life merge the apparently disparate claims of self-love and self-sacrificial love, recalling Saint Anthony's paradoxical notion that earthly play can be more godly than earthly abstinence.

Shakespeare's final Antonio, Prospero's brother, retains his affinity with the saintly type if only in that he turns it inside out. *The Tempest*'s Antonio has been tempted and won over by the demon greed, withdrawing from society in a perverse parody of saintly monasticism; now he tempts Prospero to similarly selfish revenge and hatred. Along with Caliban, he is Prospero's nemesis; as such, he stirs up much of Prospero's spiritual difficulty while also raising questions about the origins and nature of evil. Does Antonio's final silence continue to exclude him from civil society? Does it signify his lack of remorse, and, for that matter, is Prospero's forgiveness provisional, contingent on his adversaries' "being penitent" (5.1.28)? How, if at all, do either Antonio or Sebastian influence the quality of Prospero's mercy?

The constant, unresolved tension between reverence for and derision of saintliness that marks Reformation drama, literature, and art culminates in English Renaissance stage Antonios, including those of Shakespeare. Yet, as has been shown, a mixed view of saintly types can be traced as far back as Athanasius and resurfaces in numerous Northern works before the Elizabethan period. Rather than a new trend, ignited by the Reformation, this complexity likely extends from a Northern tradition that never accepted or rejected its saints out of hand. John Bale's satire on false sainthood, for example, may be far less an opposition to than a deepening of pre-Reformation sentiment. The Reformation, of course, began theologically long before Henry VIII inaugurated it politically. Nor did the English break from Rome under either Henry or Elizabeth provide for the total disappearance of Catholic ritual, belief, hagiography, or iconography from English soil. Harold Gardiner points out that English taste remained "Catholic in all essential matters" "well beyond the middle of the sixteenth century," despite whatever official doctrine the crown was dictating; the people's steady love of the medieval mystery drama during the sixteenth century testifies to this taste.[80] In "Comments on Art and Reformation," Erwin Panofsky addresses the identical issue in the arena of art, asserting that many medieval icons passed through the Reformation without losing their symbolic content, though some may have undergone a transformation in meaning.[81] Even Spenser's use in *The Faerie Queene* of Saint George as the champion of the Protestant Church illustrates the ease with which a late Elizabethan audience could tolerate not just the presence of such a relic but also the conferment of heroism on him and the adaptation of him to more modern purposes.

But the view that the Reformation did not thoroughly cut off Catholic dramatic tradition is perhaps best substantiated by the existence of a *bona fide* saint play dated about 1620. *The Virgin Martyr*, by Thomas Dekker and Philip Massinger, is, John Wasson explains, about a "genuine Catholic saint [Saint Dorothea of Caesaria] rather than a 'secular' saint or Protestant martyr," and it demonstrates the "continuing saints' lives tradition" well into the seventeenth century.[82] The play includes, moreover, a character named Antoninus—a variant spelling of Antonius[83]—who is a pagan conqueror. Wasson summarizes: "Antoninus, a bit suspiciously in the manner of a Fordian love-melancholic, unable to obtain the earthly love of Dorothea becomes a Christian and dies so that his soul can join hers."[84] Small wonder if Antoninus resembles Mark Antony in his dubious self-sacrifice, since the "suspiciousness" that Wasson spots recurs throughout the secular drama in which Antonios play fools for love. Quite possibly, such ambiguity in tone is less the invention of Protestant playwrights than their elaboration of a persistent theme in the works of their Catholic predecessors.[85]

Renaissance stage Antonios and Sebastians, whatever the source of their ability to perplex, suit perfectly the high Renaissance exploratory drama. Whether predominantly good, evil, or "suspicious," each stage Antonio and stage Sebastian has assumed from his creator a life of his own, including a capacity for raising difficult moral questions about love that defy pat answers. The undisclosed fate of the sea captain in *Twelfth Night* (5.1) and the enigmatic future of the estranged merchant of Venice (5.1) lend those Antonios a mystery that finally characterizes the mute Antonio in *The Tempest* (5.1). Indebted for their existence to medieval icons, they may never have been confined to narrow symbolic meaning, and yet they grew to evoke the intriguingly mutable lives of human beings.

2

"A foolish consistency": Antonio and Alienation in *The Merchant of Venice*

Through what is likely a lapse in memory, Shakespeare contradicts the terms of the suitors' lottery when, in 2.9 of *The Merchant of Venice*, Arragon reads the poem found inside the silver casket:

> There be fools alive, iwis,
> Silver'd o'er, and so was this.
> Take what wife you will to bed,
> I will ever be your head.
> So be gone, you are sped.
>
> (68–72)

These lines assume that Arragon is free to wive elsewhere, although he exits vowing to "keep" his "oath," presumably the one of which Portia warns Morocco in 2.1:

> You must take your chance,
> And either not attempt to choose at all,
> Or swear before you choose, if you choose wrong
> Never to speak to lady afterward
> In way of marriage.
>
> (38–42)

Thus evaporates a tantalizing opportunity to read meaning from a seemingly rich textual detail: before this contradiction was introduced, Portia's father had seemed to reach from the grave not only to control her selection of a husband but also to eradicate Italy of simpletons by denying men of superficial judgment their offspring. So suggestive is this condition of the casket choice, in fact, that, despite the evidence to the contrary in Arragon's poem, some critics maintain that it is significant in Shakespeare's imagination, consistent with, if not proof of, their larger visions of the play.

One such critic, for example, sees Portia's father's restriction on her suitors as confirming the invisible grip of patriarchy in both the play's world and Shakespeare's sphere:

> The father's authority over his daughter is projected onto the suitors, none of whom challenges the conditions imposed upon *them*—a lifetime of celibacy. In fact, both Morocco and Arragon explicitly accept this provision (II,i,38–43; II,ix,12–13), and their acceptance further confirms the potency of a shadowy, posthumous patriarchy. Readers and audience members are unlikely to question these conditions either (as the play's critical history suggests), precisely *because* . . . they occur in a fable whose mode lures us into suspending disbelief and accepting the possibility that the will could have such impact. Accordingly, the fairy-tale mode inscribes and serves the interests of a patriarchy threatened by forces of change, and simultaneously makes it difficult for the harbingers of change to protest effectively.[1]

Of the several provocative remarks in this passage, perhaps the most dubious is the implication that readers or audiences "are unlikely to question" the "conditions" of the lottery, since numerous other critics over the years have pointed out the discrepancy between the father's will and the poem awaiting Arragon inside the silver casket.[2] Herself refraining from acknowledging Shakespeare's self-contradiction, this critic builds a weighty case on oozy ground: a whole threatened patriarchy is shoring up authority with a textual inconsistency.

I would like to dwell on this small example just enough to suggest that it is paradigmatic in at least two ways. First, Shakespeare's apparently real forgetfulness could not mirror more precisely than it already does in this instance the artificially constructed patterns of change and unpredictability that characterize the fictional world in *The Merchant of Venice*. Carol Leventen may be right when, in the passage just quoted, she perceives in the play an English patriarchy imperiled by social change, but the problem of transience is more pervasive in *Merchant* than she allows. It is not specific to class or gender. It is human, an intimation of mortality. And it accounts for much about the characters' behavior and audiences' responses to it. Second, the critical urge to impose a fixed, reliable understanding on *Merchant*—of which Leventen's case is but one among hundreds—reflects with remarkable accuracy the characters' approach to coping with a world in continual change. In both cases the imported structures are of limited service in providing absolute knowledge. Human experience, like the play's script, slips through our devices for framing it.

Of all the critics who have made observations about *Merchant* similar to mine, none is more compelling or quoted more often than is Norman Rabkin:

> The power of the play is its power to create the illusion of a life that is like our lives, a world like our world, in which as in our life and our world experience tempts us to believe itself to be reducible to fundamental terms but cannot be adequately analyzed in those terms. In *The Merchant of Venice* as in the life we live outside the theater we are driven to formulate questions which—despite the fact that we manage to go on living our lives—we cannot begin to answer.[3]

Whether or not this "system" of self-contradiction, as Rabkin calls it, is fully under Shakespeare's artistic control, it is far more often acknowledged by critics than heeded.[4] It tends to be invoked, then dropped in favor of efforts to wring coherence out of inconsistency. Granted, the nature of the critical enterprise, like that of living, is to experiment with ways of managing the unmanageable. Yet, I would like to return to the problem of meaning in *Merchant* by insisting that its discontinuities be viewed as the groundwork of its design.

Then, I would like to address Antonio as a major focus of the play's ambiguities. What is an Antonio doing in *The Merchant of Venice*? He is, in Shakespeare's canon, the first character by that name of any major significance and, indeed, the titular character. What associations is Shakespeare conjuring here through use of the type?

Most obvious, I think, is the flat contradiction between Antonio's truth to the type and his identity as a merchant. When he hazards all his earthly possessions and even his body for yet another whim of his lovesick friend, he acts entirely as a Pauline wise fool, a virtual copy of Saint Anthony himself. That he has accumulated such wealth in the first place and trusts that it will prevent his forfeiture to Shylock, however, rather taints his generosity (1.3.156–59, 180–81). Not only can he afford to be liberal, but he contracts with Shylock assuming that his liberality will turn out to be relatively modest once both he and Bassanio have turned a profit. He becomes a wise fool by default, as it were. His lavish existence in Venice necessarily enmeshes him in a life of material acquisition, no matter how much, as Gratiano suspects, it may sicken him: "You look not well, Signior Antonio, / You have too much respect upon the world. / They lose it that do buy it with much care" (1.1.73–75). The Antonio of the play's title—the merchant—is something of the genuine fool, the fool "[s]ilver'd o'er," to whom Arragon is compared (2.9.68–69). Repeatedly caught between worldly and otherworldly values, he is tempted toward several hypocrisies.

In the end, Antonio's story is largely determined by his failed attempts to escape the imperfect, irreducibly complex, and shape-shifting world of which he is undeniably a part—a behavioral pattern shared by most of the other characters and to which Antonio's name and characterization call attention. The play's recurring references to love in terms of money, which critics invariably notice, contribute to this pattern.[5] Such references mark the characters' endeavors to assign value to the invaluable, to approximate the ineffable, to lend meaning to the unknowable. Such language is no sooner spoken than shown to be inadequate, thrown back on and sullied by an unavoidable human need to rely on the material—a reliance that, cruelly, rekindles the human desire to transcend the material. *The Merchant of Venice*, in other words, traces and retraces a cycle of overreaching. The play enacts a series of trials wherein characters strive to outperform the human limitations that, willy nilly, take their toll. Antonio's problem, then, is that of negotiating with and in a world that both alienates and lays fierce claims on him. And he is not alone.

I

Antonio opens the play by speaking three times in seven lines of how little he understands himself:

> In sooth, *I know not why I am so sad*;
> It wearies me, you say it wearies you;
> But how I caught it, found it, or came by it,
> What stuff 'tis made of, whereof it is born,
> *I am to learn*;
> And such a want-wit sadness makes of me,
> That *I have much ado to know myself.*
>
> (1.1.1–7; emphasis added)

Thus, he immediately establishes the play's keen interest, which runs throughout, in the inadequacy of human knowledge. As readers and audiences, our first impulse is to provide the reason for Antonio's sadness—in most cases (cases too numerous to mention individually), the cause advanced is Bassanio's imminent departure. To assume so, however, is to remain deaf to Antonio's emphasis and to the dynamic of the entire first scene, which points to the absence of adequate explanations for Antonio's melancholy.[6] In the first part of the scene, Salerio, Solanio, and Gratiano all repeatedly guess at what is ailing Antonio. Clearly, none of them wholly succeeds. In rejecting their theories, Antonio reaffirms his self-estrangement: he does not know himself.

Nor does he appear to know the world in which his ships traffic. Salerio's speech about the perils of the sea (22–40), although familiar to the point of cliché, is nevertheless compelling. What's more, it is readily accessible, indebted as it is to the popular conceit of the sea as fortune and built on two simple metaphorical vehicles, "broth" and "church" (22, 29). A rhetorical *tour de force*, it speaks true: earthly life and goods, "even now worth this, / And now worth nothing," are at the mercy of earthly change (1.1.35–36). Yet, Salerio's persuasive speech does not move Antonio, who, although manifestly steeped in what Lyon calls an "ordinary and 'worldly' world" (31), is nonetheless out of step with that world. He is imprudently confident of his "fortune" (41):

> My ventures are not in one bottom trusted,
> Nor to one place; nor is my whole estate
> Upon the fortune of this present year:
> Therefore my merchandise makes me not sad.
>
> (42–45)

Two scenes later, with like oblivion, he impawns his flesh to Shylock.

Antonio's unskillful maneuvering in a world fraught with danger is pronounced but hardly unique. If he is, as his friends assert, a "strange fellow" and "marvellously chang'd" (51, 76), then he reflects the alienation and unpredictability portended even by the well-adjusted Bassanio as he greets his friends: "Good signiors both, when shall we laugh? say, when? / You grow exceeding strange. Must it be so?" (66–67). All human attachments, the play demonstrates from the start, are precarious. Nor does Venetian Christian culture fully protect its members from social alienation. For, although to themselves they are all natives, to an Elizabethan audience they would have been considered "merchant-strangers," the term applied by Londoners from midcentury on to "foreign or alien traders."[7] The concepts of native and foreign are relative, dependent upon perspective. Whatever sense of their impregnability may be afforded to the Venetians by their luxury, leisure, and power, it is continually undermined and exposed as contingent.

The effect of such undermining is dramatic irony, the tone that, in turn, dominates the play. In the particular case of the opening scene, the audience is being prepared for the crucial irony to follow, when the Venetians, themselves "strangers" in a variety of senses, treat the Jewish usurer increasingly as a foreigner, naming him "Jew" (passim), then "stranger" (3.3.27), finally "alien" (4.1.349).[8] Moreover, one of the chief purposes of such dramatic irony is to expose ostensible binaries in *Merchant*—like Christian versus Jew, or Venice versus Belmont—as suspicious, perhaps artificial. The more an audience probes the characterization of the Christian Italians in act 1, which Shakespeare takes obvious pains to elaborate at length before introducing Shylock at all, the more they resemble their Jewish counterpart.

Take, for example, the conversation in 1.3 where Bassanio, approaching Shylock in Antonio's behalf, misunderstands Shylock's remark, "Antonio is a good man," by replying, "Have you heard any imputation to the contrary?" (12–14). Almost universally, critics have cited this passage to show the difference between Jew and Christian, who, as Shylock's retort to Bassanio implies, do not even speak the same language: "Ho, no, no, no, no! my meaning in saying he is a good man is to have you understand me that he is sufficient" (15–17). Shylock's orientation is financial, we read repeatedly in the criticism on *Merchant*, whereas Bassanio's is moral. But this interpretation is misleading because it ignores Bassanio's attitudes and language as early as 1.1. There, in fact, Bassanio's request to Antonio and his description of Portia appear every bit as mercenary as are Shylock's ruminations over Antonio's suitability as a borrower. Only Bassanio's language is dressier. It is the language of spiritual venturing put to the service of obscuring his motive, which is to gain financial independence from Antonio by attaching himself to "a lady richly left" (161). Read closely, Bassanio's plans to woo Portia through Antonio's renewed generosity are couched in metaphors that are misleadingly high-minded and big-hearted: he wants to "get clear of all [his] debts" to Antonio by "hazard[ing]" another loan from Antonio (134, 151); his object is a woman of "worth" (167); and his "thrift" promises to render him "fortunate" (175–76). Not coincidentally, *thrift* is Shylock's word for "usury," as the audience is about to hear in 1.3 (50, 90).[9]

In effect, Bassanio and Shylock do not speak differently but share the same vocabulary, which Bassanio seems better at manipulating to blur his intent. He may well be attracted to Portia's "fair" looks and "wondrous virtues"—additional elements of her "worth"—as well as to her inheritance (1.1.162–63, 167). Yet, his language of financial speculation in 1.1 fits his professed love for Antonio and Portia only uncomfortably, if at all.

The immediate purpose of the dramatic irony that such implicit comparison between Jew and Christian creates is to puncture any character's pretensions to being essentially different from any other. Such claims to distinctiveness are often made in earnest—for instance, by the duke of

Venice, as he pronounces Shylock's sentence at the trial: "That thou shalt see the difference of our spirit, / I pardon thee thy life before thou ask it" (4.1.368–69). They are also parodied by Launcelot Gobbo in 3.5. According to the clown, the conversion from Jew to Christian is of no more consequence than an increase in the price of pork (21–26). In the same scene, moreover, Launcelot is revealed to have easily crossed racial boundaries himself by impregnating the Moor (37–42). In no case are the actual similarities between apparently disparate characters more extensive, however, than in that of Shylock and Antonio, who are far less divided by cultural barriers than bound naturally by their strangeness and estrangement. The one is alienated from Christian society, the other from this world altogether.

Antonio's discomfort in this world has its positive associations with ideal charity, like that of Saint Anthony, and, generally, unlike Shylock's miserliness. The merchant's willingness to dispense interest-free loans is legendary in Venice (1.2.43–45), and his devotion to Bassanio is widely recognized within his social sphere (2.8.35–50). Indeed, a large part of the point about Antonio's willingness to practice hypocrisy in borrowing from Shylock in the first place is that his high regard for Bassanio compels him to. In this sense, he is a conventional wise fool, ruled by irrational love.[10] At the same time, however, his is an obsessive attachment to Bassanio; as Solanio says, Antonio "only loves the world for" his friend (2.8.50). Such recklessness proves at least as harmful to some other characters—Shylock and Portia especially—as Shylock's overt hostility. And perhaps not all of Antonio's indiscretions can be attributed to his heedlessness; some seem every bit as calculated as Shylock's aggressions.

Antonio's affinity with Shylock is first evinced in 1.3, where his nature is disclosed through his open hypocrisies. He will "neither lend nor borrow / By taking nor by giving of excess"—that is, unless he needs to (61–64). He will also borrow from a man he has publicly abused, both verbally and physically, and will likely mistreat again (106–31). He will, in other words, practice the usury he reviles. Presumably, he satisfies his conscience by rationalizing the interest he will owe Shylock as adequate payment for his persecution of the Jew:

> If thou wilt lend this money, lend it not
> As to thy friends, for when did friendship take
> A breed for barren metal of his friend?
> But lend it rather to thine enemy,
> Who if he break, thou mayst with better face
> Exact the penalty.
>
> (132–37)

Antonio thus justifies the contemptuous "face" with which he uses Shylock's money. Worth noting here is Shylock's unwillingness to practice hypocrisy of his own until this point. He has refused Bassanio's hollow invitation to dinner and drawn a telling comparison between himself and the prototypical trickster Jacob, alerting the careful listener to his attitude toward his would-be clients (33–38, 71–90).[11] In addition, he confronts Antonio's hypocrisy directly (106–29). Only after Antonio insists on contracting with Shylock despite his loathing does Shylock assume his own mask of "kindness" (143):

> Why, look you how you storm!
> I would be friends with you, and have your love,
> Forget the shames that you have stain'd me with,
> Supply your present wants, and take no doit
> Of usance for my moneys, and you'll not hear me.
>
> (137–41)

Shylock can match Antonio move for move, ever deepening his resemblance to him.

In fact, Shylock's shift in attitude toward the bond—from "merry sport" to earnest—hinges on another Christian hypocrisy, the central one in Shakespeare's plot (1.3.145). Having finally consented to dine with the Christians in the spirit of "hate" (2.5.14), Shylock discovers too late just how much they have "flatter[ed]" him with their invitation (2.5.13). The dinner turns out to have been a subterfuge to expedite Jessica's elopement, as Shylock bemoans to Salerio and Solanio upon entering after she has fled: "You knew, none so well, none so well as you, of my daughter's flight" (3.1.24–25). Significantly, at no time hereafter is this hoodwinking of Shylock addressed. Even though it is, in the best light, a morally questionable ruse, the Christians are never held in the least bit accountable for it. Only Shylock is reproached in subsequent scenes for his violent, vengeful reaction to it. What might have happened to Shylock's "stony" heart if a Christian or two in the trial scene had apologized for participating in the earlier scheme against him (4.1.4)? Shylock's public humiliation of Antonio—and the firm control over his nemesis that it requires—are partly, as the usurer maintains, "villainy" that the Christians "teach" him (3.1.71).

I am not excusing Shylock's vengeance, which he clearly harbors from the very beginning: he "hates" Antonio "for he is a Christian; / But more, for that . . . / He lends out money gratis" (1.3.42–44). Nor do I intend to vilify Antonio and his Christian company. Neither do I mean to ignore conventional sixteenth-century depictions of Jews as monstrous or to pass over or minimize genuine cultural differences in any society, including Shakespeare's Venice.[12] They do exist. Yet, differing cultural practices may be mistaken as human differences. I am trying to show that many of the supposed distinctions in *Merchant*, which attach themselves to categories like Christian and Jew, or victim and villain, are just such mistaken disparities. They are relatively superficial, and they invite disproof. For all the acrimony they arouse among the characters and the disagreement they elicit in audience members, attempts to validate them turn quickly into vain exercises in hair-splitting and, worse yet, detours from recognizing the dramatic irony at hand and the uses to which it is put. The profound correspondences among the characters in *Merchant* ultimately redirect the audience's attention from a cultural dilemma to a universally human one.[13] It is the larger problem of feeling at home in the inhospitable world of the flesh, beginning with the body, which, as Shylock's unpleasant analogy to his vengeful humor indicates, may easily betray and "shame" us: "Some men there are . . . / . . . when the bagpipe sings i' th' nose, / Cannot contain their urine" (4.1.47–50). The worldly world of *Merchant* imposes such severe difficulties as to encourage withdrawal from it.

Put another way, Shylock's social alienation—in some ways caused by himself as much as by others—leads him to a madness much like Antonio's folly.[14] Both become increasingly isolated, even imprisoned. As Shylock becomes enslaved to vengeance, his passion finds bizarre reflection in Antonio's passive resignation to it:

> The Duke cannot deny the course of law;
> For the commodity that strangers have
> With us in Venice, if it be denied,
> Will much impeach the justice of the state,
> Since that the trade and profit of the city
> Consisteth of all nations.
>
> (3.3.26–31)

The essential truth of these lines notwithstanding, Antonio's specific explanation as to why Shylock must take his pound of flesh, rendered nearly impenetrable by his tortuous language, provides further evidence of his maladjustment to the material world. Yes, he must be shaken here by Shylock's carnivorous presence in the scene, but his contorted syntax owes to more than his present situation. For instance, is the subject of "will impeach" the "denial of commodity" or "the denial of the course of law"? The construction is muddled. Furthermore, the reason that the court might be "impeached" for a decision against Shylock is not, exactly, that Venice relies on "all nations" for trade; more specifically, it is because Venice must protect the foreigners who have relocated in Venice and who contribute to Venetian wealth and security, as Antonio means, but only vaguely relates.[15] His wording mirrors his malaise, seen especially in his consistent impulse to deal half-heartedly with the complexities of his existence by evasion, if not altogether removing himself. His readiness to die at Shylock's hands in the trial scene is expressed in the terms of Pauline wise folly: "I am a tainted wether of the flock, / Meetest for death; the weakest kind of fruit / Drops earliest to the ground, and so let me" (4.1.114–16). As numerous sequels to this speech demonstrate, however, Antonio's self-negation is not wholly sincere: "You cannot better be employ'd, Bassanio, / Than to live still and write mine epitaph" (4.1.117–18). Antonio still has an ego; in this case, he channels it toward raising himself in others' opinions.

What Antonio projects as his wisely foolish abandonment of self-interest is actually a truly foolish sacrifice of self-protection. He would rather die self-righteous than engage with Shylock, the law, and other worldly concerns, saving whatever face he can by manipulating Bassanio's public display of gratitude toward him. Likewise, the Shylock of acts 3 and 4 foolishly forfeits whatever standing he does enjoy in Venice to satisfy his loathing, as Stephen Greenblatt writes, "against all reason and self-interest."[16] In 1.3, Shylock has appeared attuned to and adept at dealing with life's perils, enumerating the reasons that contracting with Antonio would be unwise (17–25), while Antonio blithely ignores the dangers to his ships and to himself. But by act 4, both men have lost their heads. They are equally at odds with, adrift in, this world.

Their unease, merely an extreme version of that visiting all the major characters, also emerges in Belmont. There it is handled more lightly and yet is enough in evidence to erode the apparent dissimilarities between the play's two settings. Portia's first line echoes Antonio's—both are "weary," predisposed by their fatigue in "this great world" to retreat from it (1.2.2). As reasonable as are Nerissa's objections to Portia's complaints (1.2.3–9, 27–35), we may well sense, as Portia rehearses the relentless list of suitors to whom she has extended entertainment, that her world-weariness is deserved (1.2.39–111). Being stuck in a country house with a pack of unattractive suitors (one of whom just might choose the right casket) is no one's idea of fulfillment. Yet it is one of the play's many metaphors—others including the Venetian law—for the constrictions that accompany this life. No wonder, in a sense, that Antonio is so ready to leave it.

Still, Portia seems gently mocked for traces of the same characteristics that eventually render Antonio ineffectual in the world. Foremost is her tendency to rush headlong into judgments based on shallow differences, especially race and culture. That Bassanio, a Christian Italian, eventually chooses successfully among the caskets should not be misread as the play's complicity in Portia's xenophobia (3.2). For indeed, as Sinead Cusack has written of her own challenges in performing 1.2, the script leaves little opportunity to rescue Portia from close-mindedness:

> For Portia [the problem] is to escape the effect of a spoilt brat maliciously destroying her suitors. Both in rehearsal and in performance this scene [1.2] caused me more trouble than any other. I think we finally made it work, although it was at the price of cutting out the Scotsman, and perhaps one or two others.[17]

Those "others" are all Others—foreigners who, although they may fail the casket test and make miserable husbands, are deemed "strangers" in Portia's household not on those grounds but for reasons more trivial, like, "He hears merry tales and smiles not" (1.2.123). Portia's crush on Bassanio is also implicitly derided when Nerissa omits his name, citing him as the companion of the Marquis of Montferrat (1.2.114)—an "evocative family name," writes Moelwyn Merchant, for its associations with a powerful but financially drained Italian aristocracy.[18] Marquis Boniface of Montferrat had accumulated quite a debt of his own, at the turn of the thirteenth century, while participating in the Crusades; he eventually paid what he owed Venice by scheming with King Philip of Swabia, pocketing in the process "considerable personal gain" (all in the name of Christ, of course).[19]

The dramatic irony at work in scenes where Antonio and Shylock judge each other, then, is also operating in 1.2. Portia, too, falls back on false or incomplete assumptions about what constitutes genuine difference from one person to the next and about how much difference is acceptable. Through involving her in the problem of feeling alienated in the world, Shakespeare adds a new element to the equation. Not only is she wistful by virtue of her immersion in the world, and not only does she long to skirt the difficulties of navigating this life that tire her—difficulties implicit in her father's will. But also, like Antonio and Shylock, she copes with the daunting complexities, dangers, and pain of her situation with oversimplifications: all suitors are worthless but Bassanio, who is flawless. Such a response to the complicated challenge of enlightened courtship is particularly characteristic of youths, who, as Portia herself says, "skip o'er the meshes of good counsel the cripple" (1.2.20–21). In addition, her next line implies that it is a mannerism that she will outgrow, cooling her "hot temper" and accepting responsibility for herself:

"But this reasoning is not in the fashion to choose me a husband" (1.2.21–22).

The extent to which Portia does manifest growth in discernment over the play's course is a question set in motion by her first scene. Whatever the final answer to it, Shakespeare has illustrated many times over, in act 1 and beyond, that, when faced with confusion, the human inclination is to impose an order that can only fail to contain the confusion. The unruly world defies the characters' strategies for ordering it. The ultimate effect of the dramatic irony in *Merchant* is perhaps to alienate the audience from the characters enough to confuse and delay its judgment of them, lest that judgment, too, decay quickly into false appearance.

II

Shakespeare's dominant metaphor in *Merchant* for artificial constructs that appear to promise stability is the theater. The stage metaphor recurs throughout the first scene, persistently calling attention to the affectation about Venetian manners. First, Salerio fashions an image of Antonio's argosies as the "pageants of the sea," playing "signiors and rich burghers" to the "petty traffickers," or smaller ships (10–12). That tableau of courtliness and control, however, instantly gives way to Solanio's reminder that Antonio's ships are indeed vulnerable (15–22), whereupon Salerio abandons his initial scenario and pursues another (22–40), this one more in tune with "[w]hat harm a wind too great might do at sea" (24).

Only a few lines later, Antonio makes his own comparison between the world and the stage: "I hold the world but as the world, . . . / A stage where every man must play a part, / And mine a sad one" (77–79). Like Salerio's first description of Antonio's argosies, and like Jaques's celebrated "All the world's a stage . . .," Antonio's analogy too is reductive.[20] Through casting himself in a "sad" "part" (78–79), he believes he has satisfied curiosity as to his melancholy and cleared his future of mystery. Gratiano's reply, fittingly, is to try to break down Antonio's reserve by enacting the part of the "fool"; he also accuses his friend of playing another role than he admits to, that of "sir Oracle," a man whose "wisdom, gravity, profound conceit" are merely feigned, through his deceptively august silence, in order to cloak his ignorance (92–93). When Gratiano concludes his lecture by advising Antonio to "fish not with this melancholy bait / For this fool gudgeon"—that is, for an inflated "opinion" of his sagacity—he assumes that Antonio has a choice and is not necessarily so scripted as he maintains into a certain way of life (101–2).

Bassanio follows on the heels of this speech with his own categorization of Gratiano, who, he says, "speaks an infinite deal of nothing." This is a tag that critics have, to my knowledge, never questioned but that seems dubious (114). Gratiano's depiction of Antonio appears on target. Bassanio is about to ask Antonio for money, however, and would thus hasten to smooth any feathers that Gratiano had ruffled. What's more, Bassanio, as we have seen, is himself largely performing here, play-acting, as Gratiano has just described Antonio. He would naturally want to write off the perceptiveness of Gratiano's speech. As Bassanio unfolds his plans to Antonio for wooing Portia, he sets up his characterization for the rest of the play as someone who is always, in part, putting on a show and around whom theatrical language hovers. When he later welcomes Launcelot Gobbo into service by giving him a new "livery," it is with flair purchased by Antonio's loan, which also, presumably, underwrites his final Venetian "feast" for his "best esteem'd acquaintance" (2.2.154, 171–72). In 2.9, he is said to be approaching Belmont with "(besides commends and courteous breath), / Gifts of rich value," which he cannot afford, and arriving like a "day in April . . . / To show how costly summer" is approaching (90–91, 94–95). Such are the "fair ostents of love" (2.8.44)—Antonio's words for the production he has subsidized—that later embarrass Bassanio when, having won Portia's hand and learning of Antonio's distress in Venice, he must own up to his role-playing:

> dear lady,
> Rating myself at nothing, you shall see
> How much I was a braggart: when I told you
> My state was nothing, I should then have told you
> That I was worse than nothing.
>
> (3.2.256–60)

To argue that Bassanio chooses the lead casket because he knows firsthand that "outward shows [may] be least themselves" is too cynical (3.2.73). Clearly, his character is delineated to illustrate how even the best of men—including one worthy of Portia's love—may easily be tempted to lie rather than risk rejection. He at least eventually tells her the truth about owning "nothing." And that he continues, even after his confession of his indebtedness, to deal with his discomfort through "outward shows" serves at least one positive purpose: it presents Portia with repeated perceptual tests and lessons through which she can gain experience (3.2.73). Having discovered the element of play-acting in his financial situation (3.2), she is then privy during the trial to his reneging on his vow of love to her (4.1.282–87), and after that to his forfeiting her ring for love of Antonio and for gratitude to Balthazar (4.1.450–51). These instances can only temper her earlier, girlish conviction in Bassanio's perfections, which, just before he makes his choice of caskets, she likens to those of Hercules.[21]

But, even more than providing a catalyst for both Bassanio's and Portia's maturation, Bassanio's continual reliance on theatrics to make his way in the intimidating world forms part of a much larger web in *Merchant*, where action is usually acting. I have discussed already the pressures on both the Christians and Shylock in 1.3 to alternate between honesty and hypocrisy as they formulate the bond. Other instances abound. Jessica elopes disguised, while the Christians, "with varnish'd faces," plan to put on a masque (2.5.33). Portia's father's lottery serves as a skeletal script: it repeatedly prompts suitors to write their own lines within a narrowly defined formula, and it deposits Portia within similar legal confines, which are represented by the casket that encases her picture.[22] Portia's own attempt to swindle her ring from Bassanio is a consciously staged event (4.1). But the theatrical extravaganza in *Merchant* is, of course, the trial, which Portia, with Bellario's help, carefully orchestrates.

The specifics of Portia's conduct in the trial scene temporarily set aside, we should not miss several of the episode's general traits as calculated performance. Much like the final scene in *Measure for Measure*, where Duke Vincentio secretly directs his subjects' reactions to his gestures, 4.1 of *Merchant* is also a virtual play-within-a-play. It thus necessarily reminds the audience that the larger work is also fiction, thereby inviting inspection of the characters' various uses of theatrics. In the trial scene, Portia's advance knowledge of how to overturn the bond not only buys her the time to try coaxing Shylock out of his vengeance; it also rigs the other characters' responses to the court's proceedings—or, at least, severely limits the possibilities of their responses. Shylock, for example, never truly has a chance to persuade his "second Daniel" of his cause. But even more to the point, Portia's control over the trial's outcome, artistic in its breadth and resourcefulness, alerts us to how provisional—illusory, really—are all the constructs that are relied upon to stave off social and personal disorder.[23] Countless details of the scene—from Shylock's pathetically blind trust in the law's letter to the deliberate instruction with which Portia calls upon first the duke, then Antonio, to sentence Shylock—point up how easily the verdict, but for Portia's firm hand, might have gone the other way. Having done her homework and prepared for the worst, she has guarded against loss; her strategy, akin to that of the contract or bond, is meant to minimize risk.

So is, I would argue, the love for Bassanio that Antonio flaunts in the courtroom, which is of suspicious mettle, if only because of its proximity to so many other examples of feigning, like Portia's role-playing. But Antonio himself offers more grounds for doubting his professions of liberality in love because his words and actions hint of the role-playing he has discussed with Gratiano as the play began. Furthermore, in styling himself a saint, ready to sacrifice his life for friendship, he employs the sort of absolute and ideal terms that, like Salerio's metaphor of "pageants" for "argosies" (1.1.11, 9), suggest a pose. No one can be that virtuous—not in the menacing waters of this world, vividly portrayed in *Merchant*. Like Antonio's casting of himself in the role of a sad man and like Portia's close direction of the trial, Antonio's playing the martyr seems devised to eliminate risk—the risk of not having his love returned. Significantly, this lack of risk was the factor that made Christian moralists deem usury corrupt.[24] Once again, for all of Antonio's labors to distance himself from such worldly imperfections, he appears far more like than unlike Shylock. At the same time, cultural stereotypes receive another lick: Christian liberality, hazarding in love, and perhaps even mercy, versus Jewish miserliness, legalism, and revenge seem more than ever like so many theatrical props. As for Antonio, unless the image of himself that he projects is truer than it seems, it will sooner or later crack. In this case, it is sooner, and the exposure of the man behind the staged type shows much about how the rest of *Merchant* is played out.

III

The height of Antonio's role-playing coincides with the point where he most manipulates Bassanio's emotions—that is, when his letter, horrendously timed, intrudes upon the betrothal of Bassanio and Portia, usurping center stage. As Bassanio reads the letter aloud, he may as well be reading a part from a script—in this case, a revision of his life's course:

> Sweet Bassanio, my ships have all miscarried, my creditors grow cruel, my estate is very low, my bond to the Jew is forfeit; and since in paying it, it is impossible I should live, all debts are clear'd between you and I, if I might but see you at my death. Notwithstanding, use your pleasure; if your love do not persuade you to come, let not my letter. (3.2.315–22)

The letter shows Antonio's love to be conditional. His Christian "kind[ness]," trumpeted by his loyal supporters Salerio and Solanio (2.8.35), craves Bassanio's gratitude in return. It thus represents what Thomas Wilson's *Discourse Upon Usury* refers to as "*Mentalis usura*, an usurie of the mynde, when one hopeth for gayne although no contracte be made," gain not in money but in "thankfull recompense."[25] Antonio's protestations of charity, although they surely embrace some truth about his esteem for Bassanio, also reveal, as Geary puts it, "a desperate attempt to hold on to Bassanio"[26] and thereby raise himself in Bassanio's esteem. Such angling may be read as self-interest disguised as selflessness. It compares to his statement in the next scene, 3.3, that he has "oft deliver'd from [Shylock's] forfeitures / Many that have at times made moan to me" (22–23)—a line that appropriates the religious language of salvation ("deliver'd"), that stresses the abundance of his benevolence ("oft," "Many," "at times"), and that, therefore, sets himself up to appear a kind of Christ. But Antonio's self-consciousness mars his charity.

Throughout the trial scene, Antonio continues to display what Lyon calls his "talent for the . . . self-advertising whine."[27] His demeanor of long suffering is undercut by his repeated plays for Bassanio's affection, as well as by startling reminders of how ill at ease he feels in the world. His melodramatic puns, which Portia's verbal adroitness throws into relief, again betray his distress at the prospect of not belonging:

> Most *heartily* I do beseech the court
> To give the judgment.
>
> For if the Jew do cut but deep enough,
> I'll pay it instantly *with all my heart.*
> (4.1.243–44, 280–81; emphasis added)

Such painful awkwardness portrays Antonio at his most foolish, unable to feel or to express a love that entails true risk—unconditional love—and unable to trust that he could be loved without manipulating Bassanio into it.

Antonio's masquerade as a man of infinite patience, toleration, and charity is loaded with implication in a scene that takes up the "quality of mercy" at its center. How much of what passes for Christian kindness in 4.1, the audience might well ask upon witnessing Antonio's exhibition, is the real thing? That question is urged by no character's attitude in the scene more than by Gratiano's. With a name connoting grace itself, Gratiano is the enemy of Antonio's pretensions to love, echoing Shylock's denigration of Antonio's false humility as the fraudulence of a "fawning publican" (1.3.41). Gratiano, in fact, is the entire play's enemy to theatrical spectacle. Shakespeare's alteration of *Il Pecorone*, wherein the Antonio figure (Ansaldo) marries the lady's maid, tempts an audience to think of Gratiano as a branching off of Antonio's character, a kind of twin. Both characters, indeed, expose the play-acting in *Merchant* for what it is—the one, through pretense; the other, through brutal honesty.

I believe that Gratiano has yet to be explored satisfactorily in criticism, though his behavior, especially during the trial, bears significantly upon Antonio's characterization. Gratiano is almost unfailingly regarded as, at best, a Jew-baiting boor and, at worst, proof that Christians can hate as violently as Jews. In either case, he is seen as socially coarse and strident. But depictions of him that stop here take their cue, as implied above, from Bassanio's curt dismissal of Gratiano's observations as "chaff" (1.1.116). In reality, however, not only do Gratiano's statements in 1.1 hit home, but, later, he also speaks the most eloquent lines in *Merchant*. Significantly, that same speech encapsulates most faithfully the play's constant concern with the desolation that results in a world of change and instability:

> All things that are,
> Are with more spirit chased than enjoy'd.
> How like a younger or a prodigal
> The scarfed bark puts from her native bay,
> Hugg'd and embraced by the strumpet wind!
> How like the prodigal doth she return,
> With over-weather'd ribs and ragged sails,
> Lean, rent, and beggar'd by the strumpet wind!
>
> (2.6.12–19)

In addition to prophesying the fate of Antonio's argosies, Gratiano discloses the kernel of truth in *Merchant* that perhaps comes closest to being unimpeachable: that as worldly conditions change, so do human appetites.

This gift of Gratiano's for tapping into the essence of things looks forward to another such unlikely truth-teller in Shakespeare's canon: Lucio, the "fantastic" who dogs the friar/duke throughout *Measure for Measure*. Many differences attain between the two—most especially, that Lucio receives a stiff comeuppance for slandering Duke Vincentio, while Gratiano is never judged for what he says. Yet, much as Lucio has an odd way of speaking factually about the duke (or seeming to)—even as, in ignorance of the duke, he manufactures lies about him—so Gratiano remains mysteriously incapable of forgery. And, like Lucio, he sometimes appears to mirror the truth without trying or meaning to.[28] In 2.6, for instance, just after Jessica exits to "gild" herself with "some moe ducats," Gratiano muses, "Now by my hood, a gentle, and no Jew" (49–51). Although he intends to compliment Jessica, he inadvertently characterizes Gentiles as "gilded," preoccupied with the material wealth that Jessica is now adding both to her costume and to Christian coffers.

Gratiano's irrepressible honesty, again like Lucio's, adheres where it is least wanted, though possibly where it is most needed. Duke Vincentio tries in vain to shake off this "bur," who will nevertheless "stick" (4.3.179), and although reprehensible for slurring the duke, Lucio is still valuable for what he can teach the duke about how his subjects really see him. In a sense, Lucio unveils the duke verbally and does so quite literally in 5.1, when he physically lifts the friar's hood, discovering the real duke beneath his theatrical disguise. Such, I think, is also Gratiano's dramatic function: to resist attempts to suppress truth under a veneer of civility. Bassanio suggests as much when he cautions Gratiano about being himself in Belmont and advises him to play a part instead:

> But hear thee, Gratiano:
> Thou art too wild, too rude, and bold of voice—
> Parts that become thee happily enough,
> And in such eyes as ours appear not faults,
> But where thou art not known, why, there they show
> Something too liberal. Pray thee take pain,
> To allay with some cold drops of modesty
> Thy skipping spirit, lest through thy wild behavior
> I be misconst'red in the place I go to,
> And lose my hopes.
>
> (2.2.180–89)

This is all eerily familiar. Wild? Rude? Bold of voice? Thus far, Gratiano has not born out Bassanio's adjectives, although he will fulfill all such epithets during the trial; Bassanio has reason to exaggerate here because, as a nervous suitor, he wants his "show" to be just so (185). Otherwise, he stands to lose his "hopes" (189)—yet another perfectly ambiguous word for what he could gain, financially or spiritually, through marriage to Portia. And the cost to Gratiano of dispelling Bassanio's illusion of suitability? Life as a social outcast, cut off from Portia's fortune and the conduit of Bassanio's friendship. Naturally, he agrees to "put on a sober habit," to role-play along with his benfactors (2.2.190).

Yet, ironically, Gratiano seems to have less to hide than anyone. Never mind that, until the trial scene, he appears, objectively, to be the most socially well adjusted character in Venice; never mind that Gratiano sails into marriage, which eludes Antonio. He is *persona non grata.* His very presence is seen to imperil the charades that promise wealth, stability, and prosperity amidst the flux. In the end, however, Gratiano proves unable to don a socially acceptable façade, such that his character comes to embody a principle that pervades the play—the habit of truth to assert itself. His impulse to be himself and to utter the realities that other characters may intuit, but would rather suppress, calls to mind Launcelot's words to Old Gobbo in 2.2, as he attempts, finally, to reveal himself to his father: "truth will come to light; . . . in the end truth will out" (79–80). Whatever particular truth Gratiano may impart in a given scene, he always somehow displays the darker forces at work behind the cloak of order, normalcy, and reason. Ultimately, Gratiano's truth is the same truth that spoils the masquers' play when, Antonio announces, "the wind is come about" (2.6.64)—the truth that human artifice can exert precious little control over nature's vagaries.

This trait of Gratiano's does not surface fully until 4.1, where he becomes obstreperous: "O, be thou damn'd, inexecrable dog!" (128). On the face of things, the abrupt switch in his characterization may seem puzzling: the only overt link between the Gratiano of the first three acts and that of act 4 are Bassanio's depictions, which, we have seen, do not square with the actual Gratiano on the page, who initially appears well-meaning, perceptive, and even capable of poetry.[29] How appropriate if the play's chief mouthpiece for discontinuity were himself Janus-faced, composed of irreducible and inexplicable contradictions. That possibility notwithstanding, at least one common thread does unite the earlier and later Gratianos, however sensible or vicious they may be. As in the first three acts, Gratiano can still be counted on in one way or another to demystify what he, along with the audience, sees, thereby uncovering certain truths. Once he and Bassanio have become engaged in Belmont, for instance, Gratiano does not hesitate to use the candid terms of material gain for their "success": "We are the Jasons, we have won the fleece" (3.2.240–41). In the trial scene, Gratiano is likely unaware of how effectively he continues to disrupt illusion. Yet he does so by giving frank, passionate voice to the hostility and racism that the trial as play-within-a-play and Antonio as spurious saint are concealing. Gratiano's aspersions may be vile, but, like Shylock's malicious attack on Antonio, they have the virtue of honesty. In this, Gratiano strangely, paradoxically, lives up to his name. "Mercy is not itself, that oft looks so"; Gratiano's inability to pretend is, in some sense, grace indeed. Recalling the socially repugnant fool in book 1 of *Utopia*, who blurts out the proposition that churchmen ought to minister to the needy rather than to their own desires,[30] Gratiano may well be the character in *Merchant* who most closely approximates the Pauline wise fool. In this he is a foil to the folly-fall'n Antonio.

Yet this is not to say that Gratiano's insults toward Shylock speak equally accurately for all the characters' feelings at the trial or that whatever mercy surfaces during the trial is purely sham. The perspective lent by Gratiano on the multiple, complex occurrences in 4.1 is but a wedge of the entire circle, albeit a sizable wedge. It invites examination of the court proceedings as to their real, versus their ostensible, fairness. How do we understand more precisely the degree to which Shylock's treatment under first Portia, then Antonio, translates into either justice or travesty? The letter from Bellario that introduces Balthazar to the court—another disguised script, juxtaposed against Antonio's letter to Bassanio (3.2)—not only commends the young judge's precocious achievement. It also suggests that the youth's judgment is still being tested: "I leave him to your gracious acceptance, whose trial shall better publish his commendation," writes Bellario to the duke (4.1.164–66). The pun on "trial" enables the word to refer to both the trial over which Portia will preside and the scrutiny with which the audience is urged to evaluate her judgments by virtue of participating in 4.1 as audience-accomplices.

Measuring Portia's success at dispensing authentic justice, as opposed to fakery, requires further explanation of what, exactly, she aims to accomplish in court. Foremost, as indicated at the close of 3.2, she seeks to release her husband's friend from Shylock's tyranny, as much to benefit Antonio (3.4.10–21) as to comfort Bassanio (3.2.305–6). Although her primary goal is private, however, she also clearly takes care while pursuing her own ends to preserve the law's integrity, as when she denies Bassanio's request to bypass the contract entirely and "[w]rest once the law to [her] authority" (4.1.215). Already, then, even before she enters the courtroom, she is at pains to balance private against public concerns. Once the trial is underway, she quickly confronts another, similar challenge—the summons to arbitrate between the letter and the spirit of the law, an objective all the more vexed by the demands on her from both private and public spheres.

At merely a cursory glance, Portia's predicament, caught as she is between opposing and equally valid claims, registers as difficult. Indeed, it epitomizes the situation in which all the characters in *Merchant* repeatedly find themselves: that of making impossible choices. At every turn, various characters face one impasse or another. Jessica must choose between restrictive loyalty to her father or a carefree life with a Christian, a dilemma recapitulated in Portia's deciding whether or not to abide by her father's will. Portia's line in that context—"O me, the word choose!" (1.2.22–23)—expresses her dismay at lacking, rather than having, free choice. But she will soon covet the structured choice afforded her by her father's lottery, since she will freely turn to Bellario, her father reincarnated as uncle, for preinstructions about handling the intricacies of the trial. Choice between seemingly irreconcilable options also presses upon Bassanio, dividing his loyalties between Portia and Antonio. That dilemma is more playfully refigured later, in Bassanio's double desire to keep his word to Portia and yet still reward Balthazar, who are, doubly perplexingly, one and the same (4.1, 2). Furthermore, as 3.2 begins, Bassanio, in what can only be construed as the play's near self-parody, must even choose whether and when to choose. Finally, he would rather know his fate than delay it: "Let me choose, / For as I am, I live upon the rack" (24–25). The trial scene, then, is a culmination of this pattern of impossible choice.

Launcelot Gobbo, further fulfilling his dramatic function in *Merchant* as the mirror of crucial themes, takes the parody of feeling deadlocked to new heights as he struggles with whether to exchange masters:[31]

> The fiend is at mine elbow and tempts me, saying to me, "Gobbo, Launcelot Gobbo, good Launcelot," or "good Gobbo," or "good Launcelot Gobbo, use your legs, take the start, run away." My conscience says, "No; take heed, honest Launcelot, take heed, honest Gobbo, . . . do not run, scorn running with thy heels." . . . "Bouge," says the fiend. "Bouge not," says my conscience. "Conscience," say I, "you counsel well." "Fiend," say I, "you counsel well." (2.2.2–9, 19–22)

The terms of this parody are those of the old morality drama, Launcelot the Everyman being torn between heavenly and hellish alternatives. The point of the parody is how much more troublesome is the problem of choice in the new drama, which more faithfully renders the world's complexities than do the clear-cut absolutes of moral allegory. In his own rudimentary way, Launcelot suggests the overwhelming confusion that choice entails when he scrambles his moral categories: he aligns the "fiend" with the decision to abandon Shylock, who himself is called "devil" and whose house is "hell" (1.3.98, 2.3.2). "Confusions" continue to reign in 2.2 once Old Gobbo enters and Launcelot plays the role of a befuddling God to his father's blind humankind (37). Launcelot's game of ventriloquizing his own shifting identity in his father's mind cleverly mimics all the characters' sense of dislocation as they fade in and out of apprehension, as well as the audience's continual feeling that reliable knowledge of the characters eludes them (33–101). The punch line that resolves this episode of mistaken identity in 2.2 underscores the very fluidity of identity; Old Gobbo exclaims, on feeling Launcelot's beard: "Lord, how art thou chang'd!" (99).

However humorous is Launcelot's rendition of the quandaries that human judgment visits on the other characters, the problem of choice in *Merchant* is no laughing matter. It is the plight that, perhaps more than any other condition of being human, most binds the characters together as human, underlying and belying their more superficial differences. It is, in other words, the truth behind the mask of racial, cultural, and sexual distinctions that, in this treacherous world of deceptive exteriors, transience, and myopia, to boot, everyone must not only choose but choose between two cherished possibilities, letting one go forever, and also make such choice in a mist. This is the hard, tragic fact at the core of human existence in *Merchant*. The cruel necessity of choosing blindly and with finality informs every character's experience equally and, totally without discrimination, alienates them all from their world and from one another. "Joy" is sometimes the "consequence" of judgment, as in Bassanio's happy choice of caskets (3.2.107). One false move, however, and his history would play out like Shylock's, which illustrates how easily a decisive stance, like complete faith in a bond's legality, may bring loss and sorrow. In *Merchant*, choice persistently entails the possibility of lost and irretrievable opportunity. At its most cynical, the play can even imply that neither of two choices will prove gratifying. Launcelot, again, offers a light handling of a dark notion when he tells Jessica that she is damned whether she claims kinship to Scylla, her father, or to Charybdis, her mother (3.5.15–18). Maneuvering through such narrow straits leaves a wide margin for error.

A comic vision, in which extremes are shown to be reconcilable, is not entirely alien to *Merchant*. Under a comic star, two opposites give enough to produce cosmic or social harmony, as Portia is attempting to do in the trial scene: she works to negotiate a slender pass between the Scylla of Shylock's fury, lack of pity, and adherence to an unjust law, and the Charybdis of Antonio's peculiar passivity, the Christians' readiness to dispense with the law, and her own private bias in the defendants' favor. In striving to mediate between the letter and the spirit of the law, she is hoping to vindicate Antonio through strictly legal means and, perhaps, add Shylock's education in flexibility to the bargain: she does, after all, give him plenty of time to withdraw his claim voluntarily before she subjects him to his own legalese.[32]

But what is so remarkable about Portia in the trial scene is her very willingness to take on such a formidable task, especially since, no matter how well, or comically, she satisfies the various, contrary demands upon her judgment, she will likely fall short of the mark. Her partial inadequacy is virtually guaranteed. Whatever comic impulse may inform Portia's skill at judgment or her inclination to effect peace, it will remain at odds with the tragic discontent sown in the play's first lines and cultivated thereafter. For, in addition to whatever personal failings may inhibit Portia's clearer judgment, she has been placed here, as judge, in an untenable position. If the quibble on "blood" that she plays close to her vest stacks the deck against Shylock, then Portia herself has been no less finessed. Any decision she handed down to the court would be hard-pressed to elude the circumstances handed down to her by the play: namely, the unlikelihood that any choice can fully resolve antipathy or thoroughly erase a sense of bereavement.

Put another way, Portia's judgment, no matter how wise, is bound to savor of some theatrical artificiality because she cannot hope to reach an ideal ruling—that is, a thoroughly convincing resolution. She is not so foolhardy as Antonio, whose display of spirituality is at least partly counterfeit. Her performance in court is far more substantial and credible. Indeed, her appearance at the trial exhibits genuine self-sacrifice, as opposed to Antonio's hollow shows of generosity; she has forfeited her wedding night and now risks considerable damage to everyone by taking the responsibility for Antonio that he refuses to take for himself.[33] This substitution, truly Christian in spirit, evinces her noble recognition that, come what may, someone must step up, settle the contest between Antonio and Shylock, and save Antonio's life. But the conditions of her choice—which are largely out of her control—stipulate that, in some measure, her verdict be implicated as mere pretension to truth, pretension signaled even by her theatrical costume. That disguise brings into incisive focus the bind in which Portia finds herself: she must lean on the power of fiction to perform her office and yet can never shake free of the element of fiction—of untruthfulness to the ideal of justice—in her arbitration.

Judgment in *Merchant*, particularly in the trial scene, most resembles theatrical illusion in this way, in its failure to contain all desires, to embrace all aspects of truth, to satisfy from all points of view. To be sure, some strategies minimize error and narrow-mindedness: slow and patient deliberation, mature awareness of life's impermanence, adopting the widest possible angle from which to perceive. Executed with even the best of intentions and with optimal tactics, however, human judgment is merely relative in quality. So must be, then, the quality of mercy. For this imperfection the audience is prone to hold Portia and her fellow Christians wholly responsible. Yet, if the audience, too, is invested in making the best possible judgment of the proceedings, it may benefit from carefully sorting out the factors for which the characters can be held accountable from those for which they cannot. Finally, the "poor rude world" stakes its claim on Portia as forcibly as it does on Antonio, and human nature, hers included, tends to deny the unpleasant realities of that world through substituting a fiction for them. At the same time, those realities persist, gnawing away at the fragile fictions. Although Portia's shortcomings as an individual and as a member of her culture are conspicuous, her human weaknesses encourage sympathy. If, for the former, she remains a foolish fool, then, for the latter, she becomes a wise one, undertaking a largely thankless job at considerable personal expense and at high risk of the censure that Antonio abhors.

IV

Portia's development as a character over the course of the play traces, in essence, her growing familiarity with and ease in the "poor rude world." At her youngest, in 1.2, her lack of sophistication is implied by Nerissa's more extensive worldly experience ("for aught I see," [5]) and intuition about the advantages to Portia of her father's will (27–33).[34] Even here, however, Portia's appreciation of human limitations is realistic beyond her years: "If to do were as easy as to know what were good to do, chapels had been churches and poor men's cottages princes' palaces" (12–14). Yet her awareness that human inadequacy requires compassion comes and goes. Intolerant of her suitors' gullibility, for instance, she fires off a comment to Arragon that not only puts him down but also runs counter to her own convictions: "To offend and judge are distinct offices, / And of opposed natures" (2.9.61–62). If such were the case, then human sympathy would never be able to temper rigid judgment, as Portia strenuously argues it should when promoting mercy in 4.1 (for example, 184–205). Then again, Portia's suitors, intent as they are on idealizing her into a "mortal breathing saint," do little to discourage her curt dismissals (2.7.40). For Portia, as for Morocco and Arragon, the other is not fully human.

Not until Bassanio enters in 3.2 does Portia noticeably begin to bend, growing more accepting of another's weaknesses and more modest toward her own. Without any cooling of ardor for Bassanio, she acknowledges that he stands to choose the wrong casket (1–24), and she readily forgives him his indiscretion on learning of his indebtedness (299–314). Likewise, she offers herself to Bassanio acknowledging both her merits—"the full sum of me / Is sum of something"—and her shortcomings: she is "unlesson'd . . ., unschool'd, unpracticed," though "she can learn" (157–59, 162). Such concessions to imperfection are intermixed with Portia's increased willingness to accommodate the demands on her of living in a flawed society and an unpredictable world. During Bassanio's choice of caskets, she first pronounces the warning to "tarry," to "pause"—that is, to approach choice as the perceptual challenge it is (1). She will later, of course, reprise this sound advice in the courtroom: "Tarry a little," "Soft, no haste," "Tarry" (4.1.305, 321, 346). In 3.2 she confides to the audience her attempt to heed her own counsel by curbing her "joy" at Bassanio's success:

> [*Aside*.] O love, be moderate, allay thy ecstasy,
> In measure rain thy joy, scant this excess!
> I feel too much thy blessing; make it less,
> For fear I surfeit.
>
> (111–14)

These are the words of a budding realist. Still inclined toward fantasies of Bassanio as a Herculean hero (53–62), she has nevertheless undertaken to mature from and learn through experience, as she promises Bassanio she will (149–65).

And indeed, even in 3.2, which is a prelude to the trial scene, Portia's fortitude of mind and character are clearly superior when measured against her peers'. The other characters surrounding her at the scene's end, all of whom have their own attractions, cannot compete with her impressiveness. Bassanio appears more mature when, earlier in the scene, he chooses "substance"—the real and imperfect Portia—over her effigy, a poor "counterfeit" in which she is drawn as a "demigod" (115–30). But having thus rejected mere "show" at last, his former theatrics ambush him when he is forced to confess his debt to Antonio and is once again brought low in the audience's opinion (256–63). Bassanio's good judgment has somehow outstripped his practical behavior, leaving his actual experience to catch up; he is destined now to learn through trial and error what his choice of truth over "ostent" means pragmatically. At the same juncture in the scene, Jessica has just entered with her Lorenzo (219), the couple presenting a portrait of stolen love next to the earned love of Portia and Bassanio, who seem their elders. Add to this company Antonio, who even *in absentia* makes his presence felt through his cloying letter (315–22). In a telling gesture, Portia asks to hear the letter read aloud (314). She probably craves to know what she is up against. Here again, she sets herself apart in this group of seemers, all of whom seek out ways to skirt the practical difficulties and responsibilities, the complexities of human life. Never again is the specific contrast between Portia and Antonio more lucid than at the close of 3.2: for, while Antonio can conceive of realizing his devotion to Bassanio only through sacrificing his existence, Portia intends to enlist her "little body" in the service of saving Antonio's, toward the ultimate end of physically consummating her marriage with a tranquil husband.[35]

Portia's characterization as one who braves the hard vicissitudes of life in order to enjoy its rewards reaches a turning point in 3.4. Easily deceiving Lorenzo and Jessica, she proposes to "abide" in a "monast'ry two miles off," where she may "live in prayer and contemplation" (26–32). In context, her choice to do just the opposite is crucial. Given the play's larger contention between the active life, which requires risk and flexibility, and the passive life, wherein contemplation breeds dangerous idealism, the monastery is richly symbolic. It represents the literal origins of Antonio's martyrdom, implicitly connecting his saintly behavior with the likes of Saint Anthony, and it suggests the figurative roots of his maladjustment to the material life in which he is engaged. By rejecting the monastic, contemplative life in the guise of embracing it, Portia rejects much about Antonio's values without denying his feelings their validity. She separates the man from his conduct, explicitly extolling his "spirit" (3.4.11–21), though implicitly condemning his destructive behavior by electing to participate in the life he shuns. Affirming her attachment to that life, as well as her self-conception as a servant in it, she borrows as her pseudonym the real name of her man Balthazar.

Such signs bode well. In particular, the suggestions in Portia's choices of reconciling extremes—withdrawal and engagement, censure and approval, master and servant, even male and female—adumbrate an official verdict at the trial that just might avoid the pitfall of all other judgments in the play: that of choosing one option at the exclusion of another. If Portia is indeed trying to achieve private ends without doing damage to public structures, if her deliberations are directed toward serving both the law's spirit and letter and toward bringing Jew and Christian closer to mutual understanding, then earlier scenes would seem to allow her a fighting chance to make some progress on those fronts. Her first substantive statement in the trial scene, which is actually a question, also appears to uphold the characterization of Portia/Balthazar as impartial and poised to recognize the legitimacy in each of two opposing perspectives: "Which is the merchant here? and which the Jew?" (174). What less biased opening could she employ than this one, which denies outward appearance as a factor in her arbitration? Her question indicates her readiness to look beyond misleading racial and cultural distinctions and into the pith of the arguments before her.

Yet I would argue, first, that Portia's question is far more complicated in its significance than I have just said and, second, that the question's tonal ambiguity speaks accurately for that, running throughout the scene, toward Portia's approach to judgment. For not only does her question imply her disinterestedness, but it also exemplifies her theatricality, which continually flirts with false sincerity. In fact, the most obvious point to make about her initial question is that it is a gag—and at Shylock's expense: in late sixteenth-century performance, Shylock's gaberdine and accompanying stage-Jew costuming would have stood out in a crowd of Gentiles.[36] Operating simultaneously on a more serious level, however, Portia's apparently innocent question even more subtly raises suspicions about her neutrality, since her terms for Antonio and Shylock—that is, "merchant" and "Jew"—are not comparable, the one referring to a common means of sustenance in Venice and the other to a set of religious and cultural traits that help to alienate Shylock from within Venice. Thus, Portia, from the start, throws the proceedings somewhat athwart the search for justice. She also alerts the audience to the tension, which prevails from here on out, between catering to private interests and heeding the interests of others.

One way to talk about this tension is in terms of how Portia instructs Shylock. Does she, for example, truly attempt to include Shylock's viewpoint in her consideration? Her speech on the "quality of mercy" can be read as such a gesture (184–205), a generous effort to "mitigate" Shylock's severe legal rigor (203). It also contains undeniable elements of tribalism. In a very real sense, before the trial concludes, Shylock "*must* . . . be merciful" (183; emphasis added). He can either volunteer to render mercy as an ideal Christian does, without "strain" (184), or he will be required to give it "by compulsion," legally (183). In any case, his dissent from the "[w]e" who "do pray for mercy" will not be so much as minimally tolerated. Once Portia unhinges Shylock's leverage, depriving him of legal recourse, his forfeiture of his bond and his control of his fortune, are, absolutely, enforced. One could argue that Shylock always has the opportunity, until Portia plays the trump card of her quibble on "blood" (306–7), to relent and soften his cruel demands of Antonio. And many have so argued. But the only authentic opportunity that Shylock has in the trial is to become a Christian—and not the sort of flawed, real Christian represented by other characters in the courtroom but a perfect Christian who lets go of grudges, sprinkles mercy and good will freely, has no property to speak of, and therefore can pose no threat to organized Venetian society. He is also expected to turn the other cheek to those who deceived him in promoting Jessica's elopement and who themselves make no apologies. In effect, Shylock finally has no choice at all and, as a consequence, no audible voice in Venice, no visible role in its fashioning.

All of this reasoning, of course, perverts the audience's direct experience of the scene because it rests on selective evidence. Naturally, we do not want Antonio to die, we do not want Shylock to commit a killing, and we do not want Portia to fail. But what, in our most enlightened moments, we do want instead—the execution of an unbiased justice that validates Shylock's anger as well as Antonio's right to live despite that anger—is not going to happen. Such a resolution of conflict is the stuff of fantasy, not *The Merchant of Venice*. In fact, if Portia is going to rescue Antonio, she will not—cannot—succeed completely through reconciling him to Shylock. She must resort to hard choices, choices that effectively exclude Shylock, empowering Antonio and his peers to run roughshod over Shylock's feelings of betrayal and desertion and involving Portia's final treatment of the Jew as the "alien" to whom she finally, explicitly, gives the name (349). Many of Portia's statements in 4.1 are capable of being read as judiciously inclusive of Shylock's sentiments; some of those statements may well contradict that ostensible meaning beneath their outward show.

Why Portia must make decisions that exclude and then even misrepresent some of Shylock's identity is the crucial question. Without doubt, she is compelled to her behavior partly by the peculiar weaknesses of her character that have surfaced earlier. To go from despising "all" of Morroco's "complexion" to manipulating Shylock on grounds that he is an "alien" is a fairly small move (2.7.79, 4.1.349). Moreover, Portia's objectivity toward Shylock is surely challenged by the dynamic she witnesses firsthand between Antonio and Bassanio, who needs little coaxing to switch his devotion from his wife to his friend:

> Antonio, I am married to a wife
> Which is as dear to me as life itself,
> But life itself, my wife, and all the world,
> Are not with me esteem'd above thy life.
> I would lose all, ay, sacrifice them all
> Here to this devil, to deliver you.
>
> (282–87)

Not only has Bassanio adopted Antonio's self-sacrificial stance, but he has also absorbed from Antonio the religious language of love—as in "deliver" (257)—that marks the very removal from this world and its stringent responsibilities that have brought Portia to court in the first place. Here Shakespeare seems deliberately to confound Portia's identities as both judge and wife, demonstrating how lightly the rules of either marriage or of civilization can be abandoned once they prove challenging, as they inevitably and quickly do. Bassanio would just as soon "[w]rest once the law" and "sacrifice" his material life than accept what he cannot change (215, 286). Such far-reaching denial exerts no little stress on Portia's judgment, both private and public. Something has to give or go, lest even the mere semblance of domestic and social order evaporate. That something is Shylock's personality.

Portia's capacity for resolving the controversy at all, given its magnitude, thus deserves admiration. But neither will the attentive audience be able to ignore the abundant details of the scene that tarnish the vision of Portia as custodian of law and marriage alike, because during the trial she is revealed to have compromised standards that, as a judge, she purports to defend. When Shylock denounces morally flaccid "Christian husbands" in an aside, for instance, he briefly transports us to a small but valid arena of dissent against Portia's values (295–97). He fleetingly displays how she has gone to all of this trouble for a man who will disappoint her. At moments like these, Shylock's authority weighs in equal to, if not greater than, his opponents'. Hence, when he is later defeated altogether by Portia's trick and then stripped of legal rights as an "alien," the audience perforce senses grievous loss. Venice preserved means Shylock dismissed.

Such is Shakespeare's strategy for characterizing Portia's mixed triumph in 4.1. Refusing to retreat from Shylock's savagery, as Antonio and Bassanio are wont to do, she proceeds to make good on her theatrical portrayal of a judge to a point. That point lies somewhere beyond fulfilling only her private agenda and yet falls short of accommodating the public good, in the widest sense. She may slip across that point here and there throughout the trial, but she plants herself there solidly when she dredges up "yet another hold" of the law on Shylock (347), whereupon, in Lyon's words, her perseverance at the "ceremonial formalities of the trial to the end" and her "humiliating denial of Shylock's dignity" exhibit a certain "sadism."[37] Beyond that point, then, her pose as judge is empty affectation. Yet Shakespeare enlarges on the issue of what motivates Portia's actions in the trial and of how to assess her actions with a second strategy: by implicitly comparing and contrasting them with Antonio's judgments on Shylock. The overall outcome of this additional strategy, overlayering the other, is to enhance the positive perspective on Portia's performance as arbiter. To watch the duke and Antonio follow Portia in delivering verdicts is to be reminded of the perils that confound not just Portia but anyone who presumes to pass judgment. In this context, relative to her rival Antonio, Portia seems unusually bold and competent.

Still, confusion of tone dominates as Antonio assumes judicial power. That Portia should relay it to Antonio in quite the way she does, for example, underscores her sacrifice of justice for expediency's sake: by handing over formal, legitimate control to Antonio, she seems to license Shylock's elimination from Venetian society by the very man who has most despised him. If so, she has dispensed with justice. Since Shakespeare is making up his own Venetian law to suit his purposes, he could have seen to it that Portia was legally bound to collaborate with Antonio, rather than surrender her judicial office to him; he could have written the scene so that Portia was interjecting obviously fair, friendly advice to help shape Antonio's judgments. Instead, he leaves Antonio solely to his own devices and, through Portia's acquiescence to Antonio's sentences on Shylock, portrays her as sanctioning them. Perhaps Shakespeare is generously creating the chance for Antonio to display how much he has learned about kindness through his own suffering, as Holmer and others have argued.[38] At the same time, however, Shakespeare exposes Portia to greater disapproval from her audience than she has already elicited, should that audience recoil from Antonio's responses to Shylock. It probably does.

As for those responses, neither are they clear-cut; they are not unabashedly steeped in the loathing that Antonio formerly paid Shylock or that Shylock has been directing at Antonio. For starters, that Antonio is willing to take an active step of any kind toward Shylock testifies to his renewed spiritual health; even his honest expression of spite would be preferable to utter passivity, since it would plant Antonio firmly in the world that threatens him and perhaps inaugurate a life-altering introspection. Yet the privilege over Shylock that Portia has surrendered to Antonio is absolute, in that Shylock is suddenly and thoroughly in Antonio's debt, under his control. Such conditions do not make for a true test of Antonio's moral growth any more than they justify whatever ruling he settles on Shylock, since he is now free of imperative to treat Shylock humanely. This lack of constraint coats any apparent kindness on Antonio's part with a sheen of magnanimity, as though he "droppeth" mercy "as the gentle rain from heaven / Upon the place beneath" (4.1.185–86). But for all we know, Antonio may again be feigning charity; if Shylock were at liberty to rebel against his pronouncements, Antonio might once again shrink from, rather than deal with, a challenge to his professed kindness. In truth, Antonio is taking no risk in judging Shylock, unless it be that of garnering his peers' disapproval. And since Gratiano is already being the boor, nearly anything Antonio says will seem enlightened by contrast. The only real pressure on Antonio is to keep up appearances, conforming outwardly to the rules of civilized conduct that Gratiano has, conveniently, already blurred through transgressing them himself.

Not surprisingly, then, the substance of Antonio's response to Shylock is enwrapped in equivocation:

So please my lord the Duke and all the court
To quit the fine for one half of his goods,
I am content; so he will let me have
The other half in use, to render it
Upon his death unto the gentleman
That lately stole his daughter.
Two things provided more, that for this favor
He presently become a Christian;
The other, that he do record a gift,
Here in the court, of all he dies possess'd
Unto his son Lorenzo and his daughter.

(380–90)

In fact, the very concept of halving that Antonio takes from the law on which he is putting his personal stamp suggests doubleness about his verdict. On the one hand, he hastens to meet Shylock in the middle, as though he can now see his way clear to settling his differences with his enemy by turning the other cheek. Specifically, in as much as he petitions the duke to dismiss Shylock's debt to the state of half of his wealth (380–82), Antonio opens on a note of liberality. He does not have to make this request for Shylock but, by doing so anyway, seems to favor charity over any private vendetta he may harbor. He further cancels his self-interest by turning his attention to Jessica and Lorenzo, for whom he proposes a trust founded on the other half of Shylock's estate (382–85).

Presumably, then, he intends for everyone to win: Shylock will lose little during his lifetime, since he will be sustained by half his fortune and earnings from the other half, and Jessica and Lorenzo will ultimately inherit all (388–90), including the half that Antonio, apparently, assumes he can manage to their financial benefit, despite his own recently problematic investments. This insistence on Shylock's charity not just to his flesh and blood but also to his son-in-law, is of a piece with Antonio's ultimatum that Shylock convert to Christianity (386–87). Both provisions (to borrow Antonio's word in line 386) can be interpreted as newfound broad-mindedness, a genuine attempt on Antonio's part to bridge the gulf that separates him from Shylock. Nothing about Antonio's speech invites this reading more than his choice of the word *use* to define the trust he means to establish for Jessica and Lorenzo (383). By selecting, rather than disparaging, the single word that most identifies Shylock as "alien," he would seem to be supplanting his former vituperation and rejection of Shylock's person and financial practices with a new acceptance. His diction may well indicate both forgiveness and sympathy.

On the other hand, even while Antonio employs the word, he also redefines it, much as he seeks, in effect, to recreate everything about

Shylock in his own image, even if doing so entails forcible baptism. To take control over half of Shylock's investments and to demand his religious conversion is to halt his usury altogether and to coerce his conformity with the rest of Venetian society. From this angle, Antonio's conditions for Shylock are not liberal, liberated, or liberating. They are suffocating. They step up Portia's approach to treating Shylock as an "alien" by prohibiting even that meager distinction, which, though not much, is at least Shylock's proper. Withholding even so much as alienation from Shylock, he doubly alienates him; exacting his own figurative pound of flesh, Antonio pushes Shylock into a culture where full participation is, as we have seen, a mixed blessing. Nor does Antonio's vision of Shylock's future at all obligate the existing society to include the newly converted Jew: as Antonio snidely reminds Shylock, Lorenzo "stole" his daughter (385); now he is going to be rewarded for it with everything Shylock can earn until he dies. Some incentive.

In this light, Antonio has not grown in understanding.[39] Were he truly merciful to Shylock, as the whole dramatic situation is set up here to imply he is, he would simply be merciful without meddling in Shylock's personhood. His penchant for doing so, however, recalls his attitude toward Bassanio, to whom he promises unconditional love that, in reality, involves plenty of urgent provisos. In 4.1, as well, Antonio places conditions on his "favor" toward Shylock (386), conditions so restrictive as to bind the other party in virtually total obligation to his terms. Once released from his bond to Shylock and given the chance to act freely, he even takes it upon himself to advise and manipulate the duke's decision about the half of Shylock's goods that are forfeit to the state. Portia has just told the court in no uncertain terms that the half in question is properly "for the state, not for Antonio," although "humbleness" on Shylock's part may induce the duke to lower such a large sum to only a "fine" (373, 372, 371). As though deaf, Antonio immediately presumes to address his first statement not to his own business but to whether the duke should collect all that the state is owed or just the fine (380–82); furthermore, he makes his next judgment, which does concern himself (382–85), contingent upon the duke's enactment of his opening request: thus, between lines 380 and 385 he tells the duke, in so many words, "Please reduce what Shylock owes the state so long as I am permitted to do what I wish with what he owes me." Subtly but surely, Antonio has interposed himself again where he might take over, whether or not he belongs there.

Such bids for control suggest that, even now, Antonio remains subject to his fears of exclusion. He seems threatened, rushing to alienate Shylock first, as if doing so will preclude his own dispossession. In a matter of minutes, he has pivoted from dealing with the world through emotional paralysis and death-wish to reentering the hardships and confusions of this life by stage-managing. Calm as he may outwardly seem in this scene, his inner panic would appear to endure as he dictates once again how Bassanio should demonstrate his love for his friend: "My Lord Bassanio, let [Balthazar] have the ring. / Let his deservings and my love withal / Be valued 'gainst your wive's commandement" (4.1.449–51).

Thus, a definable pattern in Antonio's characterization from beginning to end comes into focus. His eleven lines about Shylock in 4.1 go by quickly and are overly dense for a first-time audience to grasp fully, but, studied carefully, they, too, substantiate his determination to direct the play's events or to die trying. The theatrical metaphor with which he describes himself in 1.1 has become completely apt by the end of 4.1. Whether Antonio is behaving submissively or asserting himself, he is often practicing some form of passive aggression. The only occasion on which he displays his antagonism outright is in 1.3, and even there it is second-hand, glimpsed through the window of Shylock's narration and affirmed by Antonio himself, who almost, but not quite, loses his temper (106–31). Ordinarily, he is not given to confessing his feelings openly, a habit behind his hypocrisies, like professing love for Bassanio, whose wife he discounts. For his lingering social awkwardness, Antonio is pitiable. But for resorting to misleading emotional and moral theatrics, which are nothing akin to the wise folly he pretends, he verges on abusiveness. In his foolish consistency, he is, at least potentially, as dangerous to social cohesiveness as are large rocks to argosies. Here, too, he is an unrecognized version of Shylock, who differs mainly in that he wears his anger on his sleeve.

If Portia both shares in and countenances Antonio's hypocrisy toward Shylock, she does not abide it toward her marriage. Through appending the substance of act 5 to the action of the trial, Shakespeare fleshes out just how much more competent in judgment has been Portia than we may have thought or than Antonio has proved to be. She accomplishes with the ring trick far more nearly the reconciliation of opposites that also occupied her in the trial. Earlier, her choice resulted in the almost tacit exile of Shylock's variety, albeit menace, from the Venetian order. In act 5, where she forms the triple bond among herself, Bassanio, and Antonio, she comes closer to harmonizing antinomies—here, those of marital love and male friendship.[40] The most prominent feature of Portia's judgments, however, as well as all instances of choice in *Merchant*, is their relative failure or success. No single judgment is completely satisfactory. Some are simply more satisfying than others.

V

The whole of act 5 is informed by the notion of relativism. Introduced as it is by the rhapsody between Jessica and Lorenzo (1–24), the scene is designed to subvert confidence in the image of an ideal world or ideal love within it. The tragic note sounded by each reference to mythical lovers—Troilus and Cressida, Pyramis and Thisby, Dido and Aeneas, Medea and Jason—resonates with the misunderstanding that has plagued the characters' relationships prior to this point, as well as with the distrust sown by Antonio between Bassanio and Portia. Much as the sweetness in the rhapsody is qualified, but not subsumed, by the bitter, so is the ensuing music (68), symbolic of universal harmony, tempered by Portia's remark that Lorenzo recognizes her "as the blind man knows the cuckoo, / By the bad voice!" (112–13). Her self-effacing humor, while not thoroughly at odds with Lorenzo's more grandiose references to "the poet," "Orpheus," and the power of music to raise human nature (79–82), nevertheless introduces a realistic element of flawed human nature into Lorenzo's more philosophic (and naive) meditations.

Portia herself values the idealism and romanticism about Lorenzo's vision, if for no other reason than that it supplies a fixed standard of judgment and a goal for human ambition:

> A substitute shines brightly as a king
> Until a king be by, and then his state
> Empties itself, as doth an inland brook
> Into the main of waters. . . .
> Nothing is good, I see, without respect.
>
> (94–97, 99)

Even so, Portia expresses keen awareness that human action is destined to fall short of the ideal. The perspective that she brings to the scene's idealism, a perspective "season'd" by her recent experiences, repeatedly adds an antiromantic, slightly deflating dimension to the higher-flown diction and sentiments of the characters in her midst (107). The moon seems to the less experienced Jessica and Lorenzo to light the sky as though setting the stage for love. To Portia, however, this night, which is "such a night" to the others, seems hardly extraordinary: "This night methinks is but the daylight sick, / It looks a little paler. 'Tis a day, / Such as the day is when the sun is hid" (124–26). Same night, different impressions.

The difference, moreover, amounts to much. Most important, it characterizes Portia as one who can accept imperfections not by ignoring hobgoblins but by flexing standards just enough to make them attainable.

For Bassanio, her attitude means a mild chastening and the forgiveness that yields a second chance (199–255). For Antonio, it also means another chance but not a chance to interfere again in her marriage. When Antonio admits, "I am the unhappy subject of these quarrels," Portia does not disagree but lends him hospitality despite his error: "Sir, grieve not you, you are welcome notwithstanding" (239). Portia's graciousness and grace expand further, as far as they will go, while she witnesses Antonio rebind himself in friendship to Bassanio, this time spiritually instead of physically but, more to the point, to safeguard, not spoil, the marriage (249–53).

This is something of a breakthrough for Antonio, since his pledge to uphold Portia's faith in Bassanio requires his own acceptance of imperfection and, at that, a difficult form of imperfection for him to tolerate: his desire to be included is only partly realized, and his dread of being left out thus only partly allayed. Yet the necessary consequence of Portia and Bassanio's choice to wed is Antonio's loss of status. Although not rejected, he must remain second in Bassanio's regard. As if to represent the compromise at hand, Portia announces (through what agency, who knows?) that three of Antonio's original six argosies have come to port (275–79).[41]

In his last line, Antonio would seem to be commemorating not only his final ostracism from the social bonds that continuously elude him but also, for once, his unwillingness to indulge in play-acting: "I am dumb" (279). Not even a sixteenth-century audience, for whom that word had yet to connote witlessness, could be expected to hear the line without a shudder or an uncomfortable laugh. Owing to his peculiar personality and to the conditions urged on him by Portia, Antonio is still somewhat alienated. His situation, like his muteness, is embarrassing. And yet his silence, recalling the harsh choice yoked upon the resigned Shylock in 4.1, also betokens Antonio's moment of greatest happiness and fulfillment. Settling for what he has been given without another word, he finally becomes a wise fool—dumb and dumbfounded, content with his place in a world whose vastness cannot be overestimated and, when it cannot be controlled, must evoke awe. Paradoxically, Antonio now seems more at ease with his alienation.

What Portia's acceptance of such human limitation means for her is the luxury of sleeping at night without an "unquiet soul" (3.2.306). Whether she planned all along to dispose swiftly of Shylock toward expediting the retrieval of her marriage or whether she did her best and still failed to cajole Shylock out of his destructive humour, Portia never looks back. Many of us, of course, do. The aftertaste of gall is the play's most potent reminder to the audience of the fact of choice and all that it intimates—our lost opportunities and our misgivings that the wrong history is being made, inexorably, against our wishes. Perhaps, ideally, Portia could and should have refrained from conspiring to alienate Shylock. Yet she, too, is ultimately an alien, held hostage by a mutable world and the submission of her judgments to fickle standards. If she undertook another judgment in act 6, she might go on evolving, never fully reaching the "right praise and true perfection" that she herself envisions as the crown of experience (5.1.108). Finally, I do not quite think, as Lyon contends, that *Merchant* portrays "different" and incompatible Portias.[42] Rather, the play seems to me to record fictionally, though impressively realistically, a segment of time during which a capable young woman, in contrast to her foil Antonio, makes repeated, active forays into the distressing territory of judgment and, by fits and starts, becomes a bit better at an essentially impossible task. With every trial of her skills, she sees more clearly and speaks more frankly.

To censure Portia for her inadequate choices, in fact, is a form of self-disgust, unfair though understandable. *The Merchant of Venice*, a tragicomedy until the end and even after the end, assaults the audience with the inherent injustice of its own situation, so much like Portia's, in a mercurial world so much like the play's, a world that consistently makes fools of us all. By implying that apparent differences belie deep-seated likenesses, *Merchant* coaches us to think of presumed opposites as a cinch to reconcile. In the same breath, it takes back what it gives, indicating that the material, mortal world will always prove unruly, will always swerve wayward of forms like law, government, choice—even poetry and drama.

Antonio's efforts to remove himself from such frustrating contradictions or to believe his choices can evade or rise above them are, though understandable, a fruitless turn at cheating human life. That sort of arrogant callowness is the object of no little irony, as it is one last time, now in Lorenzo's response to learning of his inheritance: "Fair ladies, you drop manna in the way / Of starved people" (5.1.294–95). This unsettling line betrays the speaker as flagrantly self-absorbed, misapplying sacred terms to his own worldly needs (as has been Bassanio and Antonio's wont) and misadvertising himself as needy at all, coddled as he is at present in the lap of Portia's luxury. Lorenzo's line escapes the explicit retort that it deserves (although Portia might well wince at it). But the play isn't about to let us forget that the self-satisfied speaker is ripe for sobering, if not now, then soon. For the pattern of *Merchant* has been that of disabusing credulity and overturning such self-idealizations as Antonio's saintliness and Lorenzo's fond portrait of himself and Jessica as God's chosen. The closer Portia ventures toward acknowledging the disparity between "what were good" and what actually is, the more trust she earns from her audience and, unavoidably, the more sorrow she elicits for fading illusions. As if to ratify the abiding value of such earthiness, however, the play's last word belongs to Gratiano, who has always been most at home in the "rude world" and who concludes with a final demystification, calling a "ring" a "ring" (5.1.307). His candid reference to Nerissa's anatomy purges the air of any residual delusions about love and securely grounds spiritual faith where it is "riveted"—in the "flesh" (5.1.169).

3

"Willing love": Antonio, Viola, and Epiphany in *Twelfth Night*

Disguise in *Twelfth Night* is sheer, a thin veil like the "cypress" that, Olivia tells Viola/Cesario, "hides" her "heart" (3.1.121–22). Viola, although dressed in sturdier male clothing, almost reveals herself inadvertently at several points, as during the duel with Sir Andrew and the interviews with Olivia. Other of Shakespeare's strong, disguised women do not hover so closely on the brink of losing control: Portia commands her identity as judge, and Rosalind manipulates her boyish exterior to teach her future husband about love, only once verging on disclosing her true identity before she is ready to (4.3.156 ff.). Viola's contrasting lack of sure control over her disguise points to a major theme unique to *Twelfth Night*: that of epiphany, or the manifestation of truth. Such revelation is continually suggested in this comedy by the characters' ultimate inability to hide their true feelings and natures. The persistence of truth in coming to light parallels the manifestation of Christ and His love to the Magi at Epiphany. But before any such revelation can occur in *Twelfth Night*, many of the characters must be transformed by the Christian folly that typifies the sea captain Antonio.

This particular Antonio reopens the inquiry, begun in *The Merchant of Venice*, into the relationship between otherworldly ideals and the real constraints of this world. More specifically, as in *Merchant*, the issue here is the quality of love. Can Christian self-sacrifice, such as that foreshadowed at Epiphany, actually take root in human beings, who are prone to selfishness? How closely can romantic love, sanctified by the holy "ceremony" of marriage, approach divine love (5.1.160)?

At the same time, Shakespeare's second Antonio is far removed from his predecessor in *Merchant*, chiefly by virtue of the purity of his love.

While the earlier Antonio's feelings for Bassanio are colored by his own needs, the love that the later Antonio expresses for Sebastian may well be the most selfless Shakespeare ever envisioned. The possibility that such love may influence the practical workings of this life is greater in *Twelfth Night* than it would seem in *Merchant.* Indeed, where the merchant Antonio capitulates to the Venetian laws of commerce that he rationalizes as just (3.3.26–31), the sea captain defies Illyria's policies of trade, proclaiming them unjust (3.3.30–37, 5.1.72–76); where the former Antonio constantly shrinks from engagement in the affairs of this world, the latter cannot resist them, risking his well-being for Sebastian's companionship (2.1.45–48). Surely this activity, versus the earlier Antonio's passivity, bodes more harmony here than in *Merchant* between "what were good to do" and what good intentions can actually accomplish (*Merchant* 1.2.12–13).

Antonio's history in *Twelfth Night*, however, remains far from straightforward. Teasing out its subtleties confirms that, though problematic, his character, action, and values compose the play's moral center, at once eclipsing and providing a measure for the conduct of other characters. Even when he is offstage, his standard remains, his "willing love" presiding as the play's genius (2.3.11). Although criticism of *Twelfth Night* has traditionally (and almost without exception) placed Viola at the core of the play's moral vision, for most of the play she is not. Rather, she is the play's central interest, flanked by contrasting examples of Pauline wise folly in Antonio and Feste and with much to learn over the play's course about loving Orsino and others. In fact, Viola's stubborn grip on her disguise, which is naturally inclined to fall away, runs counter to the patterns of epiphany that dominate *Twelfth Night.*

I

Few critics of *Twelfth Night* have readily acknowledged its allusions to Christian Epiphany, apparently agreeing with Pepys' comment that it is "but a silly play, and not related at all to the name or day."[1] More recently, Anne Barton, introducing *Twelfth Night* in *The Riverside Shakespeare*, maintains that the title refers not to holy Epiphany but to

> images of Epiphany as it was kept in [Shakespeare's] own time: a period of holiday abandon in which the normal rules and order of life were suspended or else deliberately inverted, in which serious issues and events mingled perplexingly with revelry and apparent madness.[2]

Barton denies the existence of any "specific references to the Feast of the Epiphany" in the play (403), as do even the critics who see *Twelfth Night* in clearly Christian terms.

Yet the play's critical history in fact yields some scattered attempts to read it as an extended allusion to Christian Epiphany. The first and best known of such readings is that of Barbara K. Lewalski, who argues that

> Shakespeare's method resembles, and was probably formed by, . . . the tradition of Christian typology, whereby certain real historical events and personages from the Old Testament and (more significantly for the present purposes) from certain classical fictions such as the *Metamorphoses* or the *Aeneid* were seen to point to aspects of Christ and of the Gospel story without losing their own historical or fictional reality.[3]

John Hollander broadens the notion of allegory that Lewalski explains here when he notices the connection in *Twelfth Night* between revelation in general and the spirit of holy Epiphany:

> *Twelfth Night* itself, the feast of the Epiphany, celebrates the discovery of the "True King" in the manger by the Wise Men. . . . The whole of Act V might be taken, in connection with "the plot" in a trivial sense, to be the other *epiphany*, the perception that follows the *anagnorisis* or discovery of classic dramaturgy. . . . The long final scene . . . serves to show forth the Caesario-King, and to unmask, discover, and reveal the fulfilled selves in the major characters.[4]

Hollander's reference to "the other *epiphany*" summons not only Aristotle but James Joyce. Of course, Joyce's more general, yet still Christian, use of the word postdates Shakespeare by centuries. But long before Joyce redefined it, churchmen appear to have used *epiphany* in the slightly more general sense of "a manifestation or appearance of some divine or superhuman being." As early as 1667, Jeremy Taylor mentions in a sermon Christ's "glorious epiphany on the mount."[5] Thus, in the later seventeenth century, the term did not pertain strictly to the manifestation of Christ to the Magi; that Taylor used the more general meaning of epiphany in a sermon implies his congregation's familiarity with—or at least their easy adaptability to—that meaning. Although *Twelfth Night* predates Taylor's sermon by over sixty years, I do not doubt that Shakespeare's audience was equally capable of imaginatively relating the biblical Epiphany to other kinds of divine revelation, or even to revelation of truth in general. Certainly Shakespeare's imagination was up to such obvious leaps.

Ultimately, even the revelation of the characters' true identities—whether lurking, as in Viola's case, behind disguise or, as in Orsino's, behind pride and self-love—comes down to the manifestation by those characters of a Christ-like, self-sacrificial love. Paradoxically, such an epiphany transforms the lead characters even as it unveils their natural capacity for liberality of spirit: it transforms in that it removes the obstacles to selfless love. The most pervasive of those obstacles in *Twelfth Night* is rationality—more specifically, reason used for self-control and as a defense against both passion and rejection. Malvolio's lack of generosity, for which Olivia scolds him within moments of his first appearance on stage, epitomizes this barrier to love: "O, you are sick of self-love, Malvolio, and taste with a distemper'd appetite. To be generous, guiltless, and of free disposition, is to take those things for bird-bolts that you deem cannon-bullets" (1.5.90–93). But Malvolio's jealous "distemper" is not unique to him; it merely exaggerates several other characters' emotional inhibitions.

To give up that control is not only to succumb to the "very midsummer madness" that Malvolio is enticed to flirt with (3.4.56) but also to enact, in a manner, Christ's passion, the ultimate madness. How could any choice appear more foolish than Christ's willingness to die, although Himself guiltless, for the sins of others? Even others whom He does not know? Even future generations whom He has yet to meet? Indeed, Christ's self-sacrifice through the Crucifixion provides, in Pauline terms, the most radical of bases for wise folly. It requires the most essential rejection of "the wisdome of this world" in exchange for "foolishnesse with God." It is not, then, necessarily or completely opposed to the carnivalesque or to suggestions of popular, secular Twelfth Night celebrations in the play, since Christ's way represents the ultimate inversion of everyday order. Moreover, the "will" of the title, which connotes sexual desire, need not exclude nonsexual passion. The escape from restraints to love in *Twelfth Night* involves a reckless abandon of both body and spirit that imitates Christ's heedlessness toward His own danger, as in Olivia's closing lines to act 1: "I do I know not what" (1.5.308). When used in the service of debunking pride, irrationality, as in Pauline tradition, is here the mark of loving well, whether spiritually or romantically.[6]

I am arguing, then, against a strictly allegorical reading of the play's religious aspects. As Chris Hassel has demonstrated amply, *Twelfth Night* is, despite Pepys' misgivings, a Christmas play rich in suggestions of Epiphany and of Candlemas—references, for instance, to light and emphases on humility and purification.[7] Yet to subdue all of the play's elements to purely religious readings is, I think, a mistake.[8] *Twelfth Night* is, in the main, a secular play about human relationships. Allusions to Christian Epiphany function as embedded yet translucent metaphor, offering a paradigm for romantic love to imitate—or perhaps, at best, approximate. Allusions to human limitations intermingle everywhere with those to the perfectability of human love, constantly questioning whether Feste's description of virtue as "but patch'd with sin" is the best that can be said of the human heart.

II

If any figure in *Twelfth Night* calls Christ to mind, it is Antonio, whom Viola, however innocently, "den[ies]" (3.4.347). The language that Antonio speaks, as well as that which surrounds him, continually implies Christianity. He expresses his love for Sebastian in extravagant, almost unearthly terms: "If you will not murther me for my love, let me be your servant" (2.1.35–36). Later, he uses the language of religious service:

> This youth that you see here
> I snatch'd one half out of the jaws of death,
> Reliev'd him with such sanctity of love,
> And to his image, which methought did promise
> Most venerable worth, did I devotion.
>
> (3.4.359–63)

Lest this language be mistaken for the overstatement of courtly love, it should be studied further. In the act of rescuing Viola/Cesario, Antonio substitutes himself for the alleged criminal: "If this young gentleman / Have done offense, I take the fault on me; / If you offend him, I for him defy you" (3.4.312–14). He soothes Viola/Cesario in the thick of his own misfortune: "be of comfort" (3.4.338). He has "redeem[ed]" Sebastian from the tempest: "His life I gave him, and did thereto add / My love, without retention or restraint, / All his in dedication" (5.1.79, 80–82). No, Antonio's use of religious language strongly suggests that he is returning these much-abused terms to their original meaning: his actions actually bear out his description of his love. His is total sacrifice, which prompts him, completely irrationally, to give Sebastian his entire purse in case Sebastian fancies "some toy" (3.3.44). Moreover, Antonio is even more endangered than Viola by walking the streets, yet his great love induces him to expose himself boldly, undisguised and vulnerable (5.1.82–85).

Shakespeare has painstakingly developed and set off this character who in the main source of the play is hardly attractive or essential to the plot. Barnaby Riche's captain forces himself on Silla, compelling her to assume a disguise for her safety.[9] Shakespeare's departures here are considerable. Antonio is the antithesis of Riche's captain, and Viola chooses to disguise herself for vaguer reasons than Silla's, reasons seemingly more psychologically than physically threatening. Furthermore, Riche's story has only one captain, while Shakespeare's includes two. Shakespeare's replacement of the second captain for Silla's faithful servant Pedro suggests a desire to thrust attention on Antonio: the unnamed captain who initially helps Viola and who finally must be released from prison periodically echoes, and thus reinforces, Antonio's history.[10] Antonio's role as a Christ-like giver of love becomes clearer yet when Riche's moral is contrasted with the fuller treatment of love in *Twelfth Night.* Riche writes of well-deserved love. But what distinguishes Antonio's love for Sebastian is precisely that it is unearned.

Why indeed does Antonio shower his worldly possessions and physical protectiveness on Sebastian but that he fancies him? Whether the nature of that fancy is specifically homoerotic—a question that is both worthwhile to ask and difficult to answer—it is also, significantly, without clear reason and yet centered thoroughly on Sebastian's welfare.[11] It is, to adapt Orsino's phrase to this context, "foolish boldness" (5.1.70). Moreover, it is implicitly contrasted with Orsino's initial "fancy" (1.1.14)—a word that recurs throughout the play. As nearly all critics of the play observe, the object of Orsino's affection is not really Olivia but itself. Here again, Antonio's active social engagement is to the point. He neglects his own safety to enter Illyria, where he can enjoy and defend Sebastian; Orsino, resembling the Antonio in *Merchant* more than does *Twelfth Night*'s Antonio, longs for solitude (for example, 1.4.36–38), uses the language of love to admire his own cleverness and pain (as in 1.1), and would probably swoon in fright if Olivia actually took him up on his proffered love. Antonio's "fancy," by contrast, is pure sympathetic imagination; he looks beyond his desire into the needs and desires of others. His "willing love," knowing no boundaries or barriers, leads him to jeopardize his own welfare because he fears for Sebastian's safety (2.3.11–13). In this regard, Antonio is a "servant" in far more than a limited and worldly sense (2.1.35–36). He ministers to Sebastian spiritually, as Sebastian himself implies when he craves Antonio's advice toward Olivia's passion for him: "His counsel now might do me golden service" (4.3.8).[12]

For all of his affiliation with Christ, however, Antonio is not to be taken as Christ. His humanity is salient, especially when he expects something in return for his generosity toward Sebastian, even growing angry when Viola/Cesario refuses him (3.4.340–63). When he feels rejected, he resorts to material possessiveness and hurt feelings to lash out at Sebastian:

his false cunning
(Not meaning to partake with me in danger)
Taught him to face me out of his acquaintance,
And grew a twenty years removed thing
While one would wink; denied me mine own purse,
Which I had recommended to his use
Not half an hour before.

(5.1.86–92)

Although in a moment like this one Antonio may fleetingly resemble the more emotionally insecure Antonio in *Merchant,* I do not believe that the effect here is ultimately to ridicule Antonio's charity or to portray it as insincere. Rather, I think it is to portray this Antonio as the best that a universally flawed humanity has to offer. If he breaks down when the supposed Sebastian does not return his affection or his purse, he and he alone initially gives up all. If, in Antonio, divine love—love that strips down barriers—is imperfectly reflected, it is reflected nevertheless. Truly the twins' savior, though savior in a necessarily limited sense, he embodies the play's highest ideal without being allegorical, without loss of realism and believability.[13]

If this Antonio were going to be able to convey high-minded ideas without irony and yet still give Orsino cause to arrest him, then his crime would have to be handled delicately, if not ambiguously. I believe this is why mystery abounds in our knowledge of Antonio's past. Whereas several critics have called him a "pirate," as does Orsino (5.1.69), Antonio respectfully denies that identity:

Orsino, noble sir,
Be pleas'd that I shake off these names you give me.
Antonio never yet was thief or pirate,
Though I confess, on base and ground enough,
Orsino's enemy.

(5.1.72–76)

These lines may make Antonio appear the victim of a false arrest, but in truth the presentation of conflict between Antonio and Orsino never allows us to take sides. Whenever either man advances his case against the other, each appears believable and principled. For example, Antonio implies that his quarrel with Orsino has been a matter of conscience, a struggle for justice:

Seb. Belike you slew great number of his [Orsino's] people?

> *Ant.* Th' offense is not of such a bloody nature,
> Albeit the quality of the time and quarrel
> Might well have given us bloody argument.
> It might have since been answer'd in repaying
> What we took from them, which for traffic's sake
> Most of our city did. Only myself stood out,
> For which if I be lapsed in this place
> I shall pay dear.
>
> (3.3.29–37)

Antonio alone, by his own account, is unwilling to compromise his standards "for traffic's sake," as his fellow citizens have done. On the other hand, Orsino's charge of "piracy" against Antonio suggests that the captain has "stood out" against the duke for selfish gain (35). Similarly, the duke's officer indicates that the fight between Antonio and Orsino has been bloody, although Antonio maintains that the conflict never came to bloodshed (30–32, quoted directly above). Even the name of Orsino's nephew, for whose lost leg Orsino blames Antonio (5.1.63), remains ambiguous. Does Titus suggest the pagan slaughterer or Paul's friend? If the first instance were true, we would favor Antonio for subduing a menace; if we believed the second, Orsino would seem nobler, and Antonio would appear a vicious slayer of innocence. As if to compound the problem of judging ethically between these two men, Orsino himself begrudgingly commends Antonio's bravery in the face of great danger:

> A baubling vessel was he captain of,
> For shallow draught and bulk unprizable,
> With which such scathful grapple did he make
> With the most noble bottom of our fleet,
> That very envy, and the tongue of loss,
> Cried fame and honor on him.
>
> (5.1.54–59)

This sustained tension between the claims of Antonio and those of Orsino appears deliberate indeed. If nothing else, it exonerates Antonio from culpability enough to win him the audience's esteem and does so without seriously damaging our opinion of Orsino, whom we must also finally respect. Thus, Antonio can serve dramatically as a model for candor and the unobstructed giving of love—for, in other words, Erasmian folly.

Appropriately, other characters in the main plot come increasingly to imitate Antonio's manner. The earliest to follow suit are Olivia and Sebastian, the latter conjuring minimal skepticism and resistance toward

Olivia's unrestrained passion for him:

> What relish is in this? How runs the stream?
> Or I am mad, or else this is a dream.
> Let fancy still my sense in Lethe steep;
> If it be thus to dream, still let me sleep!
>
> (4.1.60–63)

Sebastian's use of the word *fancy* here reverberates with Antonio's wisely whimsical, extroverted passion for Sebastian and, like Antonio's love, contrasts with Orsino's self-involved "fancy" (1.1.14). Despite the emotional risks to himself, Sebastian chooses to ignore the reasons not to follow Olivia.

Olivia herself remains ever aware of her vulnerability to humiliation: "I . . . fear to find / Mine eye too great a flatterer for my mind" (1.5.308–9). Yet she succumbs knowingly to the loss of control and self-protection that characterizes Antonio's fearlessness: "Methinks I feel this youth's perfections / With an invisible and subtle stealth / To creep in at mine eyes. Well, let it be" (1.5.296–98). Her gradual fall to wise folly is less straightforward than Sebastian's in that, as she begins to give up tokens of her wealth to Viola/Cesario, she does so as much to entrap the page emotionally as to express her affection freely, as both the ring in 1.5 and the jewelled locket attest (3.4.208). She is initially somewhat self-centered, that is—ambivalent about loving without reciprocation. Her closing line to 1.5 comically projects her conflicting desires to abandon and yet retain control: "What is decreed must be; and be this so" (311). Yet, before long, she, like Antonio and even Sebastian, is offering herself completely to another—in this case, Viola/Cesario: "What shall you ask me that I'll deny, / That honor, sav'd, may upon asking give?" (3.4.211–12).

If all the major characters in *Twelfth Night* reflected Antonio's example so readily, the play would make a simpler statement than it in fact does about the accessibility of divine love in this world. To elaborate the real difficulties of arriving at such love, however, Feste joins Antonio as the play's other wise fool, and a wise fool with a difference, more squarely situated in the Morean complexities of the Christian humanist tradition. Feste provides another perspective than Antonio's on both charity and the values of this world. That perspective, adding range to the play's exploration of charity, does much to bring Viola's characterization into focus.

III

The end of *Twelfth Night*, where Antonio is still being held captive and Feste remains at liberty to roam, reflects on the nature of true service. Antonio seemingly lacks guile to wriggle out of his shackles; he is simply enduring the consequences of his earlier openness:

> For his sake
> Did I expose myself (pure for his love)
> Into the danger of this adverse town,
> Drew to defend him when he was beset.
>
> (5.1.82–85)

As a result of his artlessness, he is prevented from practicing the wise folly that, enchained, he merely represents. Feste, by contrast, can produce a sharp sting of conscience or coax others into seeing their own folly through artful means—songs, rhymes, and riddles—that shield him from the anger that plain-speaking can incite. Feste's manipulations of both language and disguise have power to enrich his service, which, like Antonio's "pure" expression of "love," is aimed at revealing truth. More specifically and in accord with the theme of Epiphany, Feste wears down false barriers to love and to identity. He actively attempts to teach the lesson that Antonio lives through simply adoring Sebastian "without retention or restraint" (5.1.81). But leading others to such wise folly requires of Feste a willingness to compromise the high standards that drive Antonio's actions. Both characters serve the cause of wise folly, yet Feste trades Antonio's purity of heart for some practicality, thus avoiding Antonio's imprisonment. His shrewd self-protection stands either to enhance his effectiveness as a wise fool or to taint his charity with egotism. Does Feste's pragmatism finally result in more valuable service than does Antonio's relative idealism?[14]

Throughout much of the play, Feste traverses between the modes of wise folly and foolish wisdom, sometimes making them indistinguishable and other times setting off one against the foil of the other. Take, for example, the frequent confusion over his motives. In a pinch Feste will do what he must in order to save his own skin, as in his first scene, where he employs his "[w]it" to "[m]ake" his "excuse wisely" for returning late (1.5.32, 30); in the process of tending to his own needs, however, he also ministers to Olivia's, "mend[ing]" not only her anger at him but, more to the point, her grief (1.5.74). When he receives "leave" to "prove" Olivia a "fool," he shows her the true folly of excessively mourning her brother's death, which has led to his salvation (1.5.57–72). Her misguided religious devotion to her brother's memory is also implicit in Feste's affectionate and gently mocking term for her, "madonna." In the very act of escaping punishment in 1.5, Feste prepares Olivia emotionally for the subsequent wooing episode, where she becomes susceptible to Viola's charms. Here and elsewhere, Feste serves others by serving himself.

This paradox is manifest nowhere more clearly than in Feste's dealings with money, which affirm that he is at home in the world. While Antonio surrenders his entire purse to Sebastian, Feste specializes in collecting others' funds—as much as he can entice away from them. And the enticement is crucial. For Feste's chief occupation as a wise fool is precipitating generosity—self-sacrifice—in his audiences. In his own words to Orsino, whose "bounty" he is trying to "awake": "Put your grace in your pocket, sir, for this once, and let your flesh and blood obey it" (5.1.45, 32–33). To give liberally to a fool despite his failings, Feste suggests, is a form of grace. Of course, Feste enjoys and benefits from such generosity. But, as he himself indicates about his sales pitches, his "desire of having" is not simply the "sin of covetousness" (5.1.47). Feste performs for "pleasure" as well as gain—the pleasure, presumably, of delighting other people (2.4.68). He also tells Sebastian that an "open hand" to fools gives "wise men . . . a good report" (4.1.21–23), underscoring the uncanny principle that his pursuit of self-interest is a version of charity.

Yet Feste is also capable of unadulterated selfishness that is alien to the sea captain Antonio. It surfaces in Feste's pride—the pride that, Thomas More reveals, threatens to infect the Utopians because they are so highly aware of their humility.[15] As Feste protests about himself, he can be modest about his cleverness: "Those wits that think they have thee [wit] do very oft prove fools; and I that am sure I lack thee, may pass for a wise man" (1.5.33–35). At some points, however, Feste is more self-conscious of his talents than he is self-effacing. When Maria and Sir Toby express their glee at the performance of their "most exquisite Sir Topas," for example, Feste adds a little praise of himself to theirs: "Nay, I am for all waters" (4.2.63). To cite another instance, after the others have departed in the prison scene and instructed him to quit teasing Malvolio (4.2.66–67), no doubt he stays in part because he knows he can perform the virtuoso double role of himself and Sir Topas (4.2.94–101). In this case, Feste's use of wit suggests self-admiration.

In *Twelfth Night*, then, Feste is essentially a swing character whose language and action partake in both loving service and selfish pride, sometimes simultaneously, sometimes alternately. Probably the most complex character in *Twelfth Night*, he is set up to define the poles of foolish wisdom and wise folly, as Viola notes after having sparred with him:

> This fellow is wise enough to play the fool,
> And to do that well craves a kind of wit.
> He must observe their mood on whom he jests,
> The quality of persons, and the time;
> And like the haggard, check at every feather
> That comes before his eye. This is a practice
> As full of labor as a wise man's art;
> For folly that he wisely shows is fit,
> But wise men, folly-fall'n, quite taint their wit.
>
> (3.1.60–68)

Viola is specifically referring here to Feste's intellect, his keen observance and agility of mind. But she also adumbrates the two ethical categories that prevail throughout the play and between which Feste traffics: the self-absorption of true folly and the extroversion and empathy of wise folly. The former, to borrow Feste's phrase, "shines every where" (3.1.39), and the audience comes to rely on Feste to point it out, either by ridiculing it or indulging in it.[16]

With the revelers, he does some of both. Although he himself operates outside of boundaries and rules, he understands the importance of the "modest limits of order" that Maria recommends to Sir Toby (1.3.9). He carouses with Sir Toby and Sir Andrew and joins them in sneering at Malvolio's complaints about their unruliness, but during Malvolio's duping, Feste "keeps . . . from the blow of the law" by remaining aloof (3.4.153–54). When he finally participates in 4.2, he carefully protects himself with a disguise that he does not even need to conceal his identity (4.2.64–65). This caution distinguishes him from Sir Toby, Sir Andrew, and Fabian, with whom he shares a penchant for childlike folly that is potentially freeing, yet, as Feste knows, is also potentially self-destructive. Where the other revelers are reckless, careening out of control over their schemes, Feste, much as Viola describes him (3.1.62–64), remains ever alert and ready to adjust.

As a result, he evades the escalating violence of the subplot, which is intimated toward Malvolio in the asides of the revelers as early as the letter scene (2.5):

> 'Slight, I could so beat the rogue! (33)

> Pistol him, pistol him! (37)

O, for a stone bow, to hit him in the eye! (46)

Fire and brimstone! (50)

Bolts and shackles! (56)

Shall this fellow live? (62)

These and other suggestions erupt into full-blown violence later on when Sir Toby, looking for new ways to entertain himself, exploits Sir Andrew for amusement as well as money; the imminent duel he stages between Sir Andrew and Viola/Cesario backfires when Sebastian beats the dupers into the duped (3.4, 5.1.175–76). On the one hand, even such foolery, however parasitical at its origin and harmful at its conclusion, is preferable to Malvolio's sourness.[17] If only in its indifference to practical constraints, it resembles Antonio's boundless generosity, which is itself utterly opposed to Malvolio's rigidity. On the other hand, the revelers' antics, if unchecked, are perilous and increasingly self-centered, like Malvolio's self-indulgent fantasies. Fabian's very name, deriving as it does from the late-sixteenth-century term "flaunting Fabian" and meaning "a careless fellow" or an "vnthrift," conjures both the wise and foolish folly implicit in the revelers' carefree but careless action.[18] Feste cannily removes himself from the danger it threatens, as does his cohort Maria, who remains offstage whenever physical harm may occur and engages only in the psychological aspects of Malvolio's duping—writing the letter for 2.5, pretending that Malvolio is possessed (3.4), and looking on while Feste further manipulates Malvolio in the prison scene (4.2). Maria and Feste, whose verbal adroitness suggests their tight self-control, manage to indulge in sport but to lie low when play turns to earnest. Contrary to Viola/Cesario's facile assumption that Feste is a "merry fellow, and car'st for nothing," the clown is deeply apprehensive about being made a true fool (3.1.26–27).

Yet Feste commits himself to nothing more avidly than to exposing Malvolio's foolish wisdom, and it is in this connection that his capacities for both kindness and cruelty are most obvious. Oddly, although Feste and Malvolio could hardly be more disparate temperamentally than they seem to be, the clown's rigorous attention to the details of language, societal norms, and individual personalities is not altogether unlike Malvolio's strict observance of the rules of order in Olivia's household. Woefully less astute than Feste, Malvolio nevertheless values the "respect of place, persons, [and] time" that, Viola attests, preoccupy Feste: "He must observe their mood on whom he jests, / The quality of persons, and the time" (2.3.91–92, 3.1.62–63). Furthermore, both take pride in their accomplishments. Granted that Malvolio's self-love is pride in the extreme, Feste, as we have seen, is not above accepting recompense and praise for his labors; nor does he like to lose control or face. And granted that Feste, like the rest of us, simply enjoys seeing a wise man like Malvolio "folly-fall'n," his involvement in the comeuppance is not purely impersonal (3.1.68).

In fact, Malvolio, more than any other character, plays on Feste's ego and arouses his pride; he brings out the worst in Feste, exacerbating the clown's own defensiveness. From their first interaction, Feste and Malvolio are obviously in competition for Olivia's favor and approval (1.5.73–98). In addition, the audience learns at the very last (and learns from Feste's own mouth) that he has been driven to gull Malvolio out of wounded pride:

> But do you remember? "Madam, why laugh you at such a barren rascal? And you smile not, he's gagg'd." And thus the whirligig of time brings in his revenges. (5.1.374–77)

Feste's memory is long and exact, harking back to an insult in 1.5 that is too petty to escape Olivia's criticism (90–96) but not Feste's sense of injury. Like Malvolio, he readily takes a "bird-bolt" for a "cannon-bullet" (93). What's more, in contrast with Antonio's hurt feelings over Sebastian's rejection, Feste's bruised ego seeks retaliation.

Significantly, Shakespeare discloses Feste's vendetta toward Malvolio well after the audience has already witnessed the entire plot unfold. One of the several results of this delay is that the audience, hardly suspecting that Feste harbors such a trivial grievance against the steward, is naturally curious to understand what he is up to as he enters so belatedly into the scheme against Malvolio. Indeed, the confusion surrounding Feste's objectives also arises in connection with all of the revelers' aims. The overall effect is that the revelers' motives and aims in the plot against Malvolio, which are themselves unclear, also blur the lines between wise folly and foolish wisdom, thus confusing the precise relationship between the subplot and the main action as to the theme of Epiphany.

At stake in the prison scene is precisely this issue of motive: are the revelers and Feste duping Malvolio more for his own good or for theirs? Both possibilities arise repeatedly as early as 2.3, where Maria, hatching the letter plot, calls her scheme first "revenge," then "physic" (153, 173). The words are opposed in respect to both motive and desired effect: "revenge" satisfies the avenger, who returns hurt for hurt, while "physic" heals—or in this case teaches—by responding to hurt with reform. The one is self-centered and destructive; the other is ultimately charitable, employing only whatever contrivance is necessary to recreate, improve, or transform. To force Malvolio through a process of self-recognition whereby he was humbled into perceiving the truth about his arrogance would be, in other words, in keeping with the spirit of Epiphany: he would both see himself revealed and be given a second chance. But to punish him without enlightening him as to his shortcomings would be merely persuading him to "[r]emain . . . in darkness" (4.2.57). Malvolio's puritanical self-righteousness most certainly calls for a response. The question is whether the response he receives includes a gram of the kindness that Antonio represents and to which Feste, in some situations, is prone.

An apparent mixture of "physic" and "revenge" continues to pervade the revelers' language about Malvolio in 3.4 as they plan to move him to prison. Sir Toby's proposal marks a turning point in the action and tone:

> Come, we'll have him in a dark room and bound. My niece is already in the belief that he's mad. We may carry it thus, for our pleasure and his penance, till our very pastime, tir'd out of breath, prompt us to have mercy on him; at which time we will bring the device to the bar. (3.4.135–40)

Before this point, the revelers' trickery can hardly be condemned: Malvolio has voluntarily donned his yellow stockings, cross-gartering, and "ridiculous boldness" with Olivia—and at the slightest provocation (3.4.37). He has been an agent of his own undoing just waiting for a reason to mock himself, and his hypocrisy is stunning: in his mind it is acceptable for him to wear gay yellow stockings in token of his love but not for anyone else to have fun. Once he becomes "bound" and blinded, however, he is no longer free to embarrass himself and perhaps, by extension, to discover his folly. Moreover, Sir Toby's twin motives for continuing the jest—"our pleasure and his penance"—may be either compatible or at odds. In any case, they suggest a tenuous balance between the contrary motives of exploiting Malvolio beyond his deserving, merely for "pastime," and of leaving him free to learn and to change—to repent.

At issue in this connection is the degree to which Malvolio may be thought to have asked for his fate at the revelers' hands. One can argue—and many have—that the physical conditions for Malvolio's imprisonment signify his state of mind, for which he himself is ultimately responsible. He is, in other words, bound by his own intolerance and blinded by his arrogance and short-sightedness.[19] In this respect the catechism that Feste administers as Sir Topas can be read as a potential first step for Malvolio out of his private "hell" (4.2.46):

Clo. What is the opinion of Pythagoras concerning wild-fowl?

Mal. That the soul of our grandam might happily inhabit a bird.

Clo. What think'st thou of his opinion?

Mal. I think nobly of the soul, and no way approve his opinion.

Clo. Fare thee well. Remain thou still in darkness. Thou shalt hold th' opinion of Pythagoras ere I will allow of thy wits, and fear to kill a woodcock lest thou dispossess the soul of thy grandam. Fare thee well.

(4.2.50–60)

In one light, the pretended curate is genuinely trying to serve Malvolio here by ministering to his fancy. The steward lacks the sympathetic imagination to believe in any but the most narrowly defined doctrine, and if he refuses to entertain the notion of Pythagorean metempsychosis, how can he possibly summon the wisely foolish faith to endorse the Christian God and afterlife? Were Malvolio to indulge in Feste's foolish play, doing so could conceivably free his understanding, eroding his fears, tempering his disposition, and conditioning him to love selflessly. Thus, Malvolio's refusal to engage in Feste's play is actually a kind of willful madness, as Feste's antic language implies (57–60). Feste's approach to Malvolio may well resemble his method with Olivia in that it reconciles his private aims—to humiliate Malvolio—with the more charitable agenda of helping Malvolio wise up. Likewise, Malvolio's ultimate lack of charity in vowing "revenge" may owe solely to himself—to his final inability to overcome his stunted emotional, psychological, and spiritual growth.

Certainly much else about Feste's demeanor during and after the prison scene suggests that he is playfully—and largely innocuously—inviting Malvolio to change his outlook. The very zaniness of his jokes and of his language defies over-seriousness. One measure of Malvolio's insufferable moroseness, in fact, is that he cannot hear the ridiculousness in Feste/Sir Topas's lines any more than he can see himself honestly. "Why, [the prison] hath bay windows transparent as barricadoes, and the clerestories toward the south north are as lustrous as ebony," jokes Feste to an unheeding, self-consumed Malvolio (4.2.36–38). In addition, no one in his right mind can hear Feste/Sir Topas exhort Malvolio to quit his "vain bibble babble" and keep a straight face (4.2.96–97). Even the clown's attempt in 5.1 to read Malvolio's letter madly defuses Malvolio's pique and modulates the audience's sympathies toward him (291–96). Feste, after all, serves as the agent of Malvolio's release from prison, as well as his tormentor therein. That he finally brings Malvolio the "light and paper and ink" that will save him and then "delivers" Malvolio is metaphorically suggestive in context: the fool, in his glorious ludicrousness, is presented as Malvolio's spiritual redeemer (4.2.117, 5.1.291).[20]

Still, the image of Feste as physician—as true "curate" (4.2.21)—is thrown off balance not only by Feste's final confession as to his motive of "revenge," but also by the outright cruelty about some of his behavior in the prison scene. Sir Toby and Maria's departure marks the beginning of Feste's malice (72). Although Sir Toby's instructions to Feste about how to conclude their "knavery" are clear, they lack any obvious concern for Malvolio's state of mind (4.2.68). If his intentions toward Malvolio ever included an element of sincere "mercy," as they earlier appeared to (3.4.139), such thoughts have been displaced by self-interest: the plot against Malvolio is now pure "sport" for Sir Toby and sport grown tiresome at that; he wants it aborted not for Malvolio's sake but for his own "convenien[ce]," lest he further displease Olivia (4.2.67–71). From Sir Toby's indifference to Malvolio follows Feste's pointed attack. The song "Hey, Robin" blatantly taunts Malvolio by seeming to confirm that, as he fears, Olivia has ordered his imprisonment; the lines "My ladie is unkind, perdie . . . Alas, why is she so?" predict Malvolio's later questions directly to Olivia: "Why have you suffer'd me to be imprison'd, /. . . Tell me why!" (75,77; 5.1.341–44). Yet the subtler torture about Feste's song is that, with every new dig, he pretends not to hear Malvolio's anxious cries to him; not until the final jab—"she loves another"—does he attend to Malvolio's distress, feigning sudden recognition of it: "—Who calls, ha?" (79). Feste's meanest stroke of all, however, is the question he apparently innocently directs at Malvolio before exiting to find him tools to write: "But tell me true, are you not mad indeed, or do you but counterfeit?" (113–14). Perhaps no one has ever escaped the fear of being rational while being believed irrational. Feste's meddling makes Malvolio's worst nightmare—and ours—come true, the nightmare of failing to convince someone of our sanity.

When Malvolio stomps onstage in 5.1, demanding of Olivia to know why she has mistreated him, he has not changed or grown in understanding, because he has been, as he protests, most "notoriously abus'd" (4.2.87–88). Olivia affirms as much by eventually echoing his phrase: "He hath been most notoriously abus'd" (5.1.379). The justification for his indignation gains further credence from the fact that he complains to Olivia in verse, a form that ennobles his feelings (5.1.328–44). Whatever responsibility for his misery Malvolio has brought to his situation—and the amount is not inconsiderable—the revelers have, through both passive negligence and active malevolence, drained a potentially instructive, even redemptive, plot of its ability to teach.[21] They have been every bit as reluctant to sympathize with Malvolio's feelings as he has been to imagine what theirs must be. Feste's primary goal of smoothing his feathers interferes with any ambition he and the others may have harbored to humble Malvolio into an equal; by brow-beating him into a "notorious geck and gull," Feste antagonizes Malvolio, coaching him, ironically, toward ever more extreme versions of his offensive behavior and prodding him to respond in kind. His approach is like trying to teach a child to behave better by denigrating him.

Fabian's kind-hearted attempt to rescue the outcome of the scheming from animosity "on both sides" is appropriate for the only reveler who has not himself been duped and yet who has also stopped short of participating in the prison scene (5.1.368). From his perspective, the "malice" of the plot has been "sportful" enough to warrant "laughter" rather than "revenge," and his appeal to everyone's good will betokens the values that Epiphany represents (365–66): he openly "confess[es]" the trickery against Malvolio and asks for tolerance (359). What Fabian does not know, however, is the intolerance that Feste has shown Malvolio and will momentarily show again. Nor can Fabian estimate, when he announces in passing that Maria and Sir Toby have married (364), how hard that news will register with Malvolio. The "whirligig of time" has whisked in Maria's revenge, too (376): she has appropriated and realized Malvolio's impossible dream of marrying up and, even more irksome, is now stationed above Malvolio in rank.[22] Small wonder that Malvolio shakes his fists and vows retribution. Penned in as he is by disdain, he has little choice but to act childishly, resorting pitifully to hollow threats.

Far from arguing that Malvolio is tragic, I am suggesting that, in the last analysis, he bears the impression of the revelers' selfish folly in his reactions to it.[23] Himself a foolish wise man in Pauline terms, he eventually displays the damage done when his egoism is met with further egoism in the pranksters' irresponsible freedom. His treatment at the hands of the disorderly revelers—Sir Toby, in particular—cannot jolt him into the self-awareness that he so desperately needs; such foolish fools do not perceive the consequences of their actions and can sustain interest only in their own concerns. Feste, however, is morally and intellectually equipped to convert Malvolio, as it were—to have positive and lasting influence on his self-knowledge. He is also inclined toward that task, much as he is inclined throughout the play to chip away at, rather than fortify, the other characters' inhibitions, poses, and obstacles to confronting their true selves. Yet, in Feste, whose name resonates with both the spirit of festival and with the festering of disease, wise folly becomes infected with the same foolish wisdom that plagues his adversary.[24] A self-proclaimed "corrupter of words," Feste suggestively describes his complex identity (3.1.36), which incorporates the imaginative expansiveness to exploit the liberating elasticity of language but also the peevishness to turn language caustic. As "quickly" as a "sentence" or a "chev'ril glove" may be turned the "wrong side . . . outward," so may Feste's distaste for pride and for attachment to the things of this world flip over in an instant to become the very pride it loathes (3.1.11–13). No sooner than Feste mentions "revenge" to Malvolio, therefore, than Malvolio volleys the word back at him, increasing the stakes: "I'll be reveng'd on the whole pack of you" (5.1.378). The cycle of exchanging injury for injury is potentially infinite. Only the unconditional love of Antonio, the apology of Fabian, or the "peace" that Orsino proposes to "entreat" of Malvolio can end it (5.1.380). Yet the play continually mistrusts that something so "golden" can stay (5.1.382).

The subplot of *Twelfth Night* explores the advantages and shortcomings of a practical, wise folly like Feste's while implying the limits of an ideal, Christlike folly like Antonio's. Although relatively little critical attention has yet been paid to the subplot, it is essential to how the play distinguishes among wise folly, foolish wisdom, and foolish folly, which often seem confounded. The subplot shades in and deepens the main plot, permitting the play to define genuine charity.[25] Ultimately, Feste's greater worldliness, relative to Antonio's ethereal passion, grants him freedom to be effective, but his "virtue . . . patch'd with sin," when ineffective, may easily degenerate into just plain sin (1.5.48–49). The main plot finds Viola wedged between these two models. Her project—marriage to Orsino—is a practical one, and yet to base a marriage on any but the highest ideals would be foolhardy. Her challenge is in part to negotiate, if not to resolve, the conflict between such ideals and real human practice.

For the greater part of the play, she imitates Feste more closely than Antonio—for instance, by wrapping herself in disguise for self-protection. But in her one prolonged exchange with Feste emerge the same drawbacks to his practical guardedness (and hers) that surface in the clown's dealings with Malvolio (3.1.1–68). Twice he belittles Viola/Cesario. The first time, when she means to compliment him by blithely remarking that he "car'st for nothing" (26–27), he insults her: "Not so, sir, I do care for something; but in my conscience, sir, I do not care for you. If that be to care for nothing, sir, I would it would make you invisible" (28–30). The next time, when he teases her about haunting Orsino's court as an underling—"I think I saw your wisdom there" (41)—she calls him on his edginess: "Nay, and thou pass upon me, I'll no more with thee" (42–43). That she nevertheless rewards him with a coin suggests both her typical generosity and his characteristic ability to draw it out.[26] Feste's sarcasm toward Viola/Cesario combines the familiar elements of charity and self-interest, while it reprises the question of just how bitter is his tone. He is no doubt astute enough to sense that Viola is not what she seems and may be hinting at his skepticism about her authenticity when he jokes, "Now Jove, in his next commodity of hair, send thee a beard!" (44–45). In effect, by reacting harshly to her false front, he may be resisting what is stifling both her identity and thus her expression of her feelings, urging her, whether or not deliberately, to stop pretending and to be herself. Then again, Feste's testiness may owe more to petty jealousy than to his efforts to penetrate Viola's disguise, if, as Barber has remarked, Feste dislikes his interlocutor because in their banter "he finds himself beaten at his own game."[27] If indeed the sizable element of practicality in Feste's wise folly proves to be as repressive as Viola's very pose, then she may have little choice, finally, but to turn to the luminous example of Antonio.

IV

Another possible reason that Feste pokes especially aggressive fun at Viola/Cesario stands to elucidate her characterization: Feste may be probing her identity because he senses that she is evading him. Some of his remarks in 3.1 indirectly criticize the very emotional avoidance that causes Viola to use language as a subterfuge. Feste toys with this idea when, for instance, he tells her that his program is to disseminate folly and, with characteristic cleverness, he ridicules Orsino and Olivia in one breath: "I would be sorry, sir, but the fool should be as oft with your master as with my mistress" (39–41). Feste's ambiguous line can make either of two statements. First, if "should" is taken to mean "is," then Feste says that Olivia and Orsino are too often fools, in an undesirable sense. But second, if "should" means "ought to," the line can mean that Olivia and Orsino should be wise fools more often. At this point Olivia seemingly "has no folly," as Feste remarks, because, for all he knows, she is not in love or intending to marry (32–35). Through such verbal play Feste champions emotional honesty and engagement, and through his thrusts at Viola, he may be trying to produce such effects in her. But her deft parries hold him at bay. Her calm control is enviable, but her reserve, of which her disguise becomes emblematic, subverts the spirit of Epiphany. It gets her physically close to Orsino but keeps her emotionally distant.

Twelfth Night is fundamentally concerned with Viola's growth toward emotional intimacy, which is paralleled with her moral growth toward loving well. Shakespeare continually plays her off against other characters to illustrate her progress. Initially, she has all the makings of an Antonio. She generously rewards the sea captain in 1.2, as she later does Feste (1.2.18, 3.1.43), and she lashes out at ingratitude when Antonio accuses her of it (3.4.354–57). Her willingness to woo another woman for the man she loves is also magnanimous.[28]

Yet Viola often appears self-absorbed. Nowhere is this trait clearer than when Antonio, in need of service, asks for his money back from the character he thinks is Sebastian:

> *Ant.* I must entreat of you some of that money.
>
> *Vio.* What money, sir?
> For the fair kindness you have show'd me here,
> And part being prompted by your present trouble,
> Out of my lean and low ability
> I'll lend you something. My having is not much;
> I'll make division of my present with you.
> Hold, here's half my coffer.
>
> *Ant.* Will you deny me now?
>
> (3.4.340–47)

In contrast with Antonio, who gives all of his purse, Viola offers only "half" her coffer. Next to the total altruism that Antonio has shown Sebastian in the preceding scene (3.3.38), Viola's reserve seems downright stingy. Granted, Viola is not rich; nor does she even know Antonio. Her giving anything at all under these circumstances could thus be admired. But the contrast between the two characters is evident: Viola is willing to go far for someone else, but only so far.[29]

What's more, her giving anything at all to Antonio is based partly on the condition that he has shown her "kindness": it thus differs from Antonio's irrational liberality. Similarly, although Viola has good reason in 3.4 to be stunned by the sudden possibility that Sebastian may yet live and thus to ignore Antonio's arrest, Antonio, having intervened to save her life, surely deserves more attention from her than she gives. Even if Viola exits at the close of this scene in pursuit of Antonio and the officers, she apparently does so not to aid Antonio but to discover more about Sebastian's history.

This key episode in which Viola and Antonio are contrasted evinces Viola's fear of losing control, which also characterizes Malvolio and, to a degree, Feste. That she loves both her brother and her master is obvious, but a great deal of the potential and actual destructiveness in *Twelfth Night* arises from Viola's refusal to expose herself openly to others—to give herself away. Without accusing her, I would argue that her adherence to her disguise, emblematic of her self-involvement, causes significant harm and threatens more. The bodily wounds to Sir Toby and Sir Andrew in 5.1, while owing largely to their bullying, trace back to and mirror the dangerous, unpredictable complications of Viola's decision to conceal her true identity. When her disguise entangles her in the love relationship with Olivia, she admits obliquely the undesired consequences that her deception has wrought: "Now I am your fool" (3.1.144). Yet, although she calls Olivia "proud" for hiding behind her beauty, she does not acknowledge her own pride in concealing herself (1.5.250). The pain and embarrassment that she stands to cause Olivia has, by act 3, reached considerable proportions, and her celebrated soliloquy in 2.2 makes plain that she appreciates the risks to Olivia of continuing on her course: "What will become of this? . . . / As I am woman (now alas the day!), / What thriftless sighs shall poor Olivia breathe!" (36, 38–39). Still, she persists in putting Olivia at risk. Why? Because, as she says, "My state is desperate for my master's love" (37). If she were to unmask herself now, she would make everyone furious with her. Orsino's love carries a high price, that of sacrificing Olivia's feelings.

In truth, Viola is given to rationalizing her decisions to do what she would prefer to do. In her soliloquy—a supreme manipulation, as soliloquies tend to be—she excuses herself as if her hands were tied. Never mind that she has initially elected to disguise herself, even paying the sea captain to assist her in her plan (1.2.52–59). Now that her plot has gone awry, it is not her fault but that of . . . of . . . let's see . . . yes, that's it, of "Disguise," which suddenly becomes personified, as if he had a character, and an evil one at that: "I see thou art a wickedness / Wherein the pregnant enemy does much" (27–28). Or maybe it's not Disguise that's accountable but the impressionability of an entire addle-brained gender with "waxen hearts" (30); notice, though, that women *per se* are not to blame, just their naturally inferior make-up: "Alas, our frailty is the cause, not we, / For such as we are made of, such we be" (31–32). The "Alas" is a nice touch.

In all seriousness, Viola's apology, tinged with a sexism that (one hopes) is countered by the larger play, is no more convincing than her closing refusal to take responsibility for the mess she has made: "O, time, thou must untangle this, not I, / It is too hard a knot for me t' untie" (40–41). The subtle play on "not" and "knot" suggests what Viola feels but is too self-protective to confess: that *not* to remain in disguise, whatever *knot* it creates, is simply "too hard." But to contend, as she does, that she cannot alter the course of future events is patently false. She would need only to do what she will not do: drop her disguise. Such an action would hardly constitute the impossible act of will that she describes it to be. Rather, she simply refuses to reveal herself yet, deferring to time. Not that time in *Twelfth Night* is anything less than the parent of truth, for indeed its progress works against deception and undermines attempts to cover up or ignore what lies beneath the surface. But because it steals youth, time is also the enemy of love's evasion—"Then come kiss me sweet and twenty; / Youth's a stuff will not endure," sings Feste in 2.3, a sentiment that Viola/Cesario reiterates in the next scene, where she laments that women, like roses, "die, even when they to perfection grow" (2.3.51–52, 2.4.41). Time in this play is not on the side of delay, as Viola would like to argue. In fact, resisting its pull toward revelation and emotional engagement demands a far greater act of will on Viola's part than simply letting go and being led directly to her desire.[30]

As a barrier to honesty and love, Viola's disguise thus tops the list of many other such walls throughout the play: Orsino's clichéd love language; the "beauteous wall" of appearance that, as Viola observes of hypocrites, "[d]oth oft close in pollution" (1.2.48–49); Olivia's house, wit, and veil, all of which she deploys in 1.5 to fend off Orsino's suit. Olivia, curiously, has possibly even greater reason than Viola to fear emotional involvement, since she has lost both her father and her brother within the past year (1.2.35–41). Yet Olivia succumbs to folly more readily by far than does Viola. The difference may be largely one of emotional readiness, amply displayed in both women's responses to the language of courtly love that is Orsino's stock and trade.

Like the audience, Olivia instinctively recognizes that language as pretentious and insincere—"fat and fulsome" (5.1.109). Viola, on the other hand, is drawn to it (why else would she fall for Orsino?) and appropriates it. When she first enters into Olivia's chamber and begins speaking (1.5), she sounds like an encyclopedia salesperson who has memorized her spiel and will forget it if anyone interrupts her. Hence, she must locate her addressee before fully launching into her presentation:

> Most radiant, exquisite, and unmatchable beauty—I pray you tell me if this be the lady of the house, for I never saw her. I would

> be loath to cast away my speech; for besides that it is
> excellently well penn'd, I have taken great pains to con it.
>
> (170–74)

Olivia quickly points out, however, that because Viola/Cesario has taken "great pains to study it," the speech is "more like to be feign'd" (194–96). Olivia has already sensed that this page, who has been "saucy" enough to gain entrance to her person, is inclined to ignore social convention employed for its own sake (197), and Olivia is ripe for responding emotionally to unaffected emotionalism in someone with Viola's pluck. Thus, when she finally cues Viola/Cesario to speak from the heart about how she would woo, Olivia immediately succumbs to the "willow cabin" speech (268–76), and the audience is introduced to the authentic feeling that lies just beneath Viola's façade. The "willow cabin" speech, full of natural imagery, is structured so as to move ever farther out of doors, until the most uninhibited "babbling gossip of the air" confronts Olivia with adoration for herself—"Olivia!" and Olivia alone—not some nameless, generic "unmatchable beauty" (273–74). Even more than Olivia knows, Viola "might do much" once she lowers her guard (276).

Before she can act, though, she will have to surmount her girlish infatuation with Orsino, continually represented by her unquestioning attachment to his hollow language and smothering self-pity. Her reaction to Feste's song in 2.4 exemplifies the poor judgment that results from her idolatry. "Come away, come away, death" has got to be some of the most morbid verse ever set to music, as Feste kindly suggests to Orsino (73–78), and the music that accompanies it would be anything but cheering.[31] But Viola identifies with its gloom: "It gives a very echo to the seat / Where Love is thron'd" (21–22). Her exaggerated sympathy for Orsino's pain mirrors his self-indulgence and errant conception of passion as an oppressive disease to be "relieve[d]" only by greater misery (4).

In its irrationality, Viola's love for Orsino resembles Antonio's for Sebastian and Olivia's for Viola/Cesario. It is potentially good folly. But enclosed within her, it grows melancholic, festering as another disease, which "like a worm i' th' bud / Feed[s] on her damask cheek" (2.4.111–12). During her prolonged exchange with Orsino in 2.4 about the very nature of love, she is at least objective enough to question her defense of her "concealment" (111)—"Was not this love indeed?" she asks (115)—and to challenge Orsino's wildly misled notions about forcing himself on Olivia (88–92), about men's superior capacity for passion (93–95), and (in performance, funniest of all) about women's inconstancy due to poor "retention" (96). To be fair, moreover, Viola's alter identity as Cesario is here a benefit: relying on Orsino's trust in her as a boy, she can glimpse his opinions and, as a prelude to marital intimacy, try to disabuse him of his misconceptions. Still, such intimacy, if it is to be authentic, must come to mediate the gap in gender now obscured by her disguise, while also dispelling Orsino's fatuous notions about what love is. Were she not so spellbound by Orsino's bombast, she could recognize more clearly that his silliness, not Olivia's, is truly foolish.

For Viola is, next to Antonio, the play's leading visionary. Her intelligence, like Feste's, is acute, attuned, and intuitive. She outpaces the sluggish Malvolio, who misunderstands the ring that he delivers from Olivia as surely as he misreads the forged letter (2.2, 5), and she discerns with ease why Olivia has sent her the ring (2.2.22–25). She also quickly ascertains that Antonio has mistaken her for her twin: "Prove true, imagination, O, prove true, / That I, dear brother, be now ta'en for you!" (3.4.375–76). Her understanding, forged by an "imagination" akin to Antonio's compassionate "fancy" and by her perceptiveness, foretells her surrender to wise folly when the appropriate moment arrives.

That moment comes late but seems spontaneous; caught by surprise and urged by circumstance, she is content to reveal herself in 5.1 when Orsino threatens her life:

> I'll sacrifice the lamb that I do love,
> To spite a raven's heart within a dove.
>
> (130–31)

The Christian implication of the "sacrificial lamb" is reinforced by Viola's sanguine reply:

> And I most jocund, apt, and willingly,
> To do you rest, a thousand deaths would die.
>
> (132–33)

Offering herself in Olivia's place for the fanciful reason of doing Orsino "rest," Viola virtually merges with Antonio, who has earlier substituted his life for hers. Her word "willingly" recalls Antonio's "willing love" for Sebastian, which is equally unconditional (3.3.4–13). Orsino has at least reached the point where he can express his anger openly, and she meets him there, refusing to "feign" (137). She rejects his lovelorn clichés while accepting his person. That Viola turns her cheek to Orsino at his least-deserving moment emphasizes the sheer lunacy of the love that, at long last, she reveals.[32] Where her love is brought to light is also lightness of heart.

Here lies the Epiphany in *Twelfth Night*, where the meaning of Christ's birth, His sacrifice for humanity, expresses itself in the actions of human beings. Viola's commitment of her very life to love is the play's wisest folly. Through Viola's history, then, spiritual love and romantic love are linked. Ultimately, we are not shown a world in which different types of love—say, physical and nonphysical—are qualitatively different or are opposed. Rather, Christian love, as epitomized in Antonio, works itself into the worldliest of relationships through the four lovers, principally Viola. Thus, Christian love can *inform* romantic love, enriching romantic comedy with a more serious dimension that, in Renaissance tradition, it often lacked.

Fittingly, as if induced by Viola/Cesario's self-sacrifice, the revelation and good will that Epiphany connotes reign over the plot's dénouement (5.1). Olivia "[r]eveals" her marriage (154). The sea captain who has possession of Viola's clothes is "enlarge[d]" and his role brought to light (278). Olivia adjusts amicably to the news of the twins' identity and, crossing boundaries that would impede a less generous spirit, reconceives of herself as "sister" to both Orsino and Viola (317, 326).[33] Fabian, caught up in the "wond[e]r" of "this present hour," makes his confession (355–68).

The most marvelous discovery of all, however, is the double recognition of the twins, which evokes a double resurrection. More particularly, but no less miraculously, the reunion is an icon of John 20:11–17, where Mary Magdalene encounters, but does not recognize, the newly arisen Christ. Shakespeare lavishes stage time and focuses attention on this episode because it is pivotal (209–58). The prolonged and stilted questioning that Sebastian and Viola use to identify each other falls into place when understood in light of Mary Magdalene's inability to recognize Christ, whom, in the biblical account, she initially takes to be the gardener. Once Mary accurately identifies Him as "Rabboni" ("master"), he tells her, "Touche me not: for I am not yet ascended to my Father. . . ."[34] Invoking Christ's words, Viola insists, once Sebastian has properly identified her, "Do not embrace me" (251). Her request, like Christ's, seems predicated upon not yet having consummated her true identity:

> If nothing lets to make us happy both
> But this my masculine usurp'd attire,
> Do not embrace me till each circumstance
> Of place, time, fortune, do cohere and jump
> That I am Viola.
>
> (249–53)

In both instances, that is, the speakers can be identified but have not completely fulfilled their identities—Christ, by remaining on earth; Viola, by staying disguised. Neither is willing to be physically embraced in such a liminal state, yet that each has been revealed even to an extent is cause for both awe and joy.[35]

Liminality perhaps best describes the peculiar inconclusiveness that marks this play's conclusion. Although the ending of *Twelfth Night* is usually viewed as problematic, hedging, or even dark, I would suggest that, reflecting the play's patterns of Epiphany, it be regarded as unfinished, unrevealed—or still better, *yet* to be revealed. The most striking loose ends left in 5.1 all share in common the barriers to love that, once overcome, allow the characters free expression of identity and lend the romantic plot the resolution that defines its genre: Antonio is still bound; Malvolio is still vengeful; and Viola, though not disguised, is still cross-dressed. All such conditions are reversible, and if the play itself refuses to complete the process, why, then, the script transfers to us—or, at least, to those members of the audience who wish to take responsibility for it. To answer such a call by scripting the remainder of *Twelfth Night* is to identify with Viola at her crossroads, to reenact her choice at the point where, disregarding her welfare, she hazards all for love of Orsino.[36] Perhaps most important, it is to recognize her "willing love" as a matter of free consent.

Twelfth Night envisions a place where the essence of divine love lays claim, albeit imperfectly and inconsistently, to the human spirit. Then it asks the audience whether that place is merely fictional or real. The name of the place, Illyria, is as unreal as utopia—a literal no-place. And in utopian fashion, "Illyria" sounds like "delirium," perfect nonsense. Yet, because Antonio's nearly saintly wise folly finds its way into the "real" lives of four worldly lovers, the play presents such a conclusion as viable for the audience, as well. It presents other possibilities—the unregulated liberty of the revelers, which turns in on them; the self-love of vulnerable Malvolio, for which he is held strictly accountable; the mixed openness and opportunism of Feste, through which he hurts as well as heals. In fact, by these examples, Illyria is less antithetical to what we take for reality than representative of it; if Feste's final song deposits us in the waking world of "wind and rain," then the dream world of the play, where grief rolls in on a sea of other troubles, is no less vexed and harrowing. Insofar as both characters and audience author their reality in either place, the prime choice is clear—irresistible—and, what's more, possible.

At the conclusion of the play, the questions of what will become of Antonio, Malvolio, and Viola are actually the question of what we, as audience, will. Hence the alternative title of *Twelfth Night*: *What You Will*. Literally as well as figuratively, the title proposes a choice between Epiphany—a showing of divine love in the "poor rude world"—or something other. The outcome of plot and history is reposed in the audience's control. Antonio's charity will be released into society, where it stands to do some good, or it will not. Malvolio's rancor will be assuaged, or it will not. Viola's identity will "to perfection grow," or it will not (2.4.41). But, as for Shakespeare and his actors, their "play is done" (5.1.407).

4

"The world's great snare": Antony, Cleopatra, and Game

From the moment that Antony believes Cleopatra to have given him cause to kill himself—her suspected treachery in 4.12—Antony is repeatedly subjected to the ridicule normally reserved for the most foolish of Shakespeare's fools. For example, in 4.14 he is provoked to commit suicide by the mere show of Cleopatra's death, a manipulation so transparent through familiarity that Enobarbus punctures it long before this moment (1.3.133–44). Next, calling upon his trusted servant Eros to fulfill his duty, Antony is disgraced when Eros, "[t]hrice-nobler" than his master, kills himself instead (81–84, 95, 94). Then Antony, having failed to dispatch himself with a degree of his servant's elegance, pitifully calls out to his guards to finish the deed: "Let him that loves me strike me dead" (108). Three guards refuse to comply, hinting that they, like Eros, love him too much to end his pain (108–10), whereupon Decretas cruelly increases that pain by removing the sword for purposes of self-advancement (111–13). Diomedes then enters, not to put Antony out of his misery, as Antony again requests, but to inform him that Cleopatra has had second thoughts about her bungled ruse (113–27). Diomedes is, ironically, "too late" (127). The grim humor of 4.14, arising mostly from Antony's inability to complete his own demise, peaks when Antony's guards, again protesting love for him, inadvertently crack the first of several jokes to come about Antony's dead weight: asked to bear him "where Cleopatra bides" (131), they quibble on the notion that Antony "may not live to wear" his "true followers out" and exclaim together, "Most heavy day!" (133–34).

Cleopatra reprises that jest in the next scene, 4.15, when she unthinkingly refers to the burden of hoisting Antony to the monument—"How heavy weighs my lord!"—and then recovers her fumble with a pun converting his physical weight to her sorrow: "Our strength is all gone to heaviness, / That makes the weight" (32–34). But the company of onlookers reinforce the physical gag of lifting Antony aloft with another reference to his weight: "A heavy sight" (40). In this scene, as in the preceding one, the characters' concern for Antony contains a component of ridicule—sometimes verging on terror—apparently unintended by the speakers and yet unavoidable to their auditors. Hence, for instance, when Cleopatra refuses to come down to Antony from the monument (21–29), she escapes capture (which would further dishonor Antony) even as she snubs Antony and makes necessary the visually awkward and embarrassing "sport" of lifting him (32). Similarly, in her very attempt to comfort and ennoble him as he dies, Cleopatra comically subverts his efforts to muster dignity. She interrupts him when he asks "to speak a little" so that she can "rail," and she conceives of his passing in terms of her own loss: "Hast thou no care of me?" (a line, by the way, that glances back to her tactic in 1.3.90–91 for making Antony feel guilty about returning to Rome—"O, my oblivion is a very Antony, / And I am all forgotten") (42–43, 60). She twice refutes his advice to trust Caesar and Proculeius (45–50). Never mind that she is right. Her insistence to the suffering Antony that she is right robs his death scene of grandeur, replacing tragic respectability with what Jonathan Dollimore calls "bathos."[1] Until Antony finally expires and Cleopatra has full scope to exalt him in death (62), his suffering seems as much an occasion for mockery as a cause for compassion.[2]

I am not the first reader of *Antony and Cleopatra* to sense a troublesome mixture of tone in the play's conclusion. W. B. Worthen, for example, notices that the audacious hoisting of Antony in the monument scene "threaten[s] a slapstick catastrophe, as Antony plummets to the stage" and speaks of the scene's "possibly distracting humor."[3] Brian Cheadle believes the episode to be "ludicrous" as is because of Antony's "pitifully bungle[d] suicide attempt," his "being winched laboriously aloft . . . by Cleopatra and her handmaidens," and his "utter lack of judgment" in urging the queen to trust Proculeius. Robert Ornstein, remarking on the way that Cleopatra's interchange with the clown complicates the tone of the ending, is joined by Martha Tuck Rozett, who also sees touches of the "absurd" in the final treatment of the dual protagonists. Ornstein and Rozett look forward to the commentary of Barbara C. Vincent, who studies the relationship between tragic and comic forms throughout the work. Focusing solely on the monument scene, Leslie Thomson grounds an entire reading of the play on the stage picture of Antony's cumbersome ascent to Cleopatra: "In the political world Caesar rises as Antony falls. But countering this, and complicating our response, is that as Antony falls in that context, he is raised, both literally and figuratively in another: the world of love."

Yet, with virtually no exceptions, critics seem largely uncomfortable with the dark humor in the play's closing scenes, particularly with Antony's buffoonery, which I have opened this discussion by cataloging in order to press home its abundance. Some readers altogether ignore the ridicule directed at Antony.[4] Far more reduce it to inconsequentiality. Such readings minimize the amount of mockery in the last scenes, however, as well as the effect it has on both the tragic elevation of Antony and Cleopatra and the audience's sympathetic identification with them. Fairly representative of these critics is Rosalie Colie, who, while acknowledging the proclivity of Antony's suicide and death toward foolish "excesses," argues that what we finally remember about the protagonists is their "beauty of character" and "that in such excess, life itself can reside."[5]

Even critics who assert, as I would, that a production of the play should preserve the ridiculous next to the high-minded strive for interpretations that ultimately dilute the comedy. Inevitably, these readings insist in some form on the protagonists' triumph over impediments to their love: Caesar's imperialism, other values of this world, their own character flaws. In short, critics are loath to accept and deal with the full measure of irony aimed at the tragic conclusion—a conclusion that also, admittedly, invokes inspiring romanticism. But when that romanticism is permitted, in either production or reading, to suppress the irony, Antony's characterization becomes lopsided; his seemingly total surrender to his love for Cleopatra is being forced at the last to make him appear above derision.[6]

My purpose in returning to the problem of tone, especially as it involves Antony, is to place in perspective the play's competing views of his and other characters' self-sacrificial love. Recognizing the debt of Antony's characterization to the traditions linked with Saint Anthony of Egypt clarifies the work's central issues and sharpens perceptions of Antony, Cleopatra, Caesar, and others. What's more, it opens up further discussion of how Shakespeare used many other Christian analogues in *Antony and Cleopatra*, some of them veiled to modern audiences.[7] Both the saint and the conqueror, for instance, are tempted by the flesh, and both face their trials in Egypt. Indeed, in *Antony and Cleopatra*, where a name like Eros or a gesture like crowning likely points beyond itself to added meaning, the conflicts in Antony's character, recalling those of Saint Anthony, launch anew the exploration of charity in this world. Surrounded by other characters who amplify and extend qualities of his own love—mainly Enobarbus, Cleopatra, and Octavia—Antony offers Shakespeare's most complex, if least accessible, study of folly.

I

The framing in 1.1 of Antony and Cleopatra's mutual devotion by Demetrius and Philo's negative judgment does more than establish an immediate opposition between Roman and Egyptian values. It also instantly identifies the audience with Demetrius, who remains silent until the scene's end, and it insists, through Philo's repeated imperatives, that audiences formulate their own opinions about what they, along with Demetrius, are witnessing:

> Look where they come!
> Take but good note, and you shall see in him
> The triple pillar of the world transform'd
> Into a strumpet's fool. Behold and see.
>
> (10–13)

Although Philo can count on Demetrius's affirmation of what he beholds and sees, the nature of this dramatic situation encourages the audience to look beyond the viewpoints of either the critical Romans or the spotlighted lovers. While Philo and Demetrius deplore Antony's inattention to duty and devalue his passion for Cleopatra, the audience can appreciate the lovers' extravagance from the lovers' point of view while also detecting the limitations of the entire dichotomy at hand. In the context of Renaissance tradition, Mark Antony's very name outlines the twin poles of his character: war (Mars) and love (Saint Anthony). But the love for which he dismisses the concerns of war is as worldly in its own way as is Caesarian empire.[8] In some real sense, Antony is a "strumpet's fool" (13), much as Cleopatra is also the true "fool" she fears becoming in this opening scene (42). They are prisoners of their lust and egotism. Yet, as Antony finds himself jostled between the equally worldly alternatives of Rome and Egypt, war and love, Caesar and Cleopatra, his ambivalence develops in the context of yet another dichotomy, that between the worldly and the spiritual. As his characterization unfolds, in fact, his choice becomes less and less a horizontal one between the exclusively worldly values of Rome and Egypt and more a vertical one between foolish folly—attachment to this world—and wise folly—renunciation of the world.[9]

The inadequacy of this world to provide spiritual fulfillment is continually recapitulated in paradigms that echo Antony's impossible choice between the options embodied in Caesar and in Cleopatra. For instance, Antony understands from his grief over Fulvia's passing that human desire feeds on what it lacks:

> What our contempts doth often hurl from us,
> We wish it ours again. The present pleasure,
> By revolution low'ring, does become
> The opposite of itself. She's good, being gone;
> The hand could pluck her back that shov'd her on.
>
> (1.2.123–27)

The "revolution" that Antony describes here could as easily apply to the opposition he feels between his attraction to both Rome and Egypt, as could Caesar's description to Lepidus of how popular allegiance has shifted to Pompey:

> It hath been taught us from the primal state
> That he which is was wish'd, until he were;
> And the ebb'd man, ne'er lov'd till ne'er worth love,
> Comes dear'd by being lack'd.
>
> (1.4.41–44)

Pompey himself mentions the fleetingness of desire and its objects when he complains to Menas of his delayed gratification from the triumvirate: "Whiles we are suitors to their throne, decays / The thing we sue for" (2.1.4–5). The passions of this life fade.

So widespread is this pattern of one affection giving way to another that it is parodied when Agrippa and Enobarbus mock Lepidus's vacillation between extolling first Antony, then Caesar:

> *Eno.* Caesar? Why he's the Jupiter of men.
>
> *Agr.* What's Antony? The god of Jupiter.
>
> *Eno.* Spake you of Caesar? How, the nonpareil!
>
> *Agr.* O Antony! O thou Arabian bird!
>
> *Eno.* Would you praise Caesar, say "Caesar," go no further.
>
> *Agr.* Indeed he plied them both with excellent praises.

Eno. But he loves Caesar best, yet he loves Antony.

. . . .

Agr. Both he loves.

Eno. They are his shards, and he their beetle, so.

(3.2.9–20)

If at this point we remember Pompey's claim about Lepidus's loyalties—that he "flatters both, / Of both is flatter'd; but . . . neither loves" (2.1.14–15)—this rendition of Lepidus's hyperbole conjures more cynicism than humor. And the image of the encasing and potentially suffocating beetle's shards pointedly looks forward to the "pair of chaps" that devour Pompey, Lepidus, and the civilized world until they "grind th' one the other" (3.5.13–15). Such images, in other words, suggest the peril, well known to Antony by his life's end, of taking sides, although to be in the world makes doing so unavoidable. Nowhere is that peril more clearly represented than at the celebration on Pompey's galley, whose very rocking, together with the swaying brought on by drunkenness, imitates the instability of politics—portrayed, for instance, in the ease with which Menas proposes to turn on the triumvirate and the hair's breadth that prevents Pompey from capitulating, leading Menas to desert him (2.7.61–84). Enobarbus's warning to Antony as he descends into the boat is almost too blatant a reminder of his impending doom: "Take heed you fall not" (2.7.129).[10]

Octavia, too, first frozen between her "heart" and her "tongue" in parting with Octavius (3.2.47–50), eventually finds herself embattled by irreconcilable loyalties to both her husband and her brother:

A more unhappy lady,
If this division chance, ne'er stood between,
Praying for both parts.
The good gods will mock me presently,
When I shall pray, "O, bless my lord and husband!"
Undo that prayer, by crying out as loud,
"O, bless my brother!" Husband win, win brother,
Prays, and destroys the prayer, no midway
'Twixt these extremes at all.

(3.4.12–20)

In this world, even the augurs "[s]ay they know not, they cannot tell, look grimly, / And dare not speak their knowledge," so befuddled are they as to who will prevail at Actium (4.12.5–6).[11]

Octavia's private lament also portrays the larger tragic vision of *Antony and Cleopatra*, whose characters, principally Antony, waver between choices because both guarantee tragedy. Although the Soothsayer can "read" but "a little" of the future's secrets (1.2.10–11), he can tell Antony that Caesar will always defeat him at worldly "game" (2.3.25–29), making a life with Cleopatra, even one of "dotage" (1.2.117), less repugnant than losing all to his adversary. Antony, like Octavia, has good reason for feeling paralyzed by indecision. Yet, as Antony reminds Octavia, she will have to choose between himself and Caesar: "Let your best love draw to that point which seeks / Best to preserve it" (3.4.21–22). So must Antony choose between Rome and Egypt. From an earthly perspective, his tragedy lies in the stifling absence of comic possibility. He can only fall, though he is free to choose his route.[12]

For Antony, then, the only way out is up. That is to say, the play's dichotomy between this world and the next emerges in response to the bankruptcy of material gain and physical pleasure, Antony's earthly options. Does Antony's death, then, represent a change in his love for Cleopatra and thus a severing of his foolish attachment to the world? Does he elect to join Cleopatra out of pure love? So Antony would make us believe when he reacts to the rumor of her suicide: "I will o'ertake thee, Cleopatra, and / Weep for my pardon" (4.14.44–45).[13] That his death-wish stems from love of her rather than from self-love seems confirmed by myriad details from this point on—especially by his concern for her welfare once he is gone and she is in Caesar's custody (4.15.45–48). At the same time, Antony's final motives also smack of escapism. In this he recalls the behavior of Antonio in *The Merchant of Venice*, who would bypass the hardships of this life. Antony's announcement to Eros, for instance, that "there is left us / Ourselves to end ourselves" arises not from disenchantment with worldly gain but from shame that a woman could cheat him of his "glory" (4.14.21–22, 19). Here, Antony is not resplendent in his defeat of mutability, as a romantic reading would stress. Nor does his sense of having failed to achieve glory for himself square completely with the Roman ideal of honor.[14] Rather, Antony appears self-involved at best and vindictive at worst, as when he hopes that Caesar will "hoist" Cleopatra up "to the shouting plebeians" in Rome (4.12.33–34). Ironically, he wishes on her the very humiliation that he in fact receives when he is "hoist" two scenes later.

I am suggesting, first, that the ridicule to which Antony is subject, particularly at the play's end, has two possible sources. Either he becomes a wise fool who gives up even lust for love's sake, in which case his ineptitude at such political matters as guiding Cleopatra to a Roman she can trust signals his positive spiritual removal from the world. Or his foolishness derives from his ineptitude at leaving earthly matters far behind. Or both. In the pagan Mark Antony, who forfeited one third of the world all for Cleopatra, Shakespeare's original audience would also have recognized a typological association with Christ, whose spiritual kingdom and love were about to displace the triumvirate's empire and self-interest.[15] Caesar's famed pronouncement in 4.6—"The time of universal peace is near" (4)—looks in two directions, one toward the Augustan peace and the other toward Christ's birth, so as to involve the play's action in both. I also want to suggest, then, that the intertwining of traditions in Antony's very history renders him an especially plastic version of the Antonio character-type. Shakespeare's two earlier Antonios operate exclusively within clear Christian tradition: the first, in *The Merchant of Venice*, falls short of the Christian charity he professes, and the second, in *Twelfth Night*, practices an authentic Christian charity that, as the play ends, seems indefinitely divided from the world that needs it. But Mark Antony is prevented from attaining literal Christian charity by his cultural heritage. He cannot enact what he historically predates. Still, Antony's link with Christ in the sixteenth and seventeenth centuries puts in perspective his frequent tendency toward saintly behavior. That behavior implies, at the least, a prefiguration or analogue of Christ's idea of love.[16] But it also sketches, within a pagan context, the ultimately Christian problem of reconciling the flesh and the spirit. Antony's particular wavering between self-love and selfless love preserves the distinction between earthly and spiritual empire without discrediting the claims of the former on Christian grounds. In this Antonio, Shakespeare returns to the matter that pervades *The Merchant of Venice* and marks the conclusion of *Twelfth Night*: whether worldly and otherworldly values can be married. Through the twin protagonists of Antony and Cleopatra, he also extends the question to whether they should be.

II

The opposing impulses in Antony—to respond to either his own needs or to those of others—form a method of characterization. Examples of his self-centeredness pepper the play, mixed in with those of his generosity. His initial reason for returning to Egypt is not love of Cleopatra but knowledge that he cannot win against Caesar and so may as well indulge in "pleasure" (2.3.14–15, 41). Yet later, having succumbed to Caesar at Actium, he will generously insist that Cleopatra be informed of the chance to exchange Antony for Caesar's "courtesy" toward her (3.13.13–19). Ventidius expounds on Antony's pride for an entire scene (3.1), though he might have been spared the trouble, since Antony's ego speaks for itself. When he squanders victory at Actium to fight by sea, for instance, he does so, he says, because Caesar "dares" him to (3.7.29).[17] The same Antony, however, will retreat at sea purely for love of Cleopatra (3.11.56–61), risking Caesar's and his soldiers' ridicule. Craving good opinion of himself, he is consumed by insecurity when Caesar has "[s]poke scantly" of him: "If I lose mine honor, / I lose myself" (3.4.6, 22–23). Even so, he has a penchant for learning the painful truth about himself, and to hear it he will urge on a messenger (1.2.97–111), tolerate Enobarbus's venting (for example, 1.2), and encourage Octavius to pinpoint his grievance when the two confer about Antony's "broken . . . oath" (2.2.81–98). Such frank confrontations contrast tellingly with those in which Cleopatra beats a messenger for honesty, bullying him into later flattering her (2.5, 3.3).

They also bear resemblance to the many instances in which other characters attempt to bait Antony but discover that he is too temperate to be ruffled. Caesar and Pompey both needle him about his weaknesses for things Egyptian (2.2.120–22, 2.6.62–70, 2.7.96); each time, Antony responds with equanimity. His similar forbearance with Cleopatra, whose efforts to control his emotions are at one point compared to the sport of fishing for and catching him (2.5.12–15), suggests the bounteous spirit for which Plutarch had once praised him.[18] Not that Cleopatra cannot incite Antony—she does so whenever he suspects her loyalty (3.11, 4.12). But the point is that the same man who coolly endures repeated taunting from her and others is also, in other cases, nervously dependent upon external validation of his worthiness. When his fragile ego is crushed at the sight of Thidias's lips on Cleopatra's hand, he pathetically scrambles to reestablish his identity by having Thidias whipped (3.13.85–152); when he temporarily beats back Caesar, he relishes his prowess and, in symmetry with the earlier episode, offers Cleopatra's hand to Scarus (4.8.11–13). Taken together, all of these examples conflict, portraying, by turns, one Antony who is insecure, vindictive, and enmeshed in worldly affairs but another who is self-assured, forgiving, and free of the world's fetters.

A few of Antony's scenes so conflate these two perspectives on him as to render his actions and motives thoroughly ambiguous. Yet the ambiguity is so subtly crafted that the audience may be unaware of what it does not fully understand without the benefit of reflection, which a production, fleeting as it is, cannot afford. Read closely, however, the text can account for the confusion, however subliminal it may be. In one key scene, 3.11, Antony accepts military defeat and gives up his fortune with a grace reminiscent of Saint Anthony himself:

> Friends, come hither:
> I am so lated in the world, that I
> Have lost my way for ever. I have a ship
> Laden with gold, take that, divide it; fly,
> And make your peace with Caesar.
>
> (2–6)

But the language of liberality, pure as it sounds, may issue less from Antony's humility than from his humiliation, the "shame" that, Iras says, has him so "unqualited" (44). His revulsion toward Cleopatra, whose flight at sea he holds responsible for his situation, would seem to confirm that his loss of dignity, not his magnanimity, causes him to surrender his earthly possessions (25–68). Still, his quickness to pardon Cleopatra at the scene's end reestablishes his largess.

Such comingling of perspectives on Antony's character is later recalled and yet further complicated when Antony again bids farewell, this time to "three or four Servitors" in Cleopatra's palace (4.2.10, s.d.). As Fichter has pointed out, 4.2 alludes to the Last Supper, Antony's triple plea that his followers attend him at one more "bounteous . . . meal" linking him to Christ (4.2.10).[19] Shakespeare so qualifies the link, however, that the scene might be taken as a parodic inversion of its Christian counterpart. That Cleopatra twice asks Enobarbus the meaning of Antony's behavior underscores the obscurity of his intent. Enobarbus, by now jaded toward Antony's emotional displays, reads this one as a conscious manipulation of his servants' feelings (24), a charge that, once Enobarbus voices it, Antony strenuously denies: "Ho, ho, ho! / Now the witch take me, if I meant it thus!" (36–37). Antony's next lines emphasize the charity he is claiming for himself: "Grace grow where those drops fall, my hearty friends! / You take me in too dolorous a sense, / For I spake to you for your comfort" (38–40). The difficulty of reading Antony's nature here epitomizes the same difficulty until the play's end, the precise problem, for purposes of establishing tone, being that of how to take Antony's apparent self-denial.

Enobarbus, of course, offers his own final answer to the question, and it is a persuasive one. For all of his earlier skepticism toward Antony's judgment, his former master's decision to reward his betrayal with riches defines his dying admiration for Antony's willingness to turn the other cheek (4.6, 9). His route to that conclusion is nevertheless winding, and the variables in Enobarbus's character can elucidate those in Antony's.

As exemplified in Enobarbus's skirmish with Lepidus before Caesar and Antony begin to negotiate (2.2.1–14), his chief concern is a version of Antony's: he is continually torn between meeting his own needs and fulfilling his duty to others, between self and self-sacrifice. To Lepidus he defends the practice of "private stomaching" and proceeds in 2.2 to speak his mind, dispensing with the decorum reserved for the more "courteous Antony" (8–10, 222). Lepidus correctly identifies Enobarbus's "passion" as the "plainness" that Pompey later implies is famous (2.2.12, 2.6.78). Far from acting solely as the voice of reason in reaction to Antony's irrationality, Enobarbus has his own passion, a counterpart of sorts to Antony's Cleopatra: it is truth to himself at all costs. Without this indulgence of his own, he would be unprepared to sympathize with Antony's, as he does in the celebrated "barge" speech (2.2.190–239).[20]

That sympathy notwithstanding, he must inevitably choose between the "honesty" he reveres and a "loyalty" that may spell disaster for him personally:

> Mine honesty and I begin to square.
> The loyalty well held to fools does make
> Our faith mere folly; yet he that can endure
> To follow with allegiance a fall'n lord
> Does conquer him that did his master conquer,
> And earns a place i' th' story.
>
> (3.13.41–46)

The distinctly pagan sentiments behind Enobarbus's dilemma here should not fully obscure the Pauline terms that associate it with Antony's struggle between earthly and spiritual values. His anxiety over becoming a "fool" for "faith" in Antony, together with his ambition for worldly fame, is of a piece with that one trait of Enobarbus that, more than any other, portrays him as a foolish fool—that is, his fear of love.

For all his bluster about speaking as he feels, Enobarbus repeatedly shrinks from feeling itself, using his supposed plainness—and often his sarcasm—as protection against a dreaded loss of self-control. Not surprisingly in a play brimming with misogyny, Enobarbus conceives of that loss in both himself and Antony as one of manliness. He pronounces his fear most openly late in the play, in reaction to Antony's emotional valediction to his servants: "Look, they weep, / And I, an ass, an onion-ey'd. For shame, / Transform us not to women" (4.2.34–36). Already aware of his intent to leave Antony, Enobarbus may be especially unresponsive here to his master's emotional claims on him. But such explicit resistance to acknowledging his own feeling prompts the audience to reconsider such earlier instances as his unwillingness to recognize Antony's grief for Fulvia or his derision of Cleopatra's grief over Antony's imminent departure (1.2). Not until he embraces and returns Antony's love for him is he truly honest with himself or anyone.

In fact, Enobarbus's great triumph is his foolish—indeed lethal—endorsement of Antony's unconditional love:

> O Antony,
> Thou mine of bounty, how wouldst thou have paid
> My better service, when my turpitude
> Thou dost so crown with gold!
>
> (4.6.30–33)

To accept that love is to expose his former preoccupation with truthfulness as a mere pretension and to discover real passion in rejecting self-interest.[21] Among the many desertions in this play—including those of Menas, Hercules, Decretas, and Antony—Enobarbus's stands out for illustrating the final poverty of worldly gain. Beginning with his realization that, ironically, Caesar's idea of "universal peace" does not extend to trusting renegades from Antony's camp, Enobarbus's abandonment lends him an appreciation of Antony's steadfastness (4.6.4, 11–19). He even dies remarkably like Elizabethan accounts of the despairing Judas—repulsed by lucre (4.6.23), bursting from heartbreak, and falling down in a field (4.9.12–23)—thus furthering the association between Antony's loyalty to him and Christ-like love.[22]

To understand Enobarbus's reversal as the last comment upon Antony's character, however, would be simplistic. For one thing, Antony's altruism toward Enobarbus forms, as we have seen, only part of his characterization, and, for another, as we have also seen, selfless behavior in this play often comes under its own fire. True enough, the play's world proves hostile to self-interest like Enobarbus's, also consuming Pompey, whose preoccupation with his own private concerns remains unsurpassed by any other character's egotism. Pompey directs his political negotiations with the triumvirate away from empire and toward his anxiety over Antony's acquisition of his family's home and Antony's failure to thank him for giving his mother sanctuary (2.6.26–29, 39–46); these are personal grudges that, to Menas's dismay, mean more to him than obtaining lands: "Thy father, Pompey, would ne'er have made this treaty" (2.6.82–83). Yet, if the minute attention to trivialities of personal honor, virtually caricatured in Pompey, leads to personal loss, so does utter inattention to the world and one's own place in it.

Such terms describe Octavia, in whom Shakespeare exaggerates selfless loyalty much as he does its opposite in Pompey. She has every opportunity to break faith with either Caesar or Antony and yet, much like Enobarbus, instead suffers a broken heart, hers "parted betwixt two friends / That does afflict each other!" (3.6.77–78). Likewise, Shakespeare has every opportunity to reveal just one advantage to Octavia of her unwavering commitment. But our last impression of her lies far afield of spiritual fulfillment. As Caesar and Maecenas disabuse her of her blind trust in Antony, who has betrayed her, she passively responds, "Is it so, sir?" (3.6.96), the reaction perhaps not of a woman maintaining her belief in her husband at any cost but of one slightly shaken by suddenly confronting her ignorance and trying to maintain her poise. Caesar knows how to thrive in the world that has made Octavia its victim. Her folly, spawning no strength of conviction or transcendent vision, seems awkwardly out of touch, and her discomfort in Caesar's world, although not a source of ridicule, resembles Antony's awkwardness during his protracted death.

Ridicule toward Antony persists even after he has died. In 5.1, Caesar, Maecenas, and Agrippa join the ranks of other characters, like Enobarbus, Pompey, and Octavia, whose degree of charity or self-love implicitly comments upon Antony's characterization. Under the guise of mourning Antony and commending his virtues, the three Romans actually damn him with faint praise. On hearing Decretas's news of Antony's demise, Caesar sets the tone: "The breaking of so great a thing should make / A greater crack" (14–15). Literally *saying* that Decretas has understated the significance of Antony's passing, he *implies* that Antony's influence on the world has so dwindled by the time of his death that it lacks power enough to "make / A greater crack." Agrippa and Maecenas sustain the theme of Antony's ineffectuality:

Agr. strange it is
That nature must compel us to lament
Our most persisted deeds.

Maec. His traits and honors
Wag'd equal with him.

Agr. A rarer spirit never
Did steer humanity; but you gods will give us
Some faults to make us men.

(28–33)

Caesar, ostensibly "touch'd" (33), concludes by belittling Antony into a "[d]isease" that he was compelled to "launch" (36–37).[23] Granted, the Romans' backbiting says at least as much about them as about Antony, yet, significantly, it also threatens to lower our esteem for Antony as a hero, demeaning him for his worldly failures.

The last major insight into Antony's characterization may also be the most important. It looks back to and implicitly comments upon all preceding—and conflicting—references to Antony's folly. It is his revisitation of Cleopatra in act 5 in the form of the Clown.

A production of the play in 1993 by the Shenandoah Shakespeare Express doubled the actor who played Antony in the role of the Clown, a choice that, I have come to believe, faithfully mirrors Jacobean practice.[24] If so, the doubling enriched immeasurably the original audience's association of Antony with the tradition of wise folly. The role makes literal the identification of Antony as a fool, and Cleopatra's paradoxical statement about the Clown could be applied to any of Shakespeare's wise fools, particularly Lear's natural: "What poor an instrument / May do a noble deed!" (236–37). By "noble deed" Cleopatra refers to the delivery of the asp, her means to end her life. But what truly makes the Clown "noble" takes a kinder form, which she is too single-minded to appreciate fully. Despite Cleopatra's instructing him three times to leave her (259, 261, 264), he lingers until the fourth (278). The content of his speeches in response to her repeated farewells is, overwhelmingly, concern for her well-being. Simple as he is, he knows why she has ordered him to leave the snake, and, though he cannot help boasting about his expertise on the "worm," his chief purpose is to warn her, as Antony has warned her about trusting "none . . . but Proculeius," from tempting the asp further than she intends (4.15.48):

> You must think this, look you, that the worm will do its kind. . . . Look you, the worm is not to be trusted but in the keeping of wise people; for indeed, there is no goodness in the worm. . . . Give it nothing, I pray you, for it is not worth the feeding. (262–70)

Cleopatra's rejoinder to this last direction—"Will it eat me?" (271)—combines an appreciation of the Clown's bawdry, a last pinch of the fear that the Clown hopes to elicit, and a plea for assurance that her plan will work. At this point, even he can see that she is not to be dissuaded: "I wish you joy o' th' worm" (279).

The Clown, then, reincarnates all the essential elements of Antony's character. To his lustiness he adds strict attention to Cleopatra's welfare, limited understanding of her own designs, and, above all, a gift for botching practical endeavors, shown particularly in his language: "I would not be the party that should desire you to touch [the worm], for his biting is immortal; those that do die of it do seldom or never recover"

(245–48). But even such blunders signify a capacity for higher understanding, meaning, and gesture than has as yet been attained in this life: as so many critics have remarked, the Clown's "immortal" is a malapropism that speaks more wisely than he knows and that Cleopatra returns to in earnest when she cites her "immortal longings" (5.2.281). Like Antony's suicide, a misfired shot at what Seneca calls a "becoming exit" from the world,[25] the Clown's verbal bungling briefly figures forth, in a complementary context, a fundamental discord between practical competence and charitable practice. Likewise, Antony, seeking to free himself from the constraints of this life, seems to become ever more mired in them.

As C. W. R. D. Moseley has demonstrated by studying the play's emblems of wisdom, Hercules traditionally proves wise at the crossroads when he chooses Virtue over Pleasure.[26] Hercules' desertion of Antony (4.3), in this light, can perhaps be seen as Antony's loss of prudence, a certain kind of wisdom.[27] But the Colossus to which Cleopatra compares Antony after death is, as Moseley has also shown, another Renaissance emblem for wisdom (5.2.82–92), demonstated in examples from the work of George Wither. Sometimes it is a wisdom so potent that it can subdue the unruly world under its sway, sometimes a wisdom that actually transcends the earth, like Saint Paul's "wisdome of this world," which is "foolishnesse with God."[28] This transition in emblems for Antony's wisdom tempts the audience to infer a progression in his history: the practical prudence of Hercules, witnessed in Antony's youthful worldly success, gives way to a higher, transcendent wisdom, found in his only apparently foolish surrender to love.

Though such an outline may bear some truth, it is an all too facile account of Antony's final inability to escape what Cleopatra playfully calls "the world's great snare" (4.8.18). Even if he dies for love, it may be love of himself. Even if he dies for love of another, his dignity as a martyr is significantly undermined. As we have observed, he is not alone. Even Eros, acting out his name in self-sacrifice for Antony, expresses mixed motives: "Thus I do escape the sorrow / Of Antony's death" (4.14.93–94). This is self-sacrifice of the most dubious order. Whether because Antony's martyrdom is diluted by escapism, or because his half-failed suicide represents an only half-hearted willingness to die for love, or because he is unlucky, life will not let him go without an awkward struggle. And death insists on humiliating him. Something there is in *Antony and Cleopatra* that doesn't love saintliness—or, at the least, Antony's approach to it as a fool for love. Cleopatra's enterprise is to find it out.

Hee, over all the Starres *doth raigne,*
That unto Wiſdome *can attaine.*

ILLVSTR. XXXI. *Book.* I.

I Am not of their Minde, who thinke the *Sun,*
The *Moone*, the *Planets*, and thoſe glorious *Lights*
Which trim the *Sphæres*, doe in their *Motions* run
To no more purpoſe, then to pleaſe our *Sights.*
Nor for diſtinguiſhment of *Nights*, and *Dayes*,
and the *Times*, alone.

George Wither, Colossus, 1635.
By permission of University of South Carolina Press.

When Law, *and* Armes, *together meet,*
The World *descends, to kisse their feet.*

ILLVSTR. XXIX. **Book.**

THe Picture of a *Crowned-king*, here, stands
Upon a *Globe*; and, with outstretched hands,
Holds forth, in view, a *Law-booke*, and a *Sword*:
Which plaine and moderne *Figures*, may afford
This meaning; that, a *King*, who hath regard

George Wither, Colossus, 1635.
By permission of University of South Carolina Press.

III

Over the course of the play's last scene, Cleopatra sees to it that Caesar is made every bit the foolish fool that Antony has just seemed in his final hour. Caesar covets the chance to humiliate her publicly.[29] Instead, she humiliates him privately by controlling her own destiny. Her objective—to play fortune to Caesar's luck, thus making him her fool—is clear from her first lines in 5.2: "'Tis paltry to be Caesar; / Not being Fortune, he's but Fortune's knave, / A minister of her will" (2–4).

Her success at her goal is stressed repeatedly at the point of her death, first by her lines to the asp: "O, couldst thou speak, / That I might hear thee call great Caesar ass / Unpolicied!" (306–8). After her passing, Shakespeare relies on the dramatic irony of Dolabella's lines to underline Caesar's defeat. Once the guard has announced that "Caesar's beguiled" (323), Dolabella, having secretly betrayed Caesar's trust, makes sure the audience appreciates how ridiculous the emperor appears:

> Caesar, thy thoughts
> Touch their effects in this: thyself art coming
> To see perform'd the dreaded act which thou
> So sought'st to hinder.
>
> (329–32)

and

> O, sir, you are too sure an augurer;
> That you did fear is done.
>
> (334–35)

That Caesar remains ignorant of Dolabella's role in thwarting his plans intensifies our sense of his folly: at least Antony recognizes when he has been demeaned. And because the audience knows how Cleopatra accomplished her death, Caesar's deliberate investigation of the premises—the women's bodies and the aspic's "slime" (345–48, 351–53)—appears slow and dull-witted. His embarrassing ignorance of being duped lasts until the play's closing lines, where Caesar is still commanding Dolabella, this time to accord Antony and Cleopatra the "glory" for which, unbeknownst to Caesar, Dolabella has made way (362, 365–66). Charnes writes of this moment that Caesar "swiftly translates [the lovers] from rebellious figures who escaped his control and punishment into legendary lovers" so as to minimize their political power, yet his efforts are just as swiftly undermined and implicitly derided by the audience's awareness of Cleopatra's sway, which is greater than Caesar's, over Dolabella.[30] Through Cleopatra's agency, then, Antony has accomplished vicariously what the Soothsayer declared he never would himself (2.3): he wins against Caesar in a contest for worldly control. The wheel has come full circle. Caesar is now the "strumpet's fool" (1.1.13).[31]

Nor is Cleopatra's project a simple one. Caesar plays to win. Laura Quinney has remarked on his politically deft use of messengers (who swarm around him) for purposes of both "self-dissemination" and gathering information.[32] Indeed, in his first scene, his knowledge of state affairs, kept current by a stream of messengers, clearly surpasses Lepidus's (1.4.81–83). He later indicates that he has spies on Antony (3.6.1–31), and at Actium a soldier marvels at the "speed" of his approach, which "[c]arries beyond belief" (3.7.74–75). In the last scene, when Dolabella relieves Proculeius from attending Cleopatra, he attributes to Caesar an Orwellian omniscience: "Proculeius, / What thou hast done thy master Caesar knows" (5.2.64–65). The end of Caesar's game is nothing less than total control over himself and the world—control that Cleopatra "bolts up" despite Caesar's prowess (5.2.6).[33]

At the very least, then, Cleopatra's victory over Caesar discloses a political focus and cunning that may come as a surprise after her initial characterization. Until the middle of act 3, her very reason for being seems to be her gift for oblivion, for losing herself in pleasure and luring Antony along with her. She bids him ignore Caesar in the first scene, wallows in self-pity when he determines to rejoin Caesar (1.3), and longs to "sleep out this great gap of time / My Antony is away," fantasizing that, while gone, he will "[t]hink on" her, as did Caesar and then Pompey, for whom she was "his life" (1.5.27–34). Outdoing the younger Pompey in self-indulgence, she draws the world in to her and refashions it in her own image.[34] From this inwardness ensue inversions of the natural: her professed love for Antony (or Caesar or Pompey) seems narcissistic, and her "repent[ance]" for having terrorized the messenger, once he has spoken her wishes (3.3.39), appears an ironic foreshadowing of Enobarbus's authentic change of heart, brought about by his discovery of the truth.

Perhaps Shakespeare is counting on his audience to understand that Cleopatra's ostensible retreat from the practical demands of political life is a mere façade, that her frequent threats to dissolve Egypt and Egyptians rather than see her most trivial desire unmet cloak a keen awareness of her political ambitions and of her options for achieving them. After all, when Antony first arrived in Egypt, her experience at protecting her regime from the clutches of foreign empire was extensive. Her method was also based on sexual seduction, if not love, and could therefore belie her political acumen. Her impressive capacity for self-preservation to date suggests that, in the play's early scenes, she has yet to avail the audience of her full characterization. Nor would her skill at throwing off Caesar likely spring up out of nowhere.

In any case, an apparent transition in Cleopatra's character begins occurring in 3.7, where she is inclined less to abandon and more to focusing on such outward matters as military strategy and royal responsibility. Here, she struggles between supporting Antony's bad decision to fight Caesar at sea and expressing her dissatisfaction with other of Antony's poor judgments.[35] Her line, "Celerity is never more admir'd / Than by the negligent," not only "rebuke[s]" Antony (24–25) but also looks back to Enobarbus's rebuke of her own "celerity in dying" (1.2.144). This Cleopatra almost seems beyond such nonsense. While she quizzes Enobarbus honestly about the way he has "forspoke" her presence at Actium (3)—as she will later question him again when she seeks to understand Antony's behavior (4.2)—her demeanor is less that of vamp than of pupil. She appears both motivated and quick to learn more about military and political science, as though the necessity of guarding her own interests has snapped her to attention.

Indeed, this same juncture—where Caesar's bid for control becomes ever more blatant and unavoidable, and where Cleopatra becomes more attuned to political exigencies—is also where the difficulty of penetrating the reasons for Cleopatra's conduct becomes increasingly pronounced. For a time this difficulty parallels that of discerning what prompts Antony's behavior. The challenge of sifting through the action of 3.13 epitomizes the problem of reading Cleopatra's motives, which resurfaces in the closing scene.

Any production of *Antony and Cleopatra* will present a viewpoint on Cleopatra's intentions toward Thidias in 3.13, and any viewpoint will seem slanted. If, throughout this scene, Cleopatra clearly means to remain faithful to Antony and is only toying with Caesar by playing up to Thidias, then the audience faces the vexed question of why it can detect Cleopatra's irony toward Thidias and Enobarbus cannot.[36] Maybe Enobarbus's powers of perception are imperfect—he of course fails to comprehend his own feelings toward his master—but the unwavering trait of his comments on and to Cleopatra is an incisiveness furnished by objectivity. Witness his earlier discrimination in interpreting Cleopatra's behavior, particularly in the "barge" speech, where he pinpoints her attractiveness to Antony and to all men (2.1.190–239). How, then, if Cleopatra is only having at Thidias, can we account for Enobarbus's impression that Cleopatra is betraying Antony?: "Sir, sir, thou art so leaky / That we must leave thee to thy sinking, for / Thy dearest quit thee" (63–65). To argue that Enobarbus is looking for a last reason to desert Antony or is so jealous of Cleopatra's hold over Antony that he hears what he wants to in Cleopatra's language is unconvincing. So is the explanation that Enobarbus is pulling strings in order to see Thidias punished, even though he taunts him in an aside: "You will be whipt" (88).[37]

Yet, if Cleopatra plays the scene without irony—so that she is aggressively campaigning for Caesar's good graces—it becomes equally skewed. Enobarbus's judgment may be vindicated; Cleopatra's is not. As Ornstein comments: "How foolish of this cunning woman to plan a betrayal of Antony in the presence of Enobarbus!"[38] In this reading, the audience is left disenchanted, halfway through the play, with an overtly obtuse, treacherous Cleopatra and with an Antony too credulous to be believed himself when he forgives Cleopatra's duplicity. Surely the audience is not meant at this point to feel as sour toward these protagonists as does Enobarbus (3.13.194–200). Otherwise, Enobarbus's reversal in act 4 will not work theatrically.

The very purpose of a scene like this one is, seemingly, to raise questions about what is driving Cleopatra. How can an actor playing Cleopatra claim any assurance about the tone of her response to Thidias's first gamble for her allegiance?:

> *Thid.* He [Caesar] knows that you embrace not Antony
> As you did love, but as you fear'd him.
>
> *Cleo.* O!
>
> (56–57)

Evidence of her tone is no more lucid in her longer speeches to Caesar's man:

> Most kind messenger,
> Say to great Caesar this in deputation:
> I kiss his conqu'ring hand. Tell him, I am prompt
> To lay my crown at 's feet, and there to kneel.
> Tell him, from his all-obeying breath I hear
> The doom of Egypt.
>
> (73–78)

What could only be construed as sarcasm in most other characters' mouths is here perfectly matched with Cleopatra's usual hyperbole. Once Antony has erupted over the sight of Thidias's lips on Cleopatra's hand, ambiguity continues to surround her intent toward Thidias. Although she insists that Antony has failed to apprehend her true meaning and even identity—"Not know me yet?" (157)—what incentive she could possibly have for teasing Thidias remains unstated. (Is she just having fun? Does she mean to buy time and flexibility with Caesar through persuading Thidias that she will switch loyalties? Is she hoping that Enobarbus will retrieve Antony so that the vision of her tête-à-tête will provoke him to positive action?) Furthermore, the pivot by which she turns Antony around from his anger is dubious at best: is Cleopatra's vow to sacrifice her children if she is guilty a mode of finessing him or a legitimate defense of her innocence (158–67)? How naive is Antony's response to her vow: "I am satisfied" (167)?

On paper such cruces would appear insoluble. And although in performance some stance on them would no doubt prove inescapable, something of their indeterminacy needs to be preserved in a production calculated to tap into the play's rounded portrayal of Egypt's queen. The shading of Cleopatra's plausible motives into each other—the one narrow and self-serving and the other serving Antony and Egypt's larger political cause—involves her in the play's wider inquiry into wise and foolish folly. The cryptic quality of her inner life—the mystery about what, exactly, she is up to—both resembles the uncertainty about Antony's motives and yet suggests greater self-control, more self-knowledge, and a facility exceeding Antony's at managing her worldly enterprises in tandem with her spiritual needs.

In the last analysis, Cleopatra may not fully reconcile earthly and transcendent values. But she succeeds at both toppling Caesar's designs on her and rejoining Antony in death. The intertwining of her self-preservation and her self-sacrifice continually results in further ambiguity about her objectives—when she takes on Caesar, for instance, is she satisfying herself or trying to champion Antony? Her indistinguishable motives also illuminate how she fulfills her apparently antithetical desires and energies relatively unscathed by the ridicule that dogs Antony and Caesar. Neither confining herself to Caesar's political game nor retreating from the "world's great snare," she embraces this life without deceiving herself about the limits of its rewards. Unlike any other character in the play, Cleopatra, aided by the generosity of her two attendants, accepts her own humanity and thereby (paradoxically) moves toward surpassing it. Refusing to act as a saint—insisting in fact on experiencing her suicide as the consummation of her marriage (5.2.287–313)—she nearly approaches saintliness.

IV

Cleopatra's penultimate act—her pretended suicide—matches in recklessness Antony's final deeds. Her last act, however, rejects such uncalculated behavior in favor of careful orchestration, made possible in part by what Harry Levin calls the "purest Stoicism" of her approach to real suicide.[39] Cleopatra's highly controlled leaving of this world, while necessitating an emotional removal from it, also leads her to immerse herself, characteristically, in earthly affairs. In Cleopatra, then, merge motives self-interested and otherworldly, such that we are hard-pressed to know one from the other. In Cleopatra emerges a harmony between the claims of this world and the next that would seem opposed to the conflict between those values in Antony. In Cleopatra intermingle attachment to and detachment from Caesar's game, such that her most basically human gestures may connote divinity.

Her handling of Dolabella illuminates this paradox. Caesar's intent to use Dolabella as a player in a meticulously staged drama is made increasingly clear once Caesar whisks Decretas offstage at the close of 5.1 with blatant self-promotion:

> Go with me to my tent, where you shall see
> How hardly I was drawn into this war,
> How calm and gentle I proceeded still
> In all my writings. Go with me, and see
> What I can show in this.
>
> (73–77)

Decretas, twice prompted to "go with" Caesar and "see" as Caesar would have him see, is an audience to the emperor's "show"—propaganda that Caesar has painstakingly crafted by saving his "writings" to document his innocence and generosity toward Antony.[40] That his staff has already been briefed on his program, which is also meant to subdue Cleopatra through a display of his apparent magnanimity, becomes evident moments later, when Proculeius reiterates Caesar's self-description to Decretas in his instructions to Dolabella: "Be *gentle* to her" (5.1.75, 5.2.68; emphasis added). Dolabella's role is that of prop, a surrogate for Caesar whose mission, as Caesar conceives of it, is to fulfill his master's will.

Cleopatra conquers Dolabella—and through him Caesar—by awakening his own will, which quickly supplants Caesar's in his sense of allegiance. He, of course, invites her manipulation of him with his overture to her—"Most noble Empress, you have heard of me?" (5.2.71)—by which he strays from Caesar's rigid agenda to fond thoughts of himself.[41]

Given the opportunity, Cleopatra sets immediately to degrading his lack of imagination and insisting that he indulge her in her vision of the colossal Antony (5.2.73–100). Within minutes, Dolabella is divulging Caesar's secret ambition to "lead" her back to Rome "in triumph" (5.2.109–10). For someone like Dolabella, Cleopatra's alchemy must partly consist in the flattery toward him that she implies in her praise of Antony: if she immortalizes Antony so extravagantly, Dolabella must be thinking, how might she remember the man who rescues her from Caesar?

But more significant is Cleopatra's appeal to Dolabella's feeling. Even if he never fully subscribes to her glorification of Antony (5.2.93–95), she has touched his capacity for sympathy:

> Hear me, good madam:
> Your loss is as yourself, great: and you bear it
> As answering to the weight. Would I might never
> O'ertake pursu'd success, but I do feel,
> By the rebound of yours, a grief that smites
> My very heart at root.
>
> (5.2.100–105)

Caesar's mere "show" of concern is supplanted by Cleopatra's genuine "grief," and the old joke about Antony's heaviness (recalled all the more by the internal rhyme on *great* and *weight)* is transformed into an article of true sorrow. Again paradoxically, Cleopatra profits from the good deed of converting Dolabella, who, because she helps him "feel," hastens to sacrifice his own aspirations in her service. When he reenters in 5.2, confirming Caesar's plans to abuse her, his reference to his "love" for Cleopatra as "religion" portrays him as more than a courtly lover (199): through pursuing her own ends, Cleopatra (whom even the priests bless when she is riggish) has transported Dolabella to an authentic self that he then becomes willing to abnegate in her behalf.

Such interwoven motives are for Cleopatra but a scion of those she seems to harbor for her suicide. By now, the futility of ascribing that act to *either* her devotion to Antony *or* her yen to undo Caesar is critical commonplace.[42] Indeed, here again, *through* subverting Caesar and protecting her own interests she simultaneously demonstrates her love for Antony, who can defeat Caesar in no other way than by imping his wing on hers. And here again, the final difference between Antony's and Cleopatra's dying choices is that, for whatever reason, he at least seems to renounce the world on which she relies. Her success at realizing any and all of her hopes—to defeat Caesar, to save her earthly reputation, to join Antony in perfect love—depends entirely upon her openness to the potentially corrupting experiences of human life that Antony would apparently just as soon reject. In the case of her suicide, in order to bequeath her earthlier elements to "baser life" (5.2.289–90), she must come to terms with those elements, whether by testing Caesar's vulnerability to her flirtations (5.2.111–90), manipulating Charmian and Iras with threats of public degradation (5.2.207–26), or dressing herself in her finest clothes to end her life (5.2.280–81). She is determined not to be "hoist" as Antony has been (5.2.55–57). Never completely escaping the claims of "baser life" on her image, she nevertheless transfigures the baser images of that life into something more than earthly through a stunning imposition of will.

Such transfiguration occurs nowhere more stunningly than in the complex iconography of Cleopatra's death scene, the last eighty lines or so of the play. In particular, the images of the serpent and the crown—common emblems in early seventeenth-century England—cut at least two ways. The serpent, which for a Christian audience cannot possibly elude association with the Fall, is, in this play, largely representative of fecundity.[43] But Moseley has pointed out the additional, well-substantiated connection between the serpent and wisdom:

> Snakes, whatever their other less attractive characteristics, have always been associated with subtlety, wisdom, and knowledge—Hermes' caduceus and Our Lord's "Be ye wise as serpents" [Matthew 10:16] both draw on a common and very ancient association. (According to Alciati, the frequency of whose editions shows how much he was regarded in the XVIth Century and later, the serpent was an Egyptian symbol of royalty. Shakespeare could well have been alluding to this too.)[44]

Moseley goes on to catalog several Renaissance pictorial illustrations in which great rulers, including the allegorical queen Prudence and Elizabeth I of England, are shown with serpents, symbolizing "wisdom with self-rule and political rule" (127–28). He conjectures that, finally, Cleopatra's triumph over Caesar, an "ass Unpolicied" at her "metaphorical feet," suggests the transformation of her "(apparent) conventional unwisdom" into true wisdom, facilitated by the serpent at her breast (128).

Moseley's reading of Cleopatra indicates a link between the last stage picture we have of her and the Pauline tradition of wise folly.[45] In fact, although Moseley never mentions that tradition outright, he concludes that Antony and Cleopatra's love, seemingly immoral from a Roman perspective, may constitute "a paradoxical wisdom that is no plant which grows on mortal soil."[46] In other words, he sees Cleopatra's ostensibly unwise love as a higher, transcendent wisdom.

Charmian (Sorcha Cusack) kneels while Cleopatra (Helen Mirren) is bitten by the asp. Iras (Josette Simon) can be seen lying in the foreground. From an RSC production of *Antony and Cleopatra* at The Other Place in Stratford-upon-Avon, 1982; "The Shakespeare Centre Library: Joe Cocks Studio Collection." By permission of The Shakespeare Birthplace Trust.

Anonymous (German), ***The Madonna Nursing the Infant Christ in the Presence of Angels*****, before 1500.**
By permission of Abaris Books.

Jan Provost, center panel of the *Altarpiece of the Virgin Enthroned*, c. 1500. By permission of The Royal Collection, Her Majesty Queen Elizbeth II.

Bernard van Orley, *Holy Family*, 1522.
By permission of Musées royaux des Beaux-Arts de Belgique.

I believe, however, that we can pursue the iconography of Cleopatra's death scene more specifically. When Cleopatra, crowned, enthroned, and flanked by her two votaries, describes the asp, a familiar emblem of wisdom, as a baby who "sucks the nurse asleep" (5.2.309–10), she unavoidably alludes to scores of icons, from the mid-thirteenth to well into the early seventeenth century, of *Maria lactans*—the nursing mother of Christ.[47] These images, ranging in provenance from Italy, to the Netherlands, to England, are known to date as far back as Early Christian times in Egypt, where, according to Gertrud Schiller, they "are connected with early Egyptian representations of Isis."[48] In the West, they began taking root in the late fourth century.[49] By the time they enjoyed

William Basse, *The Virgin and Child with St. John*, from etchings, 1628–48. By permission of the Rijksmuseum.

popularity during the fourteenth century and throughout the Renaissance, they had remained predominantly Northern in number and character.[50]

Gail McMurray Gibson, writing about the "complex and omnipresent . . . Marian devotion" in fifteenth-century East Anglia, discusses at length one approach to the meaning of *Maria lactans*.[51] Gibson's example is Our Lady of Walsingham chapel, site of "miraculous healings, especially after returning crusaders presented to the shrine a phial said to contain drops of milk from the Virgin's breasts" (140). Pilgrims to the shrine—a favorite of Henry VIII, who ensured its prosperity until the Dissolution—could glimpse the phial "[i]n return for a suitable offering" (140–42). This relic is emblematic of Mary's maternity, the essence of which, says Gibson, is the "principle, both incarnational and linguistic, of saving fecundity" (139).

The relationship between the nursing mother Mary and her salvific nurturance is longstanding. According to Millard Meiss,

> The representation of the Madonna suckling her Child had a special significance in late medieval art and thought. Since it showed that situation in which the Virgin was most concretely and intimately the mother of Christ, it set forth that character and power which arose from her motherhood, i.e. her role as *Maria mediatrix*, compassionate intercessor for humanity before the impartial justice of Christ or God the Father. . . . [T]he act of nursing signified moral qualities, such as benevolence and mercifulness. . . . In the Middle Ages the Virgin was believed to be the mother and nurse not only of Christ but of all mankind.[52]

Theresa Coletti concurs: "The Virgin's milk serves as an analogue to the salvific nourishment of Christ's blood, and consequently images of *Maria lactans* inevitably evoke association with the redemptive promise."[53] Nor must the nursing image involve Mary specifically to represent divine charity, though most do. For instance, the figure of *Ecclesia*, sculpted by Giovanni Pisano for the Duomo in Pisa (1302–10), envisions the Church as nursing her congregation and thus recalls Paul's metaphor for the Church's teachings: "I fed you with milk, not solid food; for you were not ready for it; and even yet you are not ready, for you are still of the flesh" (1 Cor. 3:2–3).

The implicit comparison between Cleopatra and the Virgin is far from thorough or allegorical. To assert otherwise would be patently absurd. Instead, I would argue that the comparison is selective and precise and that, furthermore, its incompleteness is essential to how it works. In Cleopatra, the worldliness of her roles as illicit lover and as ruler and as mother are never denied or forgotten.[54] Still, by virtue of her final appearance, as well as her verbal self-characterization as a nursing mother, she connects herself with the wise folly of redemptive love, or charity. Her characterization, in the fullest sense of that word, interrelates, fuses even, the secular and the holy.[55] Renaissance audiences were well-versed in how to tide the gap between such disparate traditions; as Gibson points out, Elizabethans had already long practiced the "transference of the cult of the Virgin to the political cult of the Virgin Queen."[56] One especially telling example involves the Puritan preacher Andrew Willett, who in the late sixteenth century published a book of double acrostic emblem poems whose shaped verses (what Moseley calls "figured forms"[57]) replace the visual images that normally accompany the poetry. His first poem, in praise of the dedication to Queen Elizabeth, Willett himself glosses thus:

> The Queen our Prince is a great succour to all; . . . this famous maiden denies not milk to her peoples—to them, immediately [they need it], she their sweet nurse has already sent help by her own hand.[58]

Willett's choice of metaphors—a mother's milk—evinces the post-Reformation ease with reappropriated religious iconography, in this case applied to secular (though God-fearing) politics.[59] In short, the nursing metaphor was portable, applicable in various contexts. The well-known association between Elizabeth I and the Virgin Mary no doubt also cooperated with that between Cleopatra and Elizabeth I to further the third one between Cleopatra and the Virgin.[60]

Shakespeare's Cleopatra, then, arrives at the emblem of nurse through several doors—by virtue of her association with divinity, with royalty, and with motherhood. But the particular transference of Mary's salvific love onto Cleopatra is advanced by other details—for example, her earlier appearance in the image of the pietà, the dying Antony draped across her lap (4.15.38–91).[61] In this instance, too, she is gaudy Egyptian queen, grieving the loss of a foolish soldier, yet so visionary in her eulogizing this "crown o' the earth" as to redeem his image quite. The figure of the crown, moreover, recalls vividly Antony's untarnished love for Enobarbus, whose "turpitude" the betrayed master "crown[s] with gold" (4.6.32–33). It also looks forward to Cleopatra's appearance as she prepares "again for Cydnus / To meet Mark Antony" (5.2.228–29).[62] That particular crown symbolizes her royalty but also the "bounty," like Antony's toward Enobarbus (4.6.31), about her suicide for Antony's sake. What's more, it further relates our last impression of Cleopatra to popular representations of the Virgin.

As Meiss explains, the attribution of the heavenly crown to Mary, whose "nursing . . . signifies her mercy," stems, paradoxically, from her reign as queen of humility.[63] Through refusing grace to none, she descended to the level of meanest human sin, often demonstrating her lowliness by sitting on the earth, rather than in a throne, in fourteenth-century portrayals. Her humility, however, released her to become enskied and sainted, as her identity began to combine with, as Meiss puts it, "the awesome Woman described in the twelfth chapter of the Apocalypse: 'And there appeared a great wonder in heaven; a woman clothed with the sun, and the moon under her feet, and upon her head a crown of twelve stars'" (153). This amalgam is exemplified, down to the crown of exactly twelve stars, by Albrecht Dürer's woodcut entitled "The Virgin on the Crescent." The poem that accompanies the figure preserves Mary's identity as intercessor in behalf of humanity, using her power to save her supplicants from the shifting fortunes of earthly life.

Not that Cleopatra's crown confines her to an association either with the virtue of humility or with the Apocalypse, nor that the crown itself is limited only to symbolism that is religious at base. In early seventeenth-century Europe, the crown emblem proliferated, ranging in meaning from worldly vanity, as in Wither's effigy of a naked soul rising above earth-bound fame, to political security, the theme of an emblem by Henry Peacham: two prudent serpents guard the realm (the "Soveraignes crowne"), while the poem warns would-be usurpers (like Caesar?) that their ill-considered "abuse" of "tha'nointed Diadem" will be "reuenged." Still, the majority of crowns in Renaissance emblem books connote something akin to the heavenly crown—for example, the "Vertue" of lasting love over Wanton affection in Wither's emblem of the fickle woman. Thus, the image of Cleopatra's crown points in several directions, some of them opposed to features of the humble Madonna, and some not: in a final example of this blending, the queen's momentary lure of Caesar himself with her "strong toil of grace" speaks to the universal appeal of her physical loveliness, as well as her abundant love. Caesar, perhaps in spite of himself, commemorates both in burying her next to Antony (5.2.358).

But the most suggestive detail about Cleopatra's crown is that, in the course of the strong toil that is her death, it shifts "awry" (5.2.318), faintly burlesquing those hundreds of pictures in which the Virgin's perfection remains inviolate, eternal. Every inch an earthly queen, Cleopatra must contrive to idealize her outward looks through artificial means, as by avoiding the unsightly "swelling" induced by poisons (5.2.345–46). For this vanity, she is herself lightly mocked, her crown embarrassingly, if only briefly, askew. Charmian's last act of adoration, to "mend" the crown's angle (5.2.319), portends her self-sacrifice through suicide—both gestures in which exemplary devotion mixes with

EPITOME IN DIVAE PARTHENICES MARI
AE HISTORIAM AB ALBERTO DVRERO
NORICO PER FIGVRAS DIGES
TAM CVM VERSIBVS ANNE
XIS CHELIDONII

Quisquis fortunæ correptus turbine perfers
Quam tibi iacturam fata sinistra ferunt.
Aut animæ delicta gemis. Phlegethontis & ignes
Anxius æternos corde tremente paues.
Quisquis & vrgeris iam iam decedere vita
Alterius: migrans: nescius hospitij.
Huc ades: auxilium: pete: continuoq; rogabo
Pro te: quem paui lacte: tuliq; sinu.
Ille deus rerum mihi subdidit astra: deosq;
Flectitur ille meis O homo supplicijs.

76 (131) The Virgin on the Crescent (The Life of the Virgin)
(*La Vierge assise sur le croissant, et donnant le sein à l'enfant Jésus*) c.1511 [SW.156] 203 x 196.

Albrecht Dürer, *The Virgin on the Crescent*, c. 1511.
By permission of Abaris Books.

As, to the World I nake[illegible] came,
So, naked-stript I leave the same.

12

ILLVSTR. XII. *Book. 1.*

THrice happy is that Man whose *Thoughts* doe reare
His Minde above that pitch the *Worldling* flies,
And by his *Contemplations*, hovers where
He viewes things mortall, with unbleared eyes.
What Trifles then doe *Villages* and *Townes*
Large *Fields* or *Flockes* of fruitfull *Cattell* seeme:
Nay, what poore things are *Miters*, *Scepters*, *Crownes*,
And all those *Glories* which Men most esteeme:
Though he that hath among them, his Delight,
Brave things imagines them (because they blinde
With some false Lustre his beguiled sight)
He that's above them, their meane-Worth may finde.
Lord, to that *Blessed-Station* me convey
Where I may view the *World*, and view her so,
That I her true Condition may survey;
And all her Imperf[illegible]

George Wither, The vanity of worldly pursuits, 1635.
By permission of University of South Carolina Press.

THE auntient Romans by their Temples vſ'd,
To paint a ſerpent, or ſuch hideous thing:
That holy places, might not be abuſ'd
By children, whom they told, that theſe would ſting:
And made beleue they liu'd, to that intent,
To Sacred things they ſhould be reverent.

pingo meos angues: *Perſ*;

Vile Traytor, of ſome Hyrcane Tiger bred,
Such Serpents ſtill, thy Soveraignes crowne do guard:
But think not as the other, theſe are dead,
Like child or foole: but that they are prepar'd,
With mortal ſtings, to be reueng'd on them,
That ſhall abuſe, tha'nointed Diadem.

Iovi cura eſt veneranda principis *Thracinus*.

Proditores etiam iis quos ante ponunt inviſi ſunt.

Tacitus. 1. *Annal*:

Dob:s

Henry Peacham, *Regum Maiestatem non imminuendam*, from *Minerva Britanna*, 1612. By permission of Walter J. Johnson, Inc.

A fickle Woman *wanton growne,*
Preferres a Crowd, *before a* Crowne. 7

ILLVSTR. VII. *Book.* 1.

FOole! Doſt thou hope, thine *Honours*, or thy *Gold*,
Shall gaine thee *Love?* Or, that thou haſt her heart
Whoſe hand upon thy tempting *Bayt* layes hold?
Alas! fond *Lover*, thou deceived art.
She that with *Wealth*, and *Titles*, can be wonne,
Or woo'd with *Vanities*, will wav'ring bee;
And, when her Love, thou moſt dependeſt on,
A *Fiddle-ſticke* ſhall winne her heart from thee.
To *Youth* and *Muſicke*, *Venus* leaneth moſt;
And (though her hand ſhe on the *Scepter* lay)
Let *Greatneſſe*, of her Favours never boaſt:
For, *Heart* and *Eye*, are bent another way.
And lo, no glorious Purchace that Man gets,
Who hath with ſuch poore *Trifles*, woo'd, and wonne:
Her footing, on a *Ball*, his *Miſtreſſe* ſets,
Which in a moment ſlips, and ſhe is gone.
A *Woman*, meerely with an *Out ſide* caught,
Or tempted with a *Galliard*, or a *Song*,
Will him forſake (whom ſhe moſt lovely thought)
For *Players* and for *Tumblers*, ere't be long.
You, then, that wiſh your *Love* ſhould ever laſt,
(And would enjoy *Affection* without changing)
Love where your *Loves* may worthily be plac't;
And, keepe your owne *Affection*, ſtill from ranging.
Vſe noble *Meanes*, your Longings to attaine;
Seeke equall *Mindes*, and well-beſeeming *Yeares*:
They are (at beſt) vaine *Fooles*, whom *Follie* gaine;
But, there is *Bliſſe*, where, *Vertue* moſt endeares:
And, whereſoe're, Affection *ſhee* procures,
In ſpight of all *Temptations*, it endures.

This

George Wither, Fickle woman rejecting the honor of a crown, 1635.
By permission of University of South Carolina Press.

a lower form of folly, bred of fleeting efforts to control human destiny. Doomed as may finally be the attempts of these women to manipulate Caesar and their reputations after death, their pains meet with some success.

Cleopatra never transcends this world, whatever protests she may make about discarding her earthlier "elements" (5.2.289–90). Her frank engagement in Caesar's game leads her, in some true sense, to render unto Caesar the things that are Caesar's.[64] So doing, she embraces her humanity. Though her characterization is riddled with instances of her pride, her struggle to take down Caesar while also eluding him establishes, paradoxically, her humility: she is not above playing by Caesar's rules, turning his tactics against him, or risking loss at his hands. Also paradoxically, her openness to worldly folly seems inseparable from—the very grounds for—her apotheosis of Antony and Shakespeare's of her.[65]

Shakespeare's Mark Antony reflects the saint whose name he shares by at least appearing to exchange earthly "glory" for pure love and his "pardon" (4.14.19, 45). But Shakespeare's Cleopatra recalls, in her peculiar way, Caxton's story of Saint Anthony and the bowman, in which the monk makes no apology for worldly game, which has its holy purpose (see chap. 1). In the broadest sense, Saint Anthony's wise folly traditionally includes a worldly playfulness that he is also, finally, willing to put at risk and, if need be, sacrifice. For Cleopatra, the wisdom of this world is divine foolishness in something of this uncanny sense. It is foolishness with this world in all its splendor and inadequacy—what Caesar calls "noble weakness" (5.2.344). Because her defeat of Caesar and her ennobling of Antony are forever tainted by her commitment to the goals, standards, and passions of this life, audiences will be forever tempted to take the part for the whole and respond only negatively, only to her familiarity with the mutable, corrupt world. Or they will minimize her worldliness and protest that her love for Antony cancels it or rises above it. To do either, however, is to derange the careful balance of a play that, insofar as it concerns the problems of living in and leaving this world, remains deeply suspicious of endeavors to avoid it. As Antony grows increasingly uncomfortable on earth, so does Caesar, who, recoiling from bodily pleasures (for example, 2.7.98–125), takes refuge in conquest and pride in self-control. If Cleopatra evades a good share of the folly that visits these two soldiers, it is not for lack of loving this life.

5

Prospero's "false brother": Shakespeare's Final Antonio

The essential question about the Antonio and Sebastian of *The Tempest* is why they are the direct antitheses of their saintly precursors. Saints Anthony and Sebastian, each in his own way, forfeited worldly possessions and risked their lives for love of God. All three of the earlier Shakespearean Antonios studied thus far bear resemblance to the saints at least in part, notably for sacrificing their own property, power, and safety in the name of earthly love, albeit not without encountering for their pains some measure of suspicion, or even outright ridicule. This last Antonio/Sebastian pairing, however, stands apart from the others, although both, like Saint Anthony, are tempted to evil. But these two do not pretend to have goals other than selfish gain. Steeped in the folly of worldly ambition, they are mocked not for trying and failing to realize true charity but for lacking the vision and will to make the attempt.

I would like to offer two analyses as to why these familiar characters are turned inside out in *The Tempest*. Although the explanations are not opposed to each other, the first is quick and easy, while the second is far more challenging to elaborate. The first is that the thorough subversion of virtue in Antonio and Sebastian perfectly suits the effect in *The Tempest* of looking at traditional doctrine about wise folly as if through a looking glass. Insofar as *The Tempest* concerns the relationship between this world and the next (as it does to a great extent), it urges a healthy attachment to the earthly matters that Saint Paul identifies with foolish folly, rather than detachment from the world. Most particularly, Prospero's main objective during the play is to act on spiritual principles, thereby practicing tenets that the reason knows as wisdom.

Through Prospero, that is, Shakespeare pushes to conclusion doubts about avoiding the world that pervade *The Merchant of Venice*, *Twelfth Night*, and *Antony and Cleopatra*. In Spenserian and Miltonic terms, *The Tempest* "cannot praise a fugitive and cloistered virtue" but examines the meaning and purpose of wisdom both to the individual and to society.[1] Here, true sacrifice requires engaging in affairs of state and of family, while withdrawal from such practical concerns constitutes selfishness as gross as that about Antonio and Sebastian's ambition. If, then, the wise folly of *The Tempest* lies in the mirror image of its conventional form, we should not be surprised to find in this Antonio and Sebastian obversions of their originals. Rather than invalidate the saint type, Shakespeare's final Antonio and Sebastian subject it to more extreme versions of the challenges it has encountered in earlier plays. *The Tempest*, whose philosophy owes as much to classical learning as to Christianity, might be expected occasionally to turn something Christian on its ear.[2] Prospero, perennially subject to his own temptation, has virtually replaced the conventional Anthony figure. Put another way, this Antonio and Sebastian serve the dual purpose of reflecting Prospero's constant temptation toward egoism and of elucidating, like images on a photographic negative, the unorthodox treatment in this play of the doctrine they were known to represent.

Fleshing out the longer response to my opening question will occupy the rest of this chapter. Much interest will be lavished on Prospero and his temptation, as any full-length study of *The Tempest* necessitates, but with an eye to weaving Antonio and Sebastian into the larger fabric of Prospero's ordeal. In Prospero as both man and mage is extracted the larger play's fascination with the relationship between the temporal realm and the eternal. No wonder, then, if the complexities of Prospero's characterization eclipse other characters, his brother included. Yet Antonio finally contributes a perspective as essential to the whole play and to the portrayal of Prospero as does Caliban, whose character complements Antonio's.

Discussing Prospero critically must be one of the most problematic of all tasks currently presented by Shakespeare's canon, so disparate in temperament and attitude are the approaches that critics have adopted in the last twenty-five years or so. Chiefly, what seems to have begun as a move to correct idealistic views of Prospero has evolved into a rift between those scholars who continue to insist upon Prospero's nearly unqualified virtue and others who vehemently object to idolatry of Prospero, citing his injustice toward Caliban and other characters or his subconscious tendency to resemble Caliban.[3] Although I would not presume to harmonize these opposing parties, I seek more balance between them, as well as more interrelatedness, than is typical. Harry Berger complained in 1969 that the "sentimental" version of *The Tempest* "does not hit the play where it lives."[4] But neither does a blackened Prospero or an all-out renunciation of the play's concluding optimism, however superficial it may strike us, accord with any but the most perversely distorted of its productions in the theater.[5] Anyone who has seen the play performed more than once knows intuitively that a Prospero with pretensions to flawlessness is as unsatisfying as one marked by self-deception and irredeemable heartlessness.

I would like to sweep away cobwebs without eliminating aspects of recent criticism that acknowledge tonal and moral complexity about Prospero's characterization. On the one hand, the blatant allegorical texture of *The Tempest* invites allegorical critical modes. On the other hand, the defiance of the play to settle on and carry through its own allegorical suggestiveness inevitably undermines uniformly allegorical readings. Put another way, *The Tempest* is, among Shakespeare's works, unusually susceptible to interpretation based on selective evidence and aimed at consistency. Better to admit from the start that any models—allegorical or otherwise—will fall short of resolving all ambiguities. Better, too, I think, to take initial cues from scholars whose command of medieval and Renaissance moral philosophy and whose sensitivity to the play's poetry offers them perspective on what *The Tempest* and its critics cannot, as well as can, address. Consider the example of R. A. D. Grant, describing the sense in which the work concerns Providence:

> *The Tempest* . . . dramatizes a complex of mutually sustaining meanings, a tissue of analogy in which the realms of human society and moral character owe their very autonomy to the providential pattern which both embraces and informs them. For this reason, the feats of abstraction performed by the dramatist and called forth in the critic in one case do, and in the other should, involve no loss. . . . Yet . . . neither *The Tempest* nor providential fiction . . . can be read as religious allegory or as contributing to pure theology in any immediate way, if, indeed, the latter should happen to be anything more than imaginative exercises. *The Tempest* tells us much about human life, but it has nothing to say about divinity in itself. For, whereof one cannot speak directly, thereof one must, in a manner, be silent.[6]

Grant establishes the primacy in the play of individual moral conduct in particular relation to society—of "politics" in the fullest sense of the word (255). Simultaneously, he identifies expectations that the human orientation of *The Tempest* cannot fulfill; he locates the limits of this art form and the criticism about it to articulate the truths at stake.

So, in a different key, does James Walter. Commenting on the play's allegorical dimension, he writes:

> *The Tempest* . . . develops a psychological imagery that allegorizes many distinct voices in the soul. The clear voice of reason expresses itself in categories of conceptual thought and forms of discursive language; but other, more ambiguous voices speak from a dark depth of the soul that cannot be fully articulated in language, although spectacle, music, and poetic image can convince an audience of their reality. [Walter goes on to quote Caliban's speech about the island's "noises, / Sounds and sweet airs that give delight and hurt not."][7]

Having thus pointed out the inadequacy of verbal allegory to contain entirely an audience's knowledge of *The Tempest*, Walter concludes by expanding on his definition of allegory so as to account for our experience of the play:

> The direction of allegory is counter [to that of the symbol], demystifying the perceived symbolic unity to uncover a depressing difference between signifiei and signified. But allegory also seeks to heal itself by striving to signify a more than natural plenitude of meaning. Allegory both deflates signs by calling attention to their failure and inflates them by charging them to carry more truth of experience than they properly can. (74)

His determination to entertain *The Tempest* as allegory notwithstanding, Walter's point is that the play speaks more than it or its audience can say. Both Walter and Grant are in some sense remarking that this work does not formulate accessibly all that it is about.[8]

So it is, I would argue, in the case of Antonio, whose characterization not only pushes against the theatrical tradition that bred him but also resists allegorical readings of his evil and final silence. For all the audience can surmise, Antonio is in spiritual torment as *The Tempest* closes, inwardly unresolved; then again, his recent experiences may yet to have seeped into his awareness. In any event, the mysteries lingering about Antonio at the play's conclusion suggest ongoing, if not secret, evolution in Antonio's inner spiritual narrative.

Can Prospero be discussed in this spirit? Can he be seen as a character in moral dilemma, in whom several motivations act in conflict with one another? And can even this loose paradigm be abandoned when it ceases to resonate in the drama? To pursue these questions, I propose to focus on Prospero's pride, as it shapes his fluid character, as it is complicated by his identity as an artist, and as he grapples with it while reformulating his social and political bonds—most notably, his relationship with his brother Antonio.

I

The promotion of one's attachment to the world in *The Tempest* is, like so many other features of the play, paradoxical. More than any other Renaissance work before Bacon's *New Atlantis* (1627), *The Tempest* draws on Thomas More's *Utopia*—most particularly, on the dangers of excessive pride associated with either reckless immersion in or complete rejection of private material gain and earthly power. More's Utopians illustrate the veritable impossibility of being both human and capable of avoiding possessiveness, as when, for instance, they wage imperialist war under the pretense of altruistically ensuring that another country's land be put to worthy use.[9] They have only ostensibly eradicated the vice of pride through their communism, which, conveniently, applies merely in domestic, not in international, situations: they go so far as to hoard gold that they pillage from other countries (and that they purport to disdain) in order to wage more imperialist war and to allow "some of their citezeins . . . to lyue . . . sumptuously lyke men of honoure and renowne" (121). More's irony toward their hypocrisy is further complicated by his suggestion that the pride so reviled by the Utopians—and yet to which they are prone—may not, in one light, be such a bad thing. The character of More (who has a Chaucerian way of seeming a wryly naive version of the author) puts the issue this way in the book's concluding paragraph:

> When Raphaell hadde made an ende of his tale, thoughe manye thinges came to my mind which in the manners and lawes of that people semed to be instituted and founded of no good reason, . . . yea and chieffely, in that which is the principall fondacion of al their ordinaunces, that is to saye, in the communitie of theire liffe and liuinge, without anny occupieng of money; by the whyche thynge onelye all nobilitie, magnificence, wourship, honour, and maiestie, the true ornamentes and honoures, as the common opinion is, of a common wealth, vtterly be ouerthrowen and destroyed. (143)

Though pride be the downfall of many a civilization, without it a civilization flounders for lack of shared motivation, cause, and enthusiasm.

As *The Tempest* opens, Prospero struggles with a comparable paradox. Twelve years earlier, he tells Miranda, Milan had become "[t]hrough all the signories . . . the first," and himself, "the prime duke," because of his renowned "dignity" and learning in "the liberal arts" (1.2.71–74). The very study that conferred glory on his state, however, tempted him to "[neglect] worldly ends" and to concentrate solely on his own improvement (1.2.89–90). With that retirement to solitude came contempt for those who, like Antonio, were left behind to administer the practicalities that Prospero now viewed as beneath him: Prospero "cast" the burden of governing on Antonio, scorned "all popular rate," and then was surprised when no one, least of all Antonio, remembered that he was duke in actuality (1.2.75, 92, 102–5). Succumbing to his own ambitions, Prospero inadvertently tempted Antonio to give in to his. Both men became slaves to pride—the one, by trying to transcend the world through contemplation; the other, by embracing the world's trappings.

Prospero's account of his past in 1.2 goes a long way toward consciously acknowledging his role in Antonio's temptation, as when he concedes that "[I], in my false brother, / Awak'd an evil nature" (92–93).[10] Yet occasionally his diction betrays an effort to whitewash his responsibility: his "trust" in Antonio, for example, is like a "good parent" that "begets" vice in its own too much (94–97). The subtle self-justification here joins other hints in this scene of Prospero's vestigial pride—his use of present tense when declaring that he still "prize[s] his books" more than his "dukedom" (167–68) and the gloating self-satisfaction that Ariel seems to take in fulfilling Prospero's commands, which may derive from the master himself (for example, 195–237). Taken together, these details point to the greatest difficulty that Prospero's character will face in recovering his lost dignity because, to do so, he must first retrieve his former respect for the practice of governing, a kind of socially beneficial pride, which will be constantly threatened by his proclivity to flatter himself.

The demon lurking under this mage's cloak tempts him not toward but away from the world; it lures him to think of himself as separate from his society, as beyond the jurisdiction of the limits that he, the duke, must impose on his subjects. The island on which Prospero is stranded has affinities with the desert in which Saint Anthony elected to seclude himself so as to reject the world's temptations, but if removal from the world should become for Prospero an end in itself, then Prospero's opportunity to serve will degenerate into merely self-serving escapism. Only full acceptance of his social responsibility can provide him with the antidote to his false pride: paradoxically, pride in assuming and administering political responsibility—the pride of which the character More speaks at the end of *Utopia*—carries its own means of modulation by requiring a ruler like Prospero to meet other people's needs.

Shakespeare's model for the peculiar blindness that, like Prospero's, illuminates others' weaknesses while it obscures one's own, must surely have been Montaigne.[11] Most critics to date have supposed that the playwright's main interest in "Of Cannibals" was that the essay, in Walter's words, "purports to defend the natural reasonableness of precivil life."[12] If so, then the crucial relevance of the essay to the play lies with Shakespeare's handling of Caliban's primitivism—in particular, with the question of whether Caliban's naturalness is in the end more virtuous, more civil, than the actions of civilized men like Antonio, Alonso, and even Prospero. *The Tempest* clearly plays with this question throughout—for example, when Caliban displays superior understanding to Trinculo (for example, 4.1.222–24); when he speaks in verse, while Stephano and Trinculo are given only prose; and when Antonio and Sebastian try to usurp Alonso's position, as Caliban does Prospero's (1.2).[13]

Still, I think the core of Montaigne's piece, and of Shakespeare's focus on Montaigne, is something other: it is the pride of allegedly civilized people, which renders them capable of perceiving barbarism in others' actions but not in their own. "Of Cannibals," in other words, centers on the hypocrisy of one society's hiding behind the pretense of reasonableness and civility in order to judge another society as barbaric, beneath the standards of reasonableness and civility. Montaigne abhors inhumanity in any society whatsoever; he aims not to exalt "precivil life," but to debunk civilization. Repeatedly, he signals that his subject is any society's attachment to its own practices—its self-love:

> Now (to returne to my purpose) I finde (as farre as I have beene informed) there is nothing in that nation [i.e., Brazil], that is either barbarous or savage, unlesse men call that barbarisme which is not common to them. As indeed, we have no other ayme of truth and reason, than the example and *Idea* of the opinions and customes of the country we live in. There is ever perfect religion, perfect policie, perfect and compleat use of all things.
>
> I am not sorie we note the barbarous horror of such an action [i.e., the practice of cannibalism "to represent an extreme, and inexpiable revenge,"] but grieved, that prying so narrowly into their faults we are so blinded in ours.
>
> We may then well call them [i.e., Brazilians] barbarous, in regard of reasons rules, but not in respect of us that exceed them in all kinde of barbarisme.[14]

Montaigne does not excuse truly barbaric behavior in either natural or artificial society. Instead, he laments the license that civilization gives social beings to ignore barbarity among themselves.

Montaigne's fixation on such hypocrisy offers a crucial lens on Prospero's wrongdoers and, more so, on the problems confronting Prospero himself. Shakespeare's metaphor for Montaigne's barbarity is monstrosity, visually evident in only Caliban but manifested spiritually in the "three men of sin," one of whom, Alonso, uses the metaphor in describing his former barbarity against Prospero:

O, it is monstrous! monstrous!
Methought the billows spoke, and told me of it;
The winds did sing it to me, and the thunder,
That deep and dreadful organ-pipe, pronounc'd
The name of Prosper; it did base my trespass.

(3.3.95–99)

In fact, as in Montaigne, the most potentially damaging monstrosity in *The Tempest* is that which is hidden within, protected by the signs of civilization, as is the absence of conscience in Antonio: "If 'twere a kibe, / 'Twould put me to my slipper; but I feel not / This deity in my bosom" (1.2.276–78).

Gonzalo makes clear in 3.3 that a reverse incongruity between the appearance and reality of monstrosity is possible; remarking on the spirits who serve the banquet, whom he takes to be "islanders" (29), he says: "though they are of monstrous shape, yet note / Their manners are more gentle, kind, than of / Our human generation" (31–33). Of course, these spirits are about to appear far less kind (and yet are also about to be truly kind—even Christian—for their role in Ariel's upcoming sermon?), but the significance of the example is that outward monstrosity can mask inward beauty and outer beauty can cover inner barbarity. In a more relevant instance, Caliban's misshapen form both reflects his moral deformity and belies his highly developed aesthetic sensibility: he speaks in often lovely verse, he appreciates music (3.2.135–43), and his attraction to Miranda, although acted on in a violative way, owes to his awareness that "she as far surpasseth Sycorax / As great'st does least" (3.2.102–3).

In the most relevant example, however, Prospero's identity as an artist—a maker of beauty—can obscure, especially from himself, his own capacity for monstrosity. Nowhere, perhaps, does he seem spiritually uglier than when he instructs Ariel to torment Caliban, Trinculo, and Stephano:

Go, charge my goblins that they grind their joints
With dry convulsions, shorten up their sinews
With aged cramps, and more pinch-spotted make them
Than pard or cat o' mountain.

(4.1.258–61)

Indeed, the speaker here could well be Caliban, railing at Prospero: "All the infections that the sun sucks up / From bogs, fens, flats, on Prosper fall, and make him / By inch-meal a disease!" (2.2.1–3). This implicit comparison does not defend Caliban's behavior or attribute it to Prospero; rather, it implicates the presumably learned and civilized Prospero for losing his reason and self-control.[15] From the perspective that Montaigne lends Shakespeare, what is more spiritually deformed than Prospero's vengeance here is his failure to perceive it as monstrous, a failure that hinges on his assurance of his superiority to a creature like Caliban.

The demon that distorts Prospero's vision in this way has another face—despair—which is often conflated in Renaissance literature with pride. John Faustus represents the clearest of examples here: Prospero's characterization stems partly from Faustus's attraction to magic, from his dependency on his books, which careens out of control, and, above all, from his Promethean impatience with mortal knowledge and his narcissism toward his scholarly and supernatural feats. Such pride engenders in Faustus a certainty that he alone "can never be pardoned."[16] "The Serpent that tempted *Eve* may be sav'd," he groans to the young scholars who urge him to repent, "But not *Faustus*" (13.16–17). Faustus's hardheartedness, leading to his ultimate damnation, traces back to his original sense of superiority to all others—in the case of his sinfulness, even to Lucifer.

Prospero flirts with a similar despair but one less obviously directed toward his own situation than toward those he would reform—specifically, the three offending nobles and Caliban. Of the latter, we hear him speak in terms clearly bereft of hope for change:

> A devil, a born devil, on whose nature
> Nurture can never stick; on whom my pains,
> Humanely taken, all, all lost, quite lost;
> And as with age his body uglier grows,
> So his mind cankers.
>
> (4.1.188–92)

So Prospero has felt ever since Caliban betrayed his trust—his "human care"—by trying to rape Miranda (1.2.345–48).[17]

The influence of this betrayal on Prospero's cynicism about Caliban should not be minimized.[18] Granted that Prospero's character is naturally inclined toward condescension, Caliban not only attacked his daughter but threatened her honor, a terrifying attempt at violation in any historical period but of even more ethical than physical consequence in the cultural context of *The Tempest*. In addition, that the incident reprises Prospero's earlier misplaced trust in Antonio helps explain the intensity of his reaction to Caliban: he has been deceived twice but until now has had only Caliban, not Antonio, with whom to register his grief and anger. Prospero may also be understood as projecting onto Caliban shame that properly belongs to himself. Caliban's claim that Prospero usurped the island from him implies another instance, in addition to the earlier incident with

Antonio, in which Prospero has contributed, partly unawares, to being betrayed (1.2.331–32). His usurpation has possibly encouraged Caliban's retaliation. Yet the context of Caliban's claim about Prospero's seizure of the island from him suggests that it is an afterthought, a means of justifying his own anger at Prospero's loss of faith in him (1.2.331–44). In short, if Prospero is given to despair in Caliban or in humanity generally, it is not gratuitous; he has seen much in twelve years' time to induce it.

My point is that Prospero's evident antisocial tendencies stem from various possible roots, some of them more understandable—and acceptable—than others. Moreover, those tendencies are in tension with Prospero's apparent desire to overcome them and his efforts to bring forth something better, redemptive even, from the mistakes and the pain of the past. That impetus depends on his capacity for humility and for the "human care" that he once dispensed to Caliban and clearly continues to display toward Miranda. The story of *The Tempest* is, essentially, that of Prospero's wrestling with his demons to sustain that care. As such, the play features a protagonist in moral flux. The dynamic pull between his "fury" and his "nobler reason" sees him constantly tempted to repeat his original mistake by removing himself from all that is human (5.1.26). Sometimes, he succumbs to temptation, and it is almost always with Caliban. More often, he is engaged in struggle, and the struggle is the substance of the play's drama.[19]

The clearest illustration of what remains unfixed in Prospero's character throughout the play is his behavior toward the three offending nobles—especially his intent as to how he will use them once he has them in his power. Tellingly, some critics assume that Prospero never entertains the possibility of avenging their wrongs but only wants to reform them; others, that Prospero intends revenge until his scene with Ariel at the beginning of 5.1. Both sets of critics seem sure of their views.[20] And both, I would suggest, are partly right. From the start, Prospero knows rationally that he should refrain from harming so much as one "hair" of the men on board the ship (1.2.217). What he is tempted to do is another matter. *That* he is tempted to wreak revenge bubbles up in his language (for example, he is "strook to th' quick" with "fury" over his enemies' "high wrongs," 5.1.25–26), and ambiguity as to his motives hovers around some of his actions, like teasing Alonso before finally reuniting him with Ferdinand (5.1.134–71). In short, audiences disagree about aspects of Prospero's characterization because Prospero's character is unresolved. Nuances in his lines as he deals with his anger imply that he *could* always go in the other direction—away from forgiveness and toward a wild justice connoting despair over his peers' ability to change morally.

As if Prospero's mixed motives and sometimes subtle inner conflicts did not produce enough complexity, Shakespeare adds to the problem of coming to terms with this character the challenge of discerning when he is merely acting. For all we know, he may be ever the artist, unceasingly manipulating others through manipulating their feelings and their impression of his feelings. His peevishness toward Miranda and Ferdinand, for instance, may be partly or largely feigned. Miranda indicates twice in 1.2 that his "ungentl[e]" conduct is "unwonted" (445, 497–99), confined only to this day, and Prospero himself later calls into question the authenticity of all his earlier testiness, when he explains to Ferdinand that his "auster[ity]" was meant to convey Miranda's worth and to "test" Ferdinand's worthiness (4.1.1–7). What the audience may take as evidence of Prospero's inclination toward arrogance and disrespect, then, might sometimes be an extension of his art, a show. What's more, he is likely to seem more sympathetic for whatever portion of his pride and impatience is genuine if the audience takes into account that the only day he appears onstage is also the only day on which he can make a bid for reparation. On this particular day, he would naturally be more given than usual to anxiety.

In the end, Prospero's shortcomings are considerable and of a piece: his tendencies toward pride and despair, intolerance and wrath are consistent with his exceptional learning and rigorous demands of others. His perfectionist expectations square with his difficulty in accepting human error, even one so small as his daughter's nodding off as he speaks. Shakespeare has created for this character a rich personal history suitable to his advanced years, a matrix both for the difficulties he faces when the play opens and for the factors that may mitigate the audience's view of his weaknesses.

Only his reluctance to own up to those weaknesses remains as the one serious obstacle to his successful reentry into the world. His involvement in Alonso's conversion implicitly speaks to that problem. By virtue of his concern for Ferdinand and of Antonio and Sebastian's attempt at usurping his crown, Alonso is closely paralleled with Prospero. In addition, Prospero's waverings toward despair about Caliban and the nobles resonate in Alonso's broader vacillations between faith in Ferdinand's survival and despair that "he's gone" (2.1.123; cf. 2.1.323–24, 3.3.8–10). More than anything else, what distinguishes the two men is the way they tend to acknowledge their faults: while Prospero, as we have seen, hedges on the question of his own role in his downfall (1.2.66–151), Alonso confesses and repents his wrongdoing outright, first to himself (3.3.95–102), then to Prospero: "Thy dukedom I resign, and do entreat / Thou pardon me my wrongs" (5.1.118–19). Ironically, however, Prospero has pulled the strings of Alonso's open admission. In this light, he again appears poised on the border between self-awareness and what Skura calls "self-estrangement"—here, the temptation to ignore his own reasons to repent.[21] Paradoxically, his art both prompts in others the self-knowledge essential to remorse and yet permits him the very aloofness from others that sustains his pride. How Prospero comes to manage his relationship to his art, including his apparent sense of superiority to it, constitutes much of his struggle to rejoin the society of mortals in Milan.

II

Although art in *The Tempest* is strewn with traps, it is still the means to achieving the play's highest goal, spiritual freedom. Such freedom, which assumes various forms in the play, is always paradoxical because it depends on some kind of bondage or fulfillment of obligation. Subjectively, it might be defined, for lack of better words, as service, rather than slavery—that is, a willing, generous, even foolishly self-sacrificing labor in others' behalf, as against the enforced, begrudging execution of a task at another's command.[22] Hence Caliban's sense that he is enslaved because he is made to do Prospero's chores (for example, 1.2.372–74). And hence Ferdinand's view of the same burdens as welcome. Initially pressed into service (1.2.467), Ferdinand learns to accept his labors under the influence of Miranda (3.1.63–67), who herself exemplifies liberality at every turn: "To be your fellow / You may deny me, but I'll be your servant, / Whether you will or no" (3.1.84–86).

Objectively, the same spiritual freedom can be described as mercy—unhesitating, unconditional acceptance.[23] Recalling Portia's image of mercy as "not strain'd," but falling "as the gentle rain from heaven" (*Merchant*, 4.1.184–85), Prospero twice refers to "grace" and "aspersion" as heavenly rain (3.1.75, 4.1.18). If grace is a free gift, however, it is also enjoined on humanity by both nature and Providence. To the first of those ordering principles Prospero refers when he tells Ariel that to be "kind" is an inherently human quality (5.1.21–24). And he repeatedly makes clear in his narration to Miranda in 1.2 that he sees himself as both the pawn and the instrument of "Providence divine" (159). In fact, Providence has dictated that the evil done to Prospero be converted to "loving wrong" and that Prospero rely on a "most auspicious star" to achieve his "zenith" (1.2.151, 180–84). As freely as he may choose the details of his plans to fulfill the larger aims of Providence, he is nonetheless bound in service to a higher power whose ultimate motivation is heavenly love and whose final destination is love on earth.[24]

Yet neither can Providence advance in its course unless aided by Prospero's artistic manipulations. Otherwise, it is frozen in mere potentiality. Indeed, the very function of that art is to release those who partake in it from whatever obstacles impede their spiritual freedom both to forgive and to be forgiven. Most of the artistic displays that Prospero presents to an internal audience suggest that their purpose is to realize larger charitable ends. Although the vanishing banquet of 3.3, for example, has the immediate effect of arousing despair and madness in the nobles, Ariel's assurance—"I and my fellows / Are ministers of Fate" (60–61)—establishes Prospero as a guide, channeling their present pain through the difficult, slow process of penitence, to the providential end of "heart's sorrow, / And a clear life ensuing" (81–82). "The pow'rs," says Ariel, are "delaying (not forgetting)" (73); in identifying himself as a spark of memory, he further reveals this particular spectacle of Prospero's as the catalyst by which, through time, Providence will prove effective.[25] If all goes well, the same conversion Prospero effects in the nobles, thereby helping to fulfill Providence, will also benefit himself.[26]

Prospero's leanings toward pride, however, complicate his approach to artistry, as well as to forgiveness, threatening to corrupt his art with egoism. In fact, the very nature of art in the context of *The Tempest* spawns its own complications. Although it requires the artist to relinquish ultimate control to Providence, it nevertheless demands from the artist a high degree of control and, furthermore, attracts those who can muster it. Artistry thus contains its own temptations. Practically speaking, if Prospero feels drawn toward private vengeance, his impulse would naturally stem in part from simply possessing the power to hurt through his art. In addition to whatever specific motives might lure Prospero to revenge, that is, his identity as an artist who enjoys wielding power may well augment the enticement for him of vengeance, especially since he is certain of accomplishing it skillfully, if he so chooses. As Prospero uses art to unlock the possibility of spiritual freedom in himself and others, his art must itself enact the balance between personal freedom and obedience to higher law that also characterizes willing service and mercy. For Prospero, as for any capable artist, this is a precarious balance indeed.[27]

The antidote in *The Tempest* to the pride that can thwart the most well-meaning of artists is compassion, or what Harriet Hawkins calls "empathy."[28] It is the recognition that one's pain, however acutely felt, is not unique but shared; that to punish one's malefactor does nothing to relieve suffering but only increases it; that the common lot of humanity is, at best, what Spenser calls "tickle"—uncertain—and, at worst, hellish, therefore compelling kindness, grace. Once compassion is felt, in other words, spiritual freedom is within reach. The play's logic is inescapable: if even the best human beings err, the only possible response to human error is forgiveness.

To suggest the ultimate folly of pretensions to immunity from human error and sorrow, allusions to the essential sameness of all humanity are scattered throughout the play. The opening wrangling between the nobles and the Boatswain fixes immediately on the notion that class rank is no protection against the ravages of nature:

> *Boats*. What cares these roarers for the name of king?
> . . .
>
> *Gon.* Good, yet remember whom thou hast aboard.
>
> *Boats*. None that I more love than myself. You are
> a councillor; if you can command these elements to
> silence, and work the peace of the present, we will
> not hand a rope more.
>
> (1.1.16–23)

But perhaps no more poignant reminder of common human vulnerability emerges in *The Tempest* than Ariel's detailed description of Trinculo, Stephano, and Caliban, whom he has led far afield of their designs to usurp Prospero:

> I charm'd their ears
> That calf-like they my lowing follow'd through
> Tooth'd briers, sharp furzes, pricking goss, and thorns,
> Which ent'red their frail shins. At last I left them
> I' th' filthy-mantled pool beyond your cell,
> There dancing up to th' chins that the foul lake
> O'erstunk their feet.
>
> (4.1.178–84)

Prospero responds to Ariel with sheer approval, little sensing at this feverish moment that he could be—and once was—so humbled as are now these three scoundrels: "This was well done, my bird" (4.1.184). He also portends further punishment and humiliation: "I will plague them all, / Even to roaring" (4.1.192–93). But the evocative images of these creatures' "frail shins" and their wading chin-deep in ooze seem virtual emblems of general human frailty—witness the recapitulation of the image of drowning already applied to the ship's crew, Alonso, and Ferdinand.[29] That Prospero does not recall here the time when he himself was at the mercy of a "rotten carcass of a butt" on the "roar[ing]" sea does not except him from the same helplessness he now inflicts on Caliban and fellows (1.2.146, 149). It merely confirms his difficulty at fully imagining the effects of his artistry on others. The three low characters' actions may have invited Prospero's discipline, but not his smugness.

The vision that will allow Prospero to understand others' capacity for pain and his own capacity for brutality is, again, the vision that Montaigne advocates in "Of Cannibals." Through an exploration of Prospero's art, however, *The Tempest* pushes the issue by addressing how to achieve that vision, which engenders spiritually freeing compassion. Not surprisingly, more paradoxes ensue, specifically those through which art interrelates innocence and experience. In essence, the compassion of a child, lost in adulthood, can be retrieved through art, which is itself tainted by experience.

Montaigne's conception of an inclusive outlook on all of the world's societies is manifested in purest form in the innocent Miranda. Although the audience might expect Caliban's earlier assault on her virginity to instill some skepticism in her view of humanity, her perception is instead clear of bias toward any but her former pupil. She assumes that the men on board the afflicted ship are undeserving of Prospero's punishment, and her sympathy for their agony is explicit: "O! I have suffered / With those that I saw suffer" (1.2.5–6). Unto themselves, her tenderness and generosity are ideal. Yet the practical limitations of her perspective come into focus early on and remain so throughout the play. On first seeing Ferdinand, she takes him for a "thing divine" (1.2.419), indicating that she will fall for Ferdinand not as an individual but as a member of general humanity, with whom she is barely acquainted. Only Prospero's seasoned judgment legitimates her choice of husbands (which, in light of her naiveté, is really no choice at all). Furthermore, the audience hardly needs to hear Prospero's famous retort to know that Miranda's later assessment of humanity is dangerously ingenuous:

> *Mir.* O wonder!
> How many goodly creatures are there here!
> How beauteous mankind is! O brave new world
> That has such people in't!
>
> *Pros.* 'Tis new to thee.
>
> (5.1.181–84)

Although Miranda shows signs of growing up and away from her father, as when she breaks Prospero's rule by pronouncing her name to Ferdinand (3.1.36–37), this process is still highly controlled by the hidden, protective Prospero, and it is unfinished by the play's end.[30]

In earlier plays by Shakespeare, Miranda's inattention to the perils of blind trust and her readiness to sacrifice her comfort to do Ferdinand ease might have seemed problematic but not so painfully simple as in *The Tempest*. Particularly in *Twelfth Night*, Antonio's (and later Viola's) love at all costs raises problems concerning wise folly but remains valued and desired for its idealism. And so is Miranda's natural compassion, in one light, held in high esteem. But *The Tempest* deeply distrusts an easy compassion, which, uninformed by the evil of which humanity is capable, is therefore automatic, not chosen freely.[31] Prospero's gaze, though jaded, is clearly safer. It is also profoundly of this world, born of disappointed expectations and firsthand experience with treachery. Because he is still at risk of loathing this life, his business is to recover enough of Miranda's childlike compassion to modulate his cynicism but not so much as to render his worldliness ineffectual. Gonzalo's trust and idealism, though refreshing, go too far; he is the adult incarnation of Miranda's innocence and so is prone to reflecting both wise and foolish folly in the extreme—through, respectively, his humane concern and his inability to deal with the villains who tease him for his unworldliness (2.1.1–190).[32] Prospero's partial recovery of the kindness that Gonzalo may never have lost relies in part on his fatherly love for Miranda; like other instances of parental love in the romances, this love is so fervent as to be grace indeed. What's more, Prospero often makes explicit that the image of Miranda's devotion to Ferdinand softens his heart and gives him hope—for example, while he blesses the new love between her and Ferdinand (3.1.74–76) and when he presents the pair to Alonso as a "wonder" (5.1.167–71). Not even the sight of the young lovers can erase the bitter experience that colors his view of the world, but it can restore to him some measure of joy about participating in social living: "So glad of this as they I cannot be, / Who are surpris'd withal; but my rejoicing / At nothing can be more" (3.1.92–94).[33]

Another means of rehabilitating Prospero's compassion that is equally potent to his love for Miranda lies in his art. Not coincidentally, each time he is moved by parental love, he is observing Miranda in a dramatic scene or a tableau of his own devising. The strength of natural love is somehow intertwined in *The Tempest* with the power of artifice properly employed—at least to the extent that the father's commitment to his child's welfare compels him to use art responsibly, in the service of her welfare.[34] Yet the instinctive compassion of a child, to which art can return an adult, also diverges widely, in the context of this play, from the essence of artistry, which is both learned and chosen. Prospero's art is solely the product of experience—not, as in Sir Philip Sidney's *Apology for Poetry*, innately good simply because it is natural.[35] It is thus perpetually—and vexatiously—debased by the artist's fall from grace. It is also likely, then, to be an imperfect mode of recovering lost grace. Nor is it, from this angle, much to be proud about. For whatever may be natural about art in *The Tempest* is inherently at odds with what is unnatural—morally corrupt—about the artist.

That art in *The Tempest* is the exclusive domain of postlapsarian humanity is suggested frequently—for instance, by Miranda's inability to detect Ariel's presence. Miranda herself is artless, in both the senses that she does not practice art and that she is guileless. That pun suggests at least the contrivance, and at most the corruption, about the other characters' artfulness. Indeed, even young Ferdinand's exposure to courtly society is already evident in the self-consciously artful—adult—language in which he addresses Miranda: "Most sure, the goddess / On whom these airs attend!" (1.2.422–23). Although his diction mirrors Miranda's (for example, 1.2.411–12), its deliberately crafted rhetoric is implicitly contrasted with the absence of cunning in her speeches. By his own account, Ferdinand has already known many women, experience that enables him to judge Miranda's relative merits (3.1.39–48) but also that has introduced him to the manipulative ways and discourse of politicians and usurpers, such as that of his father's company. When Antonio urges Sebastian to murder Alonso in 2.1, he applies the language of the theater to political usurpation, linking fallen society with abusive artistry. Claribel, he says, is

> she that from whom
> We all were sea-swallow'd, though some cast again
> (And by that destiny) to perform an act
> Whereof what's past is prologue, what to come
> In yours and my discharge.
>
> (250–54)

Human artifice in *The Tempest*—whether Ferdinand's, Antonio's, or Prospero's—is necessarily morally suspect because it results from experience. Hence, its moral efficacy is always in question.

Accordingly, as if portrayed as a belated appendage to human nature, art is repeatedly figured in *The Tempest* as a garment that may be worn or removed at will. Prospero identifies his magical powers with his mantle—"Lie there, my art" (1.2.25)—and political positions are seized and put on like costumes in a play, inessential features of the people who perform within them. The notion of political plotting as an act of fashionmongering is sharpened through parody when Stephano and Trinculo are distracted from their ambush of Prospero by the "wardrobe" he has displayed for them (4.1.222–54). Rosemary Wright has written persuasively on the emblematic significance of this episode: "The gaudy clothes that dangle from the branches of the [lime] tree seem almost certainly to have derived from the late Gothic device of the pedlar and the apes."[36] This device, she explains, concerns mainly the human folly of "being attracted . . . by glittering trifles," as portrayed by the apes whose keeper sleeps idly nearby while they plunder a lime tree for pretty clothes and trinkets (137). As helpful as Wright's interpretation is, I believe that the robes donned by Shakespeare's two fools also play off of Prospero's mantle in respect to the play's most fundamental warnings about human artifice. Prospero can be contrasted with Stephano and Trinculo for the legitimacy of his apparel: he is the true mage; they, only base imitators. But in all three cases art remains external, implying that it is not natural but willed, and, if willed, then threatening, since, as Sidney insisted, in the *Apology*, human will has been "infected" by the fall.[37]

But, again paradoxically, that human artifice is stained by worldly experience empowers it, in Sidney's phrase, to deliver a golden world. It cannot rise until its creator falls. Through directly encountering error, Milton would later write, comes the knowledge of error that can be deployed against itself.[38] Experience is double-edged, then, providing both the need for redemption and the means to it. A Prospero who had never known the temptation of lust could probably not conjure a masque that cautions a betrothed couple from indulging in lust (and a Prospero who had never struggled with such temptation would likely not repeat his call to abstinence so often and so adamantly, as in 4.1.14–23, 51–54, 94–98). In fact, art in *The Tempest* might yet be thought natural in the narrow sense that, quite apart from humanity, it occupies a pure realm into which experience initiates the fallen. Some attribute of Prospero's art, that is, lies beyond his ability to corrupt it or to contain it; it is that principle that permits his artistry to intersect with Providence, to instill virtue, and to awaken both conscience and compassion in folly-fallen humanity.

Such words come as close as I can force them to describing Ariel, of whom I have not yet found a thoroughly satisfactory reading.[39] Many of Ariel's traits delineate him as the pure idea, spirit, of art in nature. His singular refusal to be bound into any service other than that of his own delight removes him from the human sphere. His decided nonhumanity is, in fact, stressed; at one point, he is "but air" (5.1.21). He is, however, subject to abuse by mortal artists like Sycorax, as well as to the more benign employment of human beings like Prospero, whose freeing of him from the cloven pine metaphorically suggests the redirecting of the artistic principle from vice toward virtue. Ariel's own compassion recommends him for the task of imbuing spiritual freedom in the audience he shares with his master. He tells Prospero: "Your charm so strongly works 'em [Prospero's enemies] / That if you now beheld them, your affections / Would become tender" (5.1.17–19). In Aristotelian terms, if Prospero is the efficient cause of art in *The Tempest* and Providence the final cause, Ariel might be considered the formal cause.

Ariel's passage from unbearable slavery to Sycorax, to uncomfortable service to Prospero, to complete freedom from any earthly obligations indicates the inevitability of Prospero's forfeiting his magic, which seems to rely on a force that can be borrowed but not possessed and which, if borrowed too long, decays into ugliness. Illustrating this principle, Prospero reminds Ariel of his misery and repulsiveness after years of fruitless subjugation by Sycorax:

> Thou best know'st
> What torment I did find thee in; thy groans
> Did make wolves howl . . . .
> It was a torment
> To lay upon the damn'd.
>
> (1.2.286–90)

Confinement once made a virtual howling Caliban out of Ariel, until Prospero freed the spirit to create beauty (1.2.291–93). Prospero's profit by Ariel, however, could itself grow exploitative. Not coincidentally, Prospero has relied upon Ariel for twelve years, exactly the length of time that Sycorax had previously trapped him in the cloven pine (1.2.274–79). Prospero seems able to harness Ariel's spiritual perfection favorably only so long, up to a point beyond which lies unchecked pride and abuse, like that of Sycorax.

Racing against that terminus, Prospero treats Ariel with hints of impatience and disrespect, indications of the self-centeredness that militates against his kindness. The oddly unnatural aspect of human artistry is exposed over and again as Prospero imposes demands on an Ariel who must struggle to comply and marshals inflammatory insults, like calling Ariel "malignant thing," to enforce, ironically, the natural law of love (1.2.257). As the play draws to a close, along with the day, the pressing question is whether Prospero's collaboration with Ariel can penetrate beneath the outer garments of the chief characters to affect them internally. Before Ariel vanishes, can the clothes that Gonzalo says are "new-dy'd" and "fresh" come to represent the spiritual renewal of the men who wear them (2.1.64, 69)? What's more, will the artistry confined to Prospero's mantle make its spiritual impression on him before he discards it? Will Prospero's magic have left its indelible traces in his other art—that of his governing? Can he truly reenter this world and its society, that is, as a changed person?

Caliban tells Stephano that, if he would conquer Prospero, first to "possess his books; for without them / He's but a sot, as I am" (3.2.92–93). Of course, Caliban exaggerates: in the most negative light, Prospero does not, and could not, sink to "sot." Still, Caliban's line points in a number of provocative directions, all of which contain their grain of truth. First, what distinguishes civilized, fully human creatures from monsters is their practice of artistry. But, second and at the same time, pure art always somehow escapes human practice, as though held at a distance in a book that mortal minds can briefly touch and yet that mortal hands will eventually soil—make sottish. Finally, Caliban diminishes Prospero's stature from a self-impressed artist to the lowliness that, once Prospero fully recognizes it, can plant his humility. On Prospero's willingness to lower himself in the glass of his own imagination hinges the relative success of his art.

III

Prospero reaches a distinct turning point in *The Tempest*, where he demonstrates a seemingly new humility in respect to his own art. It comes in 4.1, when he cuts off the masque. Previous critical analyses of this scene have concentrated on the parallels between the content of the masque—Pluto's kidnapping of Proserpine behind Ceres' back—and Prospero's history: Caliban remains at large, stalking Miranda. Of greater significance, however, is what happens to Prospero as he recognizes this parallel. What starts as a thinly veiled injunction against the young couple's prenuptial love-making ends as a warning to the artist himself. While witnessing the adverse consequences of Ceres' obliviousness to Proserpine's well-being—a devastating mistake that Ceres still rues and because of which she is now more circumspect (88–91)—Prospero connects the artistic vision with his own grievous experience, recognizing his parental obligation to Miranda: "I had forgot that foul conspiracy / Of the beast Caliban and his confederates / Against my life" (139–41). He takes the moral instruction of the masque to heart, learning about his own conduct from his own art. Apparently reordering his thinking, he moves his focus from Ferdinand's responsibility to safeguard Miranda's chastity to his own.

Such re-vision, in addition to protecting Prospero from the charge of hypocrisy, shows that he is being humbled, as reflected in his metamorphosing views of his artifice. He at first glibly calls the masque "[s]ome vanity of mine art" (41), at least striking an appropriately self-effacing pose. As the masque proceeds, however, the artist and Shakespeare's audience come to understand the real sense in which the masque is vain. Now Ferdinand, repeating Prospero's youthful history, is lured by the delight of this "vision" and longs to escape into its false freedom (118): "Let me live here ever; / So rare a wond'red father and a wise / Makes this place Paradise" (122–24). The danger of art's beauty and idealization, with which Prospero has long been wrestling, is that it will distract its audience or its maker from applying its moral content where it is most needed, in the fallen world. Ferdinand's relative inexperience also obscures from his perception much of what Prospero, who has suffered the consequences of such oblivion, can learn from it. For Ferdinand, then, the masque threatens to dwindle into a vehicle of self-admiration, a trifling entertainment, a "vanity."

When Prospero suspends the masque to attend to life, he avoids such youthful error and lowers his pride sufficiently to objectify his art. But he also restores a much-needed perspective on the role of art in life, reestablishing art's purpose as that of serving life, which is to say serving social, rather than private, ends. Prospero has in this case, as in earlier ones, egotistically coached Ferdinand's idolatry with more false modesty toward the "[s]pirits, which . . . / I have from their confines call'd to enact / By my present fancies" (120–22). Yet in 4.1 Ferdinand's ill-advised attraction, so like his own toward the wonders of pure contemplation, seems to register with him. Not long after Ferdinand makes his comment, Prospero breaks off the masque, as though he suddenly comprehends the potential egoism implicit in the remark and reacts against it: "Well done, avoid; no more" (142).[40]

Prospero's ambivalence toward the uses of art, however, persists in 4.1 and is so delicately scripted as to resist verbal analysis. On the one hand, his vestigial enchantment with art for its own sake tends to draw him away from social responsibility and into the selfish pleasures of his own mind. On the other hand, the traces of his suffering coerce his attention to the needs of others, visible in his urge to abandon his borrowed magic. He is still tempted, even as late as 4.1, not to do what the virtue implicit in his own art tells him he must, so that his virtuous action, once chosen, indeed seems a narrow escape out of pride and despair into humility and faith. His speeches in the remainder of the play are riddled with comparably subtle tension. His sense of social responsibility, which prompts him to end the masque, is tinged with "anger" and "distemper"

(4.1.145), suggesting his unresolved emotions. The famous comparison that follows, between the transience of artistic illusion and that of human life, both extols artifice for mimicking reality and disparages anything human for its impermanence (4.1.146–58). Prospero's equally celebrated valedictory to magic in 5.1 alternates between boasts of his superhuman "command" over nature and more modest references to the "[w]eak" spirits he controls and to his "rough magic" (48, 41, 50).

This evidence of Prospero's remaining confusion shows that the final stage of his conversion, as he experiences it, is not mechanical. But it does occur. And it is living, in many senses—chiefly, in that it evolves erratically, unevenly. No sooner than he interrupts the masque to save his dukedom and his daughter than he regresses to enjoying his fantasies of brutalizing Caliban (4.1.258–61). In this ironic instance, he readily exchanges hard-won sympathy for the familiar dispassion he long ago showed Antonio. Yet Prospero makes clear strides toward human kindness that, like his openness to the substance of his own masque, demonstrate art's power to perform spiritual alchemy. Even if Prospero succeeded in teaching no one but himself, his example alone would legitimate his art, so far has he come in twelve years' time toward transforming his and others' mistakes into "loving wrong" (1.2.151).

Prospero's susceptibility to the moral instruction of his own art has significant implications for his use of art to teach others as well. Any art in *The Tempest* that finally proves capable of improving human nature derives its potency from invading and manipulating the audience's conscience through its emotions. But such invasiveness revives familiar reservations about Prospero's presumptuousness. Twelve years after his exile, Prospero, still wavering between pride and humility, deems necessary the use of vicarious loss to convert Alonso and to chasten Ferdinand. In Alonso's case, this strategy seems especially extreme: it is the death of a child, felt as if real because imagined to be real. No bereavement could be more painful. The exploitation of such power craves adequate justification, in addition to that already discussed—in particular, Prospero's willingness to subject himself to moral standards as high as those he expects his audience to embrace. On three additional grounds, Prospero's right to practice meddlesome artistry can be considered wise and can be distinguished from both the tyranny that marks Antonio's usurpation and his own bendings toward pride.

First, Prospero's strenuous effort to teach the characters he manipulates is called for because they repeatedly exhibit cruel and violent—inhumane—behavior, which they show no signs of amending on their own. Numerous critics have recently blamed Prospero for inciting such behavior in Caliban; some would also judge Prospero indirectly guilty of

Antonio's crimes, imagining, for example, that he seduces Antonio to attempt a second usurpation in 2.1 and, beyond that, shrewdly engineers a marriage through which Milan will pass from Prospero to Ferdinand, altogether dispossessing his maligned younger brother. Stephen Orgel argues both of these points in condemning Prospero for robbing Antonio's ability to "act of his own free will."[41] He implies that Prospero practically forces Antonio to plot against Alonso so that, "at the play's end," he will "still [have] usurpation and attempted murder to hold against his brother, things that will still disqualify Antonio from his place in the family" (111). The outcome of Prospero's machinations to rid Europe of Antonio, springing from some mysterious malignancy in Prospero's character, is, according to Orgel, that "Prospero has not regained his lost dukedom, he has usurped his brother's" (111).

But, surely, to consider so is to consider too curiously. Not only does making Prospero the villain of *The Tempest* require gyrations of reasoning about the plot that a theater audience would be hard-pressed to undertake (even during postproduction reflection), but it also rests on assumptions about the plot for which textual evidence is lacking. When Orgel states about the "conspiracy" in 2.1, for instance, that it is "certainly part of [Prospero's] project," he neglects quite another possible understanding of the episode.[42] The script divulges only two elements of the scene that are incontestably instigated by Prospero: Ariel's soporific music (184–98) and Ariel's wake-up call to Gonzalo (300–305). Why the rest occurs between lines 184 and 305 is anybody's guess. Granted, some circumstantial evidence implicates Prospero in setting up Antonio and Sebastian: Ariel likely exits just after Alonso has fallen asleep (2.1.198), perhaps depriving the other two of their chance to do the same, and that Ariel earlier agrees to follow "[a]ll points" of Prospero's "command" "[t]o th' syllable" hints that Prospero is willing every detail of the action in 2.1 (1.2.501). Other explanations of the scene, however, make more sense and require less elaborate reasoning—for instance, that Antonio and Sebastian are untouched by Ariel's music because they are wicked men, not because Prospero wills them to stay conscious.[43] Indeed, insofar as Prospero is involved at all, he seems to be discouraging the intrigue to which Antonio and Sebastian are prone, having Ariel rouse Gonzalo to "keep" all of these folks "living" (299). Furthermore, Ariel says only that Prospero "through his art foresees the danger" to Gonzalo (297), not that Prospero has caused the conspiracy. Anyone who has ever become embroiled in debating the theological distinction between foreseeing and willing events knows better than to assume they are identical.

On balance, Prospero hardly seems responsible for encouraging the second fall of Antonio, who by his own admission lacks a conscience

(276–80). The circumstances that Prospero's art brings about in this scene are intended, rather, to test the current mettle of the men whose moral turpitude was verified twelve years earlier. In this arena, although admittedly one of Prospero's designing, two of these men freely elect not merely to sin again but to descend farther than ever into sin by committing murder. No, if Prospero is to be charged with abusing his magic, it cannot be for assaying the virtue of his one-time malefactors or, for that matter, for reinforcing Ferdinand's love through similar trial (4.1.1–11). Both ploys are necessary for ascertaining responsibly the degree to which further artistry is warranted and of protecting himself and Miranda against repeated misfortune.

The second consideration in determining the legitimacy of Prospero's severe and invasive tactics with the nobles is whether his art remains in line with providential ends in this most crucial of cases. Here, too, I think that Prospero's motives have lately been misunderstood. Not that he thoroughly skirts and resists the temptation to vengeance. As we have seen, his failures to teach Caliban give rise to a strong, desperate desire to punish Caliban and his cohorts. Nor is he above relishing the power in which he holds the nobles when it is at its apex: "At this hour / Lies at my mercy all mine enemies" (4.1.262–63). Indeed, the very revenge within Prospero's grasp is itself a metaphor for the ultimate tyranny of one person over another. Yet to read most of his artistic endeavors with the nobles as fostered mainly by pride is to misjudge him. Prospero's foremost objective is to awaken the faith that ushers in grace.

Greenblatt stops short of understanding Prospero's motives completely, I believe, when he writes that Prospero aims merely to arouse anxiety. Although Greenblatt marshals some historical evidence to argue that anxiety in itself was seen by theologians of the time as a "necessary precondition of the reassurance of salvation," in *The Tempest* the majority of anxiety that Prospero elicits is neither an end in itself nor a direct path to salvation.[44] Rather, it is a form of role-playing whose immediate goal is to evoke one's compassion for others' suffering and, promptly thereafter, remorse for the suffering one has caused others. Such contrition may eventually lead to conversion and salvation, as Prospero hopes it will (5.1.28–30). While Prospero's art works to promote just such remorse, it simultaneously encourages faith, itself the complement of grace, by stimulating the sympathetic imagination. Both goals—the arousal of contrition and of faith—cooperate with Providence.

The banquet scene in 3.3 details how Prospero's art seeks to conjure both the suffering that leads to penitence and salvific faith in the "three men of sin." Kermode identifies this scene as one of temptation, which it surely is, both by virtue of its allusion to Job 20:23, 27[45] and because it parallels the temptation of Christ in the wilderness. But the belief that the illusory banquet stirs in the minds of those who are tempted by it is also an important component in the process of repentance, which can become mired in despair. Indeed, although Ariel subverts the hungry men's pleasurable expectations when he and his spirits dismantle the banquet, thus making the impact of his austere sermon all the greater, the sinners' faith has, immediately before, already been exercised. It therefore stands ready to modulate the "ecstasy" brought on by "their great guilt," freshly remembered in response to Ariel's accusations (108, 104). Moreover, the belief that the nobles express as they approach the banquet is one of pure awe, admiration; it retrieves a measure of their lost innocence. They are drawn not to the feast as flesh but to the apparition as wonder:

> *Seb.* A living drollery. Now I will believe
> That there are unicorns; that in Arabia
> There is one tree, the phoenix' throne, one phoenix
> At this hour reigning there.
>
> *Ant.* I'll believe both;
> And what does else want credit, come to me,
> And I'll be sworn 'tis true. . . .
>
> *Gon.* If in Naples
> I should report this now, would they believe me?
>
> (21–28)

Sebastian speaks truer than he realizes by calling the image a "living drollery." The art here is, in a real sense, living because it acts upon the souls of its audience. This faith in the reality of Prospero's illusion will prove key in the final scene, where the same characters' faith will be tested one last time, principally by being confronted by the apparent mirage of Prospero's person. The newfound credulity of Sebastian and Antonio at the banquet, a credulity for which Gonzalo had earlier appeared to them such a fool (2.1), will remain in their memory even after Ariel has interrupted it to plunge them into the "desperat[ion]" of self-recognition (104).[46]

A similar interaction in Prospero's artistic methods between implanting grief and allaying it informs nearly every facet of his overall design. To cite another example, Ariel's song for Ferdinand moves him, uncannily, in two opposed ways: it convinces him, first, of his father's fictional death and, second, of Alonso's "sea-change / Into something rich and strange" (1.2.401–2). In actuality this is his father's ultimate destiny, although, unbeknownst to Ferdinand, it will be delayed. The song, then, is another "living drollery," acting as a catalyst in Ferdinand's mind and spirit. It introduces him—prematurely and yet none too soon—to faith in a beauty beyond death's sadness.

Prospero's extreme measures for touching off complex spiritual chemistry in the nobles, then, are authorized both by the ambitiousness of his project and by the enormity of his audience-subjects, who grow ever greedier, ever more callous. As Friar Francis advises in *Much Ado about Nothing* when he proposes to counterfeit Hero's death by slander: "to strange sores strangely they strain the cure" (4.1.252). Still, Prospero's methods are less severe than those of revenge tragedy, wherein the solution to awakening people to the pain they have caused is to inflict real pain, by maiming, killing, and psychologically torturing. Prospero seeks to share his injury by reviving or implanting it in the fantasies of those who have hurt him and could do so again. On the other side of their horrific imaginings, moreoever, lies the possibility of regret for the torment they have caused Prospero and of human compassion born of shared grief. Through his artistry, Prospero offers his brother Antonio a great gift—the imaginative capacity required for sympathetic understanding.

The third and final problem to address about the extraordinary lengths to which Prospero takes his artistry is also the most crucial and the most difficult to resolve. It is that of whether the results of his labors justify his strategies, which often edge on high-handedness. To what degree and in what sense do Prospero's efforts produce the most desirable effect: an inward turning in his artistic and political subjects toward spiritual freedom in this world?

Alonso, Sebastian, and Antonio compose, in that order, a spectrum of possible responses to Prospero's manipulations. Alonso so obviously undergoes and, at various points, articulates his reversal that further commentary than that already included here is superfluous. For his sincere "heart's sorrow," expressed both to Prospero and to his son (5.1.116–19, 197–98), and for a "clear life ensuing" (3.3.81–82), he is given a "second life," embodied in his recovered son Ferdinand (5.1.195).

Sebastian's case, although less overt than Alonso's, is not, in the end, as cryptic as is often asserted. When he first awakens from his trance, his faith in Prospero's virtue—and, by extension, his own heart's sorrow—are still unsound, as his aside evinces: "The devil speaks in him" (5.1.129). Prospero's magical ability to hear his doubt, however, unites with the tableau of the children playing chess to induce his long-awaited conversion to faith: "A most high miracle!" (5.1.177). Whether because this last of Prospero's spectacles owes more to palpable reality than to illusion, or because the sight of restored, loving children melts down Sebastian's resistance, he is brought to testify, as it were, before our eyes.[47]

Antonio's reaction to Prospero's stratagems is silence. It is, therefore, impenetrable: although we can safely assume that, were he fully converted, his lines would indicate as much, neither does he speak to the contrary. He makes one more lame joke before the play closes, implying less defiance of than indifference to Prospero's high hopes that he will transform (5.1.265–66). But the actor playing Antonio has little to go on as to Antonio's inner feelings and thoughts. Earlier, during the banquet scene, he showed clear evidence of being spiritually moved. But in 5.1, however affected he may be internally, he stops short of voicing the ecstasy that seizes Sebastian and Alonso. Taken together, then, these three fellows suggest a range of outlook, from faith to skepticism.

Less mystifying than Antonio's reserve, I believe, is Caliban's promise: "I'll be wise hereafter, / And seek for grace" (5.1.295–96). Even in view of his fear of Prospero's punishment—"I shall be pinch'd to death" (5.1.276)—and despite Prospero's threatening tone in the lines that precede his claim to reform, his pledge rings true because punishments, real or portended, have not changed him in the past. The distinguishing mark of his earlier vituperation for Prospero, in fact, is that it is involuntary, compulsive—necessitated by his anger and capable of drowning other consideration: "His spirits hear me, / And yet I needs must curse. . . . For every trifle they are set upon me" (2.2.3–4, 8). In the play's last scene, rather than pretending to win Prospero's "grace," Caliban is at long last reflecting the lessons that experience teaches: "What a thrice-double ass / Was I to take this drunkard for a god, / And worship this dull fool!" (5.1.296–98). Clearly, what Prospero has taken as Caliban's inability to learn has been in truth the inadequacy of Prospero's art to teach—or, at the least, to teach effectively. In this regard, Caliban remains the virtual emblem of Prospero's pride.

With this reversal in Caliban's attitude toward Prospero's moral discipline comes, first, the audience's increased awareness that Caliban's brutality to date has been a form of the same innocence that vexes Miranda's comfortable and effective engagement in the real, fallen world. Perhaps what truly reaches Caliban, as the play's underplot unfolds, is not so much Prospero's intervention—the tempting wardrobe on the lime tree, for instance—but, more, the direct exposure, independent of the pedagogy that Prospero has arranged for him, with men who have far less to recommend them as rulers than does his master. Through his interaction with Trinculo and Stephano, that is, Caliban has had opportunity to see for himself, absorbing naturally—and, as he perceives of it, freely—the broader truth about his presumed slavery to Prospero. Whether or not Prospero's relative inattention to Caliban toward the day's end largely accounts for the latter's change (and it may), the outcome of that change lies chiefly in Caliban's altered understanding of service and freedom. As he discovers for himself that Stephano and Trinculo are false idols (for example, 3.2.63–67), his trust in the "freedom" they can supply him by "destroy[ing]" Prospero wanes (2.2.186–87, 4.1.224). It is replaced by another kind of trust, that in the "grace" that follows from being "wise"—in this case, wisdom gained through partaking in the folly of this world (5.1.296–98). Surely Prospero, at his most lucid, would prefer that Caliban's service issue from such freedom and trust, rather than from the bondage of punishment or from forcible instruction. Prospero's forbearance toward Caliban represents a small relaxation of his grip but just enough of a release to initiate a reversal in how the two characters interact. Caliban arrives morally where, with Prospero's continued guidance, he can begin to choose his submission freely, as Miranda and Ferdinand come to do (5.1.293–94).[48]

But the spell by which Prospero has sought to control Caliban is actually broken earlier, just several lines above Caliban's professed conversion, when Prospero makes public his affinity with his nemesis: "this thing of darkness I / Acknowledge mine" (5.1.275–76). This begrudging acceptance has been variously interpreted; it has even been seen as Prospero's admission of his responsibility for making Caliban into a cursing, rapacious creature.[49] In the play's larger moral context, however, with special regard to the role that Montaigne's "Of Cannibals" plays in shaping that context, Prospero's self-recognition pertains to his resemblance to Caliban, to his own proclivity to behave barbarically, monstrously. That awareness being in place, Prospero is positioned to abandon pride, better understand the quality of mercy, and return to Milanese society balancing political control against self-control. In Prospero's shift to reentering the world by accepting his human failings and needs lies his chance at spiritual freedom.[50]

Reminiscent of Duke Vincentio before him, Prospero seems in this and other cases to be taken surprise by his own artistry, only to discover himself more influenced by his art than is his audience. When the earlier duke's attempts to reform Vienna meet with disappointment, he adapts accordingly, a process that continues throughout the play. In contrast, Prospero's transformation, from avoiding the world to participating in it, has already in large part occurred when the play begins. Thus, Prospero reacts to moments of defeat less by changing than by adjusting. *The Tempest*, then, records the last hours of a seasoned character's moral growth. Yet much the same process transpires in both dukes. They simultaneously release pride and are released from it by becoming attentive audiences to the artifice they create, thus willingly humbling themselves. Even for Prospero, however, this process is ongoing, always heading toward and yet never reaching resolution. He begins and ends in some tension, albeit tension that gradually finds certain mitigation. The refusal of *The Tempest* to resolve all difficulties being granted, the play nevertheless portrays a progression. Prospero fails very little in his broader aims, obviously moving others to feel more deeply, if not inspiring Antonio to repent. Such fruits help to vindicate his meddling; though Prospero's means are imperfect, they are minimally presumptuous. And they work.[51]

Paradoxically (one last time), more evidence that Prospero's invasive strategies have left their imprint on the creator himself emerges in his restraint from foisting them any further on Antonio. Like his tentative acceptance of his kinship to Caliban, this ultimate step on Prospero's part involves some hesitation. As act 5 opens, Prospero is clearly thinking of his mercy toward all three offenders as conditional: "They being penitent, / The sole drift of my purpose doth extend / Not a frown further" (28–30). Characteristically, he has as yet given no thought to the possibility that his "so potent art" might not work a minor miracle of repentance on absolutely everyone (5.1.50). Then again, the "solemn air" that he has played to "cure" the spellbound men's "brains" is "heavenly music," justifying Prospero's faith in its efficacy (5.1.58–59, 52). When even divine assistance stops short of realizing his hopes, however, Prospero affirms the free nature of mercy, which is not itself unless rendered unconditionally. He must deal spontaneously with his failure to convert Antonio as easily as Alonso was changed. Addressing the awakened Antonio, he reveals his intent to release his brother from his debt, even if Antonio remains unreformed: "I do forgive thee, / Unnatural though thou art" (5.1.78–79). Prospero still feels the pangs caused him by his brother's betrayal, for which Antonio has yet to express open regret, and this unresolved tension darkens his pardon with tints of his own frailty: "For you, most wicked sir, whom to call brother / Would even infect my mouth, I do forgive / Thy rankest fault—all of them" (5.1.30–32). Strained though it may be by his own vulnerability and judgmentalism, it is nevertheless free and freeing grace.[52] What is possibly even more remarkable about the scene's end than Prospero's generosity is his self-restraint; once Antonio seems spiritually static, Prospero refrains from further prodding—from trying to stir up his guilt, bring about his confession, or renew his faith in a power beyond his own ego.

Prospero's forfeiture of control over the likes of Antonio—an act paralleling his abjuration of his magic—represents the key risk required of him as he makes his way back to worldly affairs. Experience has taught him that he cannot afford to set an unregenerate Antonio loose, particularly without the borrowed powers that have helped him manage and contain Antonio's treachery on the island. Yet Prospero has no other choice than to trust Antonio even as he moves to trust himself. Such irrational faith—a version of Saint Anthony's wise folly—spiritually exonerates Prospero, too. At the same time, it makes possible—inescapable—his commitment to the worldly prospect of serving Milan. In *The Tempest*, to adapt Saint Paul's words, wisdom with God is, in large measure, the foolishness of this world.

IV

As in all English Renaissance plays where Antonios take substantial roles, in this one, too, arises the problem of reconciling unbounded love with all-too-real boundaries, boundaries imposed upon human beings by virtue of their corruption in their corrupt sphere. In Prospero's brother, whose literary-theatrical heritage immediately attaches him to the conception of wise folly, a shift occurs: he becomes the object, rather than the donor, of charity. As successor to Antonios whose extravagant love issues from a source beyond our ken, this Antonio confronts us with the opposite mystery, the unfathomable origin of evil. Miranda's early comment—that "Good wombs have borne bad sons" (1.2.120)—explains little more about Antonio's unplumbed depths than does his silence in the last act. From first to last, he is an inscrutable and perhaps intractable force to be reckoned with, the acceptance of whose elusiveness is the ultimate phase in Prospero's return to social responsibility.[53] Antonio's unruliness stands for all the reasons that Prospero veers away from ruling: he cannot be contained by Prospero's idealism and theorems. Yet, if Prospero waited until he could predict and mold every subject's actions, he would never again govern Milan.

Failing to command Antonio absolutely, he can nevertheless, as Montaigne would have it, minister to his own capacity for monstrosity, a recognition implicit in his grace toward Antonio, however tense, and crucial in recreating himself as both brother and ruler. In this light, even Prospero's brother remains true to the type of the Renaissance stage Antonio. His capacity to inspire love as intact as that of the Antonio in *Twelfth Night*, he merely serves Prospero unwittingly and probably unwillingly. The Antonio in *The Tempest*, then, is a "false brother" in many senses of the epithet (1.2.92). He is not only deceitful, as Prospero literally intends, or even, in Prospero's more figurative sense, just unbrotherly. Finally, he is also Prospero's shadow—not illusory but insubstantial relative to Prospero's active charity. By the play's end, Antonio has ceased to be the agent determining Prospero's course, or fueling his emotions, or alleviating his sense of blame for his predicament. Once Prospero becomes answerable for his own choices, Antonio fades into obscurity, set free to determine his own course. Deprived of so much as a word about his dumbness, he makes the Antonio in *Merchant* appear positively well-adjusted. He has, indeed, changed places with Prospero and lags behind Caliban, his spiritual paralysis rendering him a social outcast.

If Prospero is not, in the end, his subjects' equal, he is close, as is manifest in his warm summons to all of them: "Please you draw near" (5.1.319). Prospero's strong toil of grace is punctuated by such moments when he lets go of attempts to dominate what he cannot control and rebinds himself, in humility, to the collective effort of civilizing humanity. The narrative of his renewed commitment repeatedly implies that "temporal things," in Walter's words, "are all means through which we shape our souls to an order of love."[54] In *The Tempest*, to ignore this world, which entraps the likes of Antonio and Caliban, threatens to enslave Prospero in the disarray of self-love. As Montaigne quotes Saint Augustine: "*He who praises the nature of the soul as the sovereign good and condemns the nature of the flesh as evil, truly both carnally desires the soul and carnally shuns the flesh; for his feeling is inspired by human vanity, not by divine truth*."[55] The emphasis on the spirituality of the flesh is apt. Prospero's great achievement is restoring some, if not all, equilibrium to his political life and social outlook—in a sense, making the word flesh.

Prospero's Epilogue concentrates into his plea for freedom the moral process he has undergone. The pattern of thought here is elegantly simple: he has given up the power he could use against his offenders, releasing them from his debt; now, he asks the audience not to level that same power against him by judging him ill for his mercy but to deliver him from blame. As he has overlooked cause to censure Antonio, he begs that his faults, too, will be pardoned.[56] To do otherwise is to neglect willfully the sense of the play. The Epilogue has power to dislodge the audience from passivity because it confronts us with our own need for unconditional love, a discomforting prospect. Much as Prospero might have permanently displaced his own vices onto Antonio or Caliban, so we can hold him accountable for all the imperfections that dissatisfy us at the play's end. We can keep clinging to a trivial kind of power by quibbling over blame.

Or, as the Epilogue urges, we can begin again. Doing so requires us to recognize in ourselves the demons that still plague us even as Prospero dissolves into thin air. The last action of *The Tempest* consists in returning us, too, to the material world, nagging questions, imperfections, and all. Yet, through its portrayal of Prospero's experience, the play also carefully cultivates the audience's sense of belonging to that humble world. Permitting Antonio's crimes to go unrepented and his own "crimes" to be publicly displayed (Epilogue, 19), Prospero at once throws himself at our mercy and aligns himself with Providence. To do as he requests is to retreat from pride, "dancing up to th' chins" in the "filthy-mantled pool" that is our present home.

Conclusion: "No way out but through": Shakespeare's Antonios and the Wisdom of This World

I shan't catch up in this world, anyway.

—Robert Frost, "A Servant to Servants"

Shakespeare's fancy for naming characters Antonio and Sebastian, and thus for availing himself of the tradition that they represent, spanned his career, dating to some of his earliest works. The constable Anthony Dull in *Love's Labor's Lost* must be the most clownish of such fools, yet even he knows a *haud credo* from a pricket (4.2.11–12). Recalling Saint Anthony's wisdom in simplicity, Dull exposes, through his dialogue with Holofernes, the foolish pretentiousness of the schoolmaster's worldly wisdom and the true wisdom of his own unlettered folly (4.2). His malapropisms—"collusion" and "pollution" for "allusion" (4.2.41–49)—suggest an understanding beyond his own ken of his more learned peers' affectations, which they brandish to intimidate him. In the audience's last encounter with Dull, he has not "understood" one word in the scene, yet good-naturedly offers to supply entertainment at the upcoming performance (5.1.149–55).

Such liberality of spirit—whether it is straightforward, feigned, or problematic—is the quintessential trait of Renaissance stage Antonios. It also marks the lovelorn Julia, one play earlier, in *The Two Gentlemen of Verona.* Disguised as a boy named, tellingly, "Sebastian," she irrationally subjugates her own feelings for her beloved Proteus to those of Proteus for her rival Silvia. Aware of treading the line between sense and nonsense, she describes her action in the mixed terms that often, in Shakespeare's plays, speak true of boundless generosity:

Alas, poor fool, why do I pity him
That with his very heart despiseth me?
Because he loves her, he despiseth me;
Because I love him, I must pity him.

(4.4.93–96)

Fully aware that love has made a "fool" of her, she perseveres on her irrational course. In her self-sacrifice—which does have its limits, since she intends to woo Silvia too "coldly" to let Proteus "speed" (4.4.106–7)—she prefigures the likes of Viola/Cesario: reflecting Antonio in *Twelfth Night*, Viola not only woos another woman for, but also gives her very life to, the man she loves. In her obsessiveness, moreover, Julia looks forward to the likes of Marston's lunatic Antonio, a dubious martyr disguised to wreak revenge and of Middleton and Rowley's Tony, the false fool in *The Changeling*, who is bent on procuring Isabella's illicit love.

In turn, all such characters look back to Saints Anthony and Sebastian—more particularly, to the complex of issues concerning saintliness that their long, winding histories entail. Not surprisingly, all four of the Shakespearean plays in which major Antonios appear could be called seriocomic: they defy (and raise questions about) generic categorization, and, more to the point, they vex critical efforts to reflect faithfully the confusion of tone and the general irresoluteness that attend them throughout, especially as they draw to a close. The mixed saintliness of most Antonios, as well as the insoluble mysteries about what motivates a good many of them, is at home in such hybrid plays, where aesthetic unity often takes second place to laboring over intellectual and moral problems. Much as Saint Anthony once wrestled with his demons, so these plays take on life and death temptations—struggles between egoism and self-sacrifice; spiritual bondage and personal freedom; revenging impulsively and loving before it is too late.

The terrain on which these trials are played out is nothing shy of heaven and earth. More often than not, those locales are metaphorical or internalized, but in any incarnation they stand for disparate values, attitudes, and approaches to living. More specifically, most Antonios attempt to navigate their way to greater fulfillment than this world alone affords. Would-be purists—though wise men, folly-fallen—they evoke both sympathy in response to their pains and dissatisfaction for their failures. Confounded in their otherworldly ambition, then, are their moral complexity and their capacity to arouse in their audience both admiration and distaste.

Audiences' sympathies for stage Antonios are often enhanced by the nature of the material world that they encounter. In *The Merchant of*

Venice, both the natural and social aspects of this world are at best indifferent, and at worst hostile, to characters' idealizations; try as they might to behave consistently, according to a fixed notion of value, their trust in such systems is quickly brought to ruin, sometimes dragging them behind. Any claim to saintliness in this world is doomed from the start, destined to expose itself as vanity. So much the more, then, is the merchant Antonio set up to seem a hollow saint and his professions of perfect love bound to appear presumptuous. Not so Shakespeare's next Antonio, the one in *Twelfth Night*. His world, although another worldly world of luxury and recklessness, lends itself to ideal love in imperfect human form. It hosts far lesser kinds of love, too, and even instances of malice, and yet its very mania, while no less menacing than the vicissitudes of *Merchant*'s world, allows—indeed, encourages—emotional abandon. Here characters may more freely and safely will their refuge in wise folly than in self-interest.

The quasi-historical world of *Antony and Cleopatra* is, like its ahistorical counterpart in *The Tempest*, fraught with politics, the source of temporal power. Antony himself is trapped in the inexorable transition between real political and even theological eras, in large part victimized by his lack of viable, satisfactory options and thus tempted to indulge his whims moment to moment. The perils of this world—namely, transience and the absence of means to cope with it—are those of *Merchant* writ even larger. Here Mark Antony, like the Venetian merchant before him, is hard-put to reconcile wisdom and folly.

Prospero's brother has long been indulging his temptations to increase his earthly store. That Prospero has acted unawares as Antonio's tempter, however, pointedly recalls the considerable degree to which the characters themselves cooperate, even if unwittingly, in creating their own difficulties. The world of *The Tempest*, though subject to natural disasters and social injustice, is by far the most propitious to characters who, if not precisely saintly, would be kind. What inhibits Prospero, Antonio, and to an extent even Caliban is seated within the characters themselves—seated so deeply, in fact, that Prospero must exert himself simply to assist, rather than thwart, the established course of "Providence divine" (1.2.159). The world of *The Tempest* is bent upon carrying out the high-minded principles that Prospero can more readily understand than practice, so much so that it virtually reduces Antonio's recalcitrance to impotence. Where human misery prevails at all as the play concludes, it owes to inhumanity—that is, to demons still lingering within the human characters.

For indeed, Shakespeare's four Antonios all share in directing their own life's course, though to different degrees and with varying success.

The partial exception to that statement would be the sea captain in *Twelfth Night*, who, as the play closes, is prevented from freely performing acts of love, ironically, by the very society that his example would most benefit. Yet, even bound as he is, Antonio has made his choice of "willing love," and the stark contrast between his humility and the three other Antonios' pride accounts for much of the discomfort that the others are likely to induce, both within and outside their plays. While immune to neither resentment nor brawling with Orsino at sea, *Twelfth Night*'s Antonio nevertheless sacrifices all—his possessions and life—for Sebastian's sake. He thus realizes divine love in an impoverished world, augmenting the welfare of others; he also accentuates how removed from that world, by contrast, are a host of related characters, some of them other Antonios.

Prospero's removal from the world, although a traditional form of wise folly, easily degenerates to Pauline foolish wisdom, mirroring Antonio's pride, which is itself a foolish folly with the world. In much the same vein, the embattled Antonio in *Merchant* hesitates to acknowledge his indebtedness to the world in which he participates, yet is, willy nilly, held accountable in that world, especially by his sense of alienation. Mark Antony, too, is torn between such pride and humility. Sometimes longing to escape the trappings of the world, as when he returns Enobarbus's treasure, he is also in the world's thrall, hastening both to preserve its trappings and to escape the shame and embarrassment of losing them—empire, reputation, and all. The ridicule that marks his death suggests his double temptation—not only the folly of loving this life, which inevitably ends in disgrace, but also the arrogance and futility of attempts to elude the disgrace that is this life's due. Although in relation to the next world, the here and now may pale in glory, importance, and desirability, it is not to be wasted, misprized, or discarded lightly.

Knowing how to receive it and husband it without selling one's soul to it is rarely the province of Shakespeare's Antonios. Rather, those skills tend to lie with certain women in the plays—specifically, with Portia, Cleopatra, and, to a point, Viola. Each in her own way risks substantial loss and ventures her well-being to make good on her love in this life. Such hazarding may well be greatest where it is least exalted: of all of Shakespeare's female protagonists, perhaps none works so tirelessly as Portia to actualize ideals like justice; unjustly, however, her world is probably Shakespeare's most defiant toward establishing absolute ideals. For her active efforts to secure her marriage and maintain Venetian order, she thus receives in recompense what may appear small praise. By comparison, Cleopatra, investing no small amount of "toil" herself in trumping Caesar, coasts into the play's final grandeur. Though wedded to this world, she inherits nonetheless the dignity and divinity that belong to saints themselves. Her saintliness is qualified, to be sure, yet sometimes in the way that Saint Anthony's imperfections are occasionally shown to amplify his humility: she admits to the pleasures of the flesh, welcomes them, and still keeps them in perspective. Viola begins more timidly but ends boldly. Although sorely tempted to avoid the worldly problems that she has helped produce, she ultimately reclaims her identity and responsibility with the clearest of self-sacrificial gestures; offering up her life, she finds love in this world and is poised in the end to let her wise folly "walk about the orb" (3.1.38). Finally, both Portia and Cleopatra effectively rescue Antonios, while Viola's self-discovery redeems Orsino's love and hers.

Why these women should prove so much better prepared than their male counterparts to enact grace is another question altogether. Suffice it to mention that, in *The Tempest*, the redemptive victory goes to a man, though not Antonio. Because in *The Winter's Tale* that same salvific magic was again a woman's—Paulina's—Prospero's ultimate reconciliation of spirit and flesh is all the more remarkable. His passage through the slender corridor of faith into renewed acceptance of his own and his society's limitations is no less moving—and perhaps more so—for his set-backs. Like Len in Frost's "Servant to Servants," these characters appear to reach an understanding that "the best way out is always through." And like Len's nameless wife, who is a-weary of this great world, they also seem to realize that, being human, they won't "catch up in this world, anyway." But to let go of mortality because it is ultimately going to win, as Mark Antony seems to do, is to give over this world and life itself for the wrong reasons—out of despair and pride. Rather than do so, as they are sometimes inclined, characters like Portia, Cleopatra, and Prospero plot as best they can to play out, often playfully, some version of spiritual truth. And if, so doing, their performance falters, they ultimately refuse to fall back on the gross fakery of unearned martyrdom. Through their ordeals as makers of meaning, they also point beyond themselves to the playwright, whom they represent. Their challenge—to transform an ideal like love into something alive and breathing—is also, of course, his.

Shakespearean plays that feature Renaissance stage Antonios explore the best that can be hoped for in this process of giving shape to mere notion. Just how particular—restricted—must saints on earth finally be? And how sullied must remain human representations and enactments of a higher love? As has been shown, the relative ease and success with which Antonios, Sebastians, and other characters in their sphere are able to carry out their desires depends on an array of variables: most notably the peculiar combination of their disposition, as well as their world's, and the nature of whatever powers govern both. In the midst of such flux, however, a few constants emerge. Foremost, perhaps, they include the willingness and ability to manage and live with paradox. Shakespeare's saintliest saints eventually surrender enough control to love openly and yet not so much as to forgo responsibility or practical obligations. Witness Cleopatra's fusion, through her suicide, of total devotion to Antony and yet also defeat of Caesar. Or take Portia's facing up to the hard necessity of choosing between an adequately resolved trial or a satisfactorily resolved marriage; for all of the flaws in her action, her accomplishments far exceed the impotent gestures of Antonio, whose self-involvement far exceeds hers. Consider also Viola's movement from sham servant, a false front that spiritually binds her, to true servant, to which she is delivered when she rejects her servant's disguise and, through willing love, claims her freedom.

Although by fits and starts, the four plays at hand chart a growing conviction that this world is not to be dismissed for the purposes of seeking out higher truths but is, rather, to be esteemed for its capacity, albeit humble, to embody truths. More and more, the plays portray the foolish folly of undertaking to swindle this life of the commitment it warrants, the appreciation it deserves. As Montaigne quotes Seneca, "*The life of a fool is joyless, full of trepidation, given over wholly to the future.*"[1] So Prospero, at the last, is forced to see that his philosophical books and supernatural powers breed idle speculation; they are, in a strange sense, inferior to the immediate company of scoundrels like Antonio, if Prospero intends to acquire meaningful knowledge and to exercise significant power. His human limitations repeatedly brought home to him through his failures to reform both Caliban and, finally, his false brother, he learns that his knowledge and power, too, are limited—limited mainly to knowledge of and power over himself. Paradoxically, such belongings are both minimal and vast, as is his grace, which, hard-won and belated, releases him legitimately from bondage to the world that he so disdains and has been striving to evade. The unconditional mercy that he extends to Antonio firmly secures his humanity, which includes his own humble need to be forgiven. It is almost as if the Prospero of act 5 completes act 5 of *Twelfth Night*, surrendering control he never truly had over an imprisoned Antonio. Nor is it likely accidental that both *Twelfth Night* and *The Tempest* end with assertive attempts to puncture the conventional barrier between fiction and life, obliging the audience to acknowledge that bringing love into the world is not the province of fantasy but the essence of real living. By insisting on response from the audience, that is, these plays forestall the audience's evasiveness even as they validate their own substantiality and purpose.

"We seek other conditions," writes Montaigne in "Of Experience," "because we do not understand the use of our own, and go outside of ourselves because we do not know what it is like inside."[2] Such a statement aptly characterizes the motives of several Shakespearean Antonios—especially the merchant, Mark Antony, and Prospero's "false brother"—but also Prospero himself. Indeed, to attend or read *The Tempest* without thinking of Montaigne's "Of Experience" is nearly as difficult as to miss the play's debt to "Of Cannibals." For Prospero, who can hide from his own humanity as readily as make himself invisible, learns through his pain about the folly of pride, much as, Montaigne confesses, he is himself reborn through suffering the stone: "Put the case this way, that nature is bearing and pushing you into that glorious school, which you would never have entered of your own free will" (837).

As Montaigne sees it, possibly the prime lesson of nature's school applies not only in Prospero's instance but to Shakespeare's Antonios as well—that is, that the flesh does not exist, as pure saints would have it, to be denied. Instead, the pleasure it lends, although not an end in itself, steers humanity toward recognition: our mortality is finally beyond our control, and yet, although we cannot manipulate it, we can choose to endure it at its worst, enjoy it at its best, and then let be:

> When I dance, I dance; when I sleep, I sleep; yes, and when I walk alone in a beautiful orchard, if my thoughts have been dwelling on extraneous incidents for some part of the time, for some other part I bring them back to the walk, to the orchard, to the sweetness of this solitude, and to me. Nature has observed this principle like a mother, that the actions she has enjoined on us for our need should also give us pleasure; and she invites us to them not only through reason, but also through appetite. It is unjust to infringe her laws. (850)

To give over to this life, Montaigne implies, takes our minds off of ourselves, preparing us, paradoxically, to give ourselves away.

As so many English Renaissance Antonios suggest through examples both sound and spurious, the end of this life is not to efface the self any more than it is to allow the self to swell. Rather, self-sacrifice is a matter of cultivating self so as to invest one's self in love. Shakespeare's four Antonios, materializing in plays and dramatic situations that press across boundaries between fiction and life, collaborate in making such love felt. Through acts self-centered and generous, they reach across borders within the plays to elicit passion, and they advance upon our experience, dispelling doubt that the only way through is grace.

Notes

All quotations from Shakespeare come from *The Riverside Shakespeare*, gen. ed. G. Blakemore Evans (Boston: Houghton Mifflin, 1974).

Introduction

1. From here on out, primarily for convenience, I shall refer to all four characters as Antonio. Although the more common name for Mark Antony is his Anglicized surname, he is occasionally called Antonio in both *Antony and Cleopatra* and *Julius Caesar* and was often referred to by that name, of course, in other Renaissance works. Several plays evince the easy interchangeability of the names Anthony and Antonio; in *Much Ado about Nothing*, for example, the character named Antonio is twice called "Anthony" (5.1.91 and 100).

2. Whether or not these characters were immediately identifiable by appearance as well as name I cannot tell from the plays themselves. The only references to the dress of Antonios are the obvious ones that occur in plays like Middleton and Rowley's *Changeling* and Marston's *Antonio's Revenge*, where the Antonios pretend to be fools or madmen; some of those, we can probably safely assume, would have been appareled accordingly. (The association between the Renaissance stage Antonio and fools is elaborated in chap. 1.) In any event, I wish to draw a parallel between at least the aural effect of the name and the visual effect of, for instance, a conventional stage property or a costume like a typical stage Jew's. As demonstrated by the work in this area of such scholars as Alan Dessen and G. K. Hunter, recovering theatrical cues to the Elizabethan audience can help in reimaging an Elizabethan theatrical experience. See especially Dessen's *Elizabethan Stage Conventions and Modern Interpreters* (New York: Cambridge University Press, 1984) and his more recent *Recovering Shakespeare's Theatrical Vocabulary* (New York: Cambridge University Press, 1995). See also Hunter's "Flatcaps and Bluecoats: Visual Signals on the Elizabethan Stage" (*Essays and Studies* 33 [1980]: 16–47), which offers an excellent discussion of such visual signals as clothing and typified physical gestures, conventions within which individual actors still had considerable freedom of expression. In *Recovering Shakespeare's Theatrical Vocabulary*, Dessen conceives of the study of lost staging vocabulary as I do the uncovering of traditions surrounding stage Antonios and Sebastians: as the work of an "archaeologist" (3).

3. Barbara K. Lewalski, "Thematic Patterns in *Twelfth Night*," *Shakespeare Studies* 1 (1965): 176.

4. Maurice Hunt, "Love, Disguise, and Knowledge in *Twelfth Night*," *C.L.A. Journal* 32 (1988–89): 491.

5. I borrow the term "self-conscious" from Helen Hackett, who discusses the advantages and drawbacks of new historicist methods in the epilogue to her book *Virgin Mother, Maiden Queen: Elizabeth I and the Cult of the Virgin Mary* (New York: St. Martin's Press, 1995). Acknowledging that the new historicism has "opened up fascinating new interpretations," she continues:

> Even so, it can be insensitive to topical detail, and to the Elizabethans' own sophistication and self-consciousness. In the present study, I have aimed to give some recognition of Elizabethan thinkers' own theorisations of their cultural practices. (236)

My own attempts to represent not only "theorisations" but also actual stage practice will reveal ambivalences toward some new historicist approaches in nearly every chapter. Similar qualms about the relevance of contemporary theorizations to Elizabethan culture lead me to conceptualize the handling of generosity very differently from William Flesch's interesting book *Generosity and the Limits of Authority: Shakespeare, Herbert, Milton* (Ithaca: Cornell University Press, 1992), which noticeably overlaps with mine in subject matter but not interpretation.

1: "Wise men, folly-fall'n": Characters Named *Antonio* in English Renaissance Drama

1. Although the extent to which Antonio the sea captain is significant to *Twelfth Night* may be debatable, I believe he is crucial to the play's moral vision. For elaboration, see chap. 3.

2. John Webster, "The Duchess of Malfi," in *Drama of the English Renaissance*, ed. Russell A. Fraser and Norman Rabkin (New York: Macmillan, 1976), 2:2.2.68.

3. R. P. Corballis, "The Name Antonio in English Renaissance Drama," *Cahiers Elisabéthains: Études sur la Pré-Renaissance et la Renaissance Anglaises* 25 (1984): 65. Subsequent references in this paragraph refer to Corballis.

4. Thomas Middleton, *Women Beware Women*, ed. J. R. Mulryne (London: Methuen, 1975), 4.1.1–6, quoted in Corballis, "The Name Antonio," 70.

5. Saint Anthony of Egypt is also known as Saint Anthony the Abbot, the Great, and the Hermit. He is not to be confused with Saint Anthony of Padua, a later medieval figure. Interestingly, however, some of the miracles attributed to the Paduan Anthony recall those of the Egyptian monk—particularly those involving the revival of people presumed dead. He was also, like his predecessor, a patron of the poor. Yet in temperament the two saints were entirely opposed, since Anthony of Egypt valued monastic solitude above all else, while Anthony of Padua was known for his charismatic sermons, which drew sizable congregations to the churches where he preached.

6. David Hugh Farmer, *The Oxford Dictionary of Saints* (Oxford: Clarendon Press, 1978).

7. See, e.g., Robert C. Gregg, trans. and ed., *The Life of Antony*, by Athanasius, Classics of Western Spirituality (New York: Paulist Press, 1980).

8. See, e.g., *The Ecclesiastical History of Sozomen*, in *Nicene and Post-Nicene Fathers of the Christian Church*, ed. Philip Schaff and Henry Wace, 2nd series (Grand Rapids, Mich.: Eerdmans, 1952), 2:248–49.

9. St. Augustine, *The Confessions*, trans. Sir Tobie Matthew, rev. Roger Hudleston (London: Burns & Oates, 1954), 8, 6–8.

10. See, e.g., Gregg, *The Life of Antony*, 84.

11. See, e.g., William Caxton, trans., *The Golden Legend*, by Jacobus de Voragine, facsimile ed. by William Morris (Hammersmith: Kelmscott, 1892), 1:332.

12. Much of my historical material on the Antonite hospitals in Vienne and London comes from Rose Graham, "The Order of St. Antoine de Viennois and Its English Commandery, St. Anthony's, Threadneedle Street" (*Archaeological Journal* 34 [1927]: 341–406) and *A Picture Book of the Life of St. Anthony the Abbot* (by Jean Macellard [Oxford: Roxburghe Club, 1937]).

13. Corballis, "The Name Antonio," 61–64.

14. The iconographic Tau cross probably arises from the shape of the crutch that Anthony used in his legendary old age (Graham, *Picture Book*, 42). His book most likely represents his retirement to the contemplative life.

15. Graham, *Picture Book*, 34.

16. Information on the iconography of Saint Anthony may be found, for example, in Louis Réau's *Iconographie de l'art chrétien* (vol. 3 [Paris: Presses Universitaires de France, 1959]).

17. Laurinda S. Dixon, "Bosch's 'St. Anthony Triptych'—An Apothecary's Apotheosis," *Art Journal* 44 (1984): 120–21.

18. Weidetz's is but one of countless northern European images of Saint Anthony surrounded by amputated limbs, fires, and patients in agony. Even a glance through catalogs of late medieval and early Renaissance prints (e.g., in *The Illustrated Bartsch*) reveals this preoccupation.

19. Graham, "Order of St. Antoine," 390.

20. Graham, *Picture Book*, 4.

21. Ibid., 4.

22. Graham, "Order of St. Antoine," 390–91.

23. Ibid., 389.

24. Richard Marius, *Thomas More: A Biography* (New York: Knopf, 1984), 168.

25. Leland Miles, ed., *A Dialogue of Comfort against Tribulation*, by Thomas More (Bloomington: Indiana University Press, 1965), xliii–vii.

The parallels between More's Vincent and the history of Saint Vincent are striking. Both men are young and articulate, and Saint Vincent shows the same filial attachment to an elderly bishop that More's Vincent does to the aged Anthony. Furthermore, Saint Vincent confronts his imprisonment and martyrdom with courageous resignation—the very attitude that More's Anthony seeks to inspire in his young nephew.

26. Miles, *Dialogue of Comfort*, xxx; Marius, *Thomas More: A Biography*, 477.

27. E. Margaret Thompson, *The Carthusian Order in England* (New York: Macmillan, 1930), 518, 522–23.

28. More witnessed the Carthusian monks' ghastly torture from his window in the Tower. No doubt the sight contributed to the fear of his own fate, which prompted his composition of the *Dialogue of Comfort*.

29. Corballis mentions in passing the phenomenon of this pairing in English Renaissance drama, but he does not try to analyze why it so often recurs ("The Name Antonio," 65).

30. Réau, *Iconographie de l'art chrétien*, vol. 3, bk. 3, p. 1190.

31. Ibid., 3:3:1192. As I hope the discussion in this chapter will make clear, that Antonio, Sebastian, and Adrian are all three characters in *The Tempest* is most likely not accidental.

32. For this and other explanations of Sebastian's link with healing, see ibid., 3:3:1190–94.

33. Ibid., 3:1:104.

34. Ibid., 3:3:1194.

35. Corballis, "The Name Antonio," 66; Réau, *Iconographie de l'art chrétien*, 3:1:102.

36. Hippolyte Delehaye offers a host of instances in which such distortion is known to have occurred in hagiography because of popular sentiment or misunderstanding of a saint's legend (*The Legends of the Saints*, trans. Donald Attwater [New York: Fordham University Press, 1962]). See especially chap. 2, part 2, and also pp. 18–19, on the substitution of an abstraction for the individual saint.

Recent criticism has placed much attention on the homoerotic/homosocial suggestions in both *Merchant* and *Twelfth Night*. See, for example, the work of Alice N. Benston, Keith Geary, Robert Kimbrough, Helene Moglen, Karen Newman, Joseph Pequigney, Bruce R. Smith, and Valerie Traub, among many other authors. Smith and Kimbrough also stress the androgynous overtones of Viola's disguise and behavior as Cesario (Smith, *Homosexual Desire in Shakespeare's England* [Chicago: University of Chicago Press, 1991], 151; Kimbrough, *Shakespeare and the Art of Humankindness: the essay toward androgyny* [Atlantic Highlands, N.J.: Humanities Press International, 1990], 114–20). At issue for Antony in *Antony and Cleopatra* also seems to be his sexual identity. Specifically, his lust for Cleopatra, according to the Roman perspective, has jeopardized his masculinity. On this matter, see especially Janet Adelman, *Suffocating Mothers: Fantasies of Maternal Origin in Shakespeare's Plays, "Hamlet" to "The Tempest"* (New York: Routledge, 1992), 174–92.

37. Marius, *Thomas More: A Biography*, 342.

38. See, e.g., Graham, *Picture Book*. The story is also represented on an enamel plate, made by Léonard Limousin in 1536 for the Antonite Order at Vienne, and now in the British Museum.

39. Caxton, *The Golden Legend*, 333.

40. Geneva Bible, 1 Cor. 3:18–19.

41. This paradoxical attitude toward the world is reflected in works by both Erasmus and More. For example, scorn for earthly ambition, possession, and power appears throughout Erasmus's *De Contemptu Mundi* (trans. Thomas Paynell [Gainesville, Fla.: Scholars' Facsimiles and Reprints, 1967]), which exalts the "solitary life" reminiscent of Saint Anthony's desert asceticism. Yet, in *Praise of Folly* (London: Reeves & Turner, 1876), Erasmus also promotes a childlike participation in this life. Indeed, it is precisely because worldly riches hold so little value that one should not take this world overly seriously but should instead approach life foolishly.

42. Caxton, *The Golden Legend*, 339.

43. Ibid., 342.

44. Erasmus, *In Praise of Folly*, 188–89.

45. C. G. V. Harcourt, *Legends of St. Augustine, St. Anthony, and St. Cuthbert, Painted on the Back of the Stalls in Carlisle Cathedral* (Carlisle: C. Thurnam, 1868), #14.

46. Gregg, *The Life of Antony*, xvi.

Saint Sebastian earned his own resemblance to Christ through such attributes as his young martyrdom and his powers of revival. Interestingly, Italian Renaissance painters often portray the suffering of Christ tied to a Roman column like that to which Saint Sebastian is bound in other works from the same period: the visual comparison is unmistakable. That English Renaissance stage Sebastians can also suggest Christlike features is evident in, for instance, Lewalski's essay, "Thematic Patterns in *Twelfth Night.*" Lewalski sees in Viola and Sebastian the two salient traits of Christ: Viola suffers passively, and Sebastian triumphs physically.

47. Helen Tanzer, ed., *Praise of Folly*, by Desiderius Erasmus, facsimile ed. with the marginal drawings of Hans Holbein, 1515 (Basle: H. Oppermann, 1931), 31.

48. Ibid., drawing 74.

49. Further evidence of this point entails the fact that nearly every European language includes at least one diminutive for the name of Saint Anthony, each of which means "fool" (e.g., Italian *toni*="babbeo" [Carlo Battisti and Giovanni Alessio, *Dizionario etimologico italiano* (Florence: G. Barbèra, 1950–57)]). The dating of this meaning is made difficult in most cases because etymological dictionaries do not as yet exist for many of these languages. But the *Oxford English Dictionary* (Oxford: Clarendon Press, 1989), as Corballis points out ("The Name Antonio," 61), must surely be too late in attributing the English "Tony" (="fool") to *The Changeling*, 1623 (the new *OED* takes the same position). Granted, Middleton and Rowley are the first English writers known to have used the precise nickname *Tony* for one who literally becomes a fool through disguise. Still, an earlier date is suggested by the fact that, in *The Changeling*, Lollio recognizes *Tony* as a proper appellation for a fool: "Tony, Tony, 'tis enough, and a very good name for a fool" (in *Drama of the English Renaissance*, ed. Russell A. Fraser & Norman Rabkin [New York: Macmillan, 1976], 1.2.103–4). What is more, a much earlier date than 1623 is indicated in the second entry for the German *Tone* (also *Toni*) in Grimm, which connects the meaning of "fool" to the early sixteenth-century Reformation: Swabian Protestants once derided Catholic masons with the shortened form of Saint Anthony's name, quite possibly as early as the first Peasant Revolts (from 1523 on).

50. See, e.g., W. W. Greg, ed., *The Book of Sir Thomas More*, Malone Soc. Reprints, 1911 (Oxford: Oxford University Press, 1961), 2.299–300, 9.1117–18, 11.1354.

51. Ibid., 9.1018–22.

52. Ibid., ll. 111–20 of C's contribution to Addition 2.

53. Margo Todd, "Humanists, Puritans and the Spiritualized Household," *Church History* 49 (1980): 19.

54. Another motive for Renaissance playwrights' elevation of More and his work was likely the Puritans' disparagement of him. See, e.g., the contemptuous comments collected in Jackson Campbell Boswell's catalog (*Sir Thomas More in the English Renaissance: An Annotated Catalog*, vol. 83 [Binghamton: Medieval and Renaissance Texts and Studies, 1994]) by such figures as John Calvin (item #102), John Foxe (#232), William Tyndale (#647, 650–51), and Andrew Willet (#693).

55. Marius, *Thomas More: A Biography*, 167–68.

56. Ibid.

57. Thomas More, *Utopia*, ed. J. Churton Collins, trans. Ralph Robynson (Oxford: Clarendon Press, 1904), 79–80.

58. Because Erasmus's well-known pun on More's name connects More to foolishness (Latin *more*="fool"), the fool in *Utopia* may be something of an authorial mouthpiece for the author in promoting Christian charity. Yet More seems intent on making his fool's manner so unattractive as to cast doubt on his viewpoint. Alison Chapman, while an undergraduate at Davidson College, admirably addressed such ambiguity about More's fool in an unpublished paper ("The Fool and Hythloday: Unliked and Unlikeable," 1986).

59. Réau, *Iconographie de l'art chrétien*, 3:3:1192.

60. Mantegna's celebrated *Saint Sebastian* epitomizes the Italian Renaissance combination of idealization and naturalism that prevents the martyr from convincing us of this torment and hence of his humanity (Louvre, Paris). Blood trickles from his wounds; one arrow protrudes realistically from just beneath the skin's surface; and another arrow has grazed his right leg, leaving behind a blemish. Still, for all these manifest causes of pain, Sebastian seems to hurt less than he actually should. His grimace implies that he is not immune to human suffering, while it simultaneously suggests an ecstasy that transports him from the realm of human pain to another of spiritual pleasure.

61. E.g., Alessio Baldovinetti, *Madonna with Child and Saints*; Lorenzo Monaco, *Coronation of the Virgin* (both in the Uffizi Gallery, Florence).

62. Graham, *Picture Book*, 140.

63. Geoffrey Galt Harpham, *The Ascetic Imperative in Culture and Criticism* (Chicago: University of Chicago Press, 1987), 26–27.

64. See, e.g., act 5 of *Antonio's Revenge* (by John Marston, ed. G. K. Hunter, Regents Renaissance Drama Series [Lincoln: University of Nebraska Press, 1965]).

65. Cf. to Grünewald's panel, e.g., the roughly contemporary *Saint Anthony and Saint Paul* by Giovanni Girolamo Savoldo (c. 1480–1548; Accademia, Venice), who also emphasizes the dissimilarity between Saint Paul's sackcloth and Saint Anthony's lavish robes.

66. This interpretation is substantiated by contrasting Cranach's *Temptation* (1506) with Martin Schongauer's (c. 1475), on which Cranach's is clearly based. Schongauer's Anthony is not really troubled or harassed by the demons. He is more medieval and saintly than Cranach's.

67. Ruth Mellinkoff has shown this point in another way: in studying *The Concert of Angels—Nativity*, another panel of the Isenheim Altarpiece, she has discovered that the dark, feathered angel with the peacock's crest is Lucifer and, in calling his appearance "gangrenous," she associates bodily disease with the spiritual disease that would infect humanity after the Fall (*The Devil at Isenheim: Reflections of Popular Belief in Grünewald's Altarpiece*, California Studies in the History of Art, Discovery Series 1 [Berkeley: University of California Press, 1988], 22).

68. Grünewald further illustrates the singular saving power of Christ with two other panels in the Isenheim Altarpiece: Christ's grisly wounds in the *Crucifixion* are healed in the *Resurrection* panel. Thus pilgrims to Isenheim were instructed that they, too, would be restored after death, through faith in Christ.

69. Thomas J. Heffernan, *Sacred Biography: Saints and Their Biographers in the Middle Ages* (New York: Oxford University Press, 1989), 123.

70. Clifford Davidson, "The Middle English Saint Play and Its Iconography," in *The Saint Play in Medieval Europe*, ed. Clifford Davidson, Early Drama, Art, and Music Monograph Series, 8 (Kalamazoo: Medieval Institute Publications, Western Michigan University, 1986), 35.

71. Lynette R. Muir, "The Saint Play in Medieval France," in *The Saint Play in Medieval Europe*, ed. Clifford Davidson, Early Drama, Art, and Music Monograph Series, 8 (Kalamazoo: Medieval Institute Publications, Western Michigan University, 1986), 171, 173.

72. Kathleen C. Falvey, "The Italian Saint Play: The Example of Perugia," in *The Saint Play in Medieval Europe*, ed. Clifford Davidson, Early Drama, Art, and Music Monograph Series, 8 (Kalamazoo: Medieval Institute Publications, Western Michigan University, 1986), 181, 186, 192–94.

73. Peter Happé, "The Protestant Adaptation of the Saint Play," in *The Saint Play in Medieval Europe*, ed. Clifford Davidson, Early Drama, Art, and Music Monograph Series, 8 (Kalamazoo: Medieval Institute Publications, Western Michigan University, 1986), 214.

74. Ibid., 211.

75. Gordon Kipling, *The Triumph of Honour: Burgundian Origins of the Elizabethan Renaissance* (The Hague: Leiden University Press, 1977), 124.

76. I borrow the useful term *transformation* from Huston Diehl ("Graven Images: Protestant Emblem Books in England," *Renaissance Quarterly* 39 [1986]: 49–66), who coins it specifically to describe the remaking of Catholic icons into images that Protestants could accept. For further information on the substitution of Elizabeth I for Catholic saints, see John Ransome Phillips, *The Reformation of Images: Destruction of Art in England, 1535–1660* (Berkeley: University of California Press, 1973), e.g., p. 119: "The destruction of the sacred image of Christ and his saints was paralleled by the curious rise of the 'sacred' image of Elizabeth the Queen."

77. John Wasson, "The Secular Saint Plays of the Elizabethan Era," in *The Saint Play in Medieval Europe*, ed. Clifford Davidson, Early Drama, Art, and Music Monograph Series, 8 (Kalamazoo: Medieval Institute Publications, Western Michigan University, 1986), 243–44.

78. The best-known and most comprehensive analysis of this ambiguity is no doubt Norman Rabkin's "Rabbits, Ducks, and *Henry V*," reprinted as "Either/Or: Responding to *Henry V*" in *Shakespeare and the Problem of Meaning* (Chicago: University of Chicago Press, 1981). The view that Shakespeare's tone toward Henry V is more complicated than Wasson allows would also be supported indirectly by David Jeffrey, who attributes specifically to the English saint play the psychological realism in characterization that would eventually distinguish the even more fully drawn characters of Shakespeare and his contemporaries. Where there is psychological realism, so will there likely be multiple perspectives on a single character ("English Saints' Plays," in *Medieval Drama*, ed. Malcolm Bradbury and David Palmer, Stratford-upon-Avon Studies 16 [London: Edward Arnold, 1973], 77–82).

79. Happé, "Protestant Adaptation," 218.

80. Harold Gardiner, *Mysteries' End: An Investigation of the Last Days of the Medieval Stage*, 1946 (rprt., New Haven: Yale University Press, 1967), 47–48.

81. Ervin Panofsky, "Comments on Art and Reformation," in *Symbols in Transformation: Iconographic Themes at the Time of the Reformation* (Princeton: The Art Museum, Princeton University, 1969).

82. Wasson, "Secular Saint Plays," 252.

83. *Harper's Latin Dictionary* (New York: American Book, 1879).

84. Wasson, "Secular Saint Plays," 253.

85. There is actually a separate saint, Antoninus of Florence, who died in 1459. Unlike Anthony, however, Antoninus seems to have been little known in sixteenth-century England, probably because he was not canonized until 1523. Hence my conjecture that Dekker and Massinger's Antoninus is a variation of Anthony. Curiously enough, however, even if the playwrights were alluding to Antoninus, some parallels still hold: Antoninus was a latter-day ascetic and yet fraternized with the Medicis and taught that "money invested in commerce was true capital; therefore it was lawful and not usury to claim interest on it" (Farmer, *Oxford Dictionary of Saints*). He was not altogether removed from the world.

2: "A foolish consistency": Antonio and Alienation in *The Merchant of Venice*

1. Carol Leventen, "Patrimony and Patriarchy in *The Merchant of Venice*," in *The Matter of Difference*, ed. Valerie Wayne (Ithaca: Cornell University Press, 1991), 71.

2. See, e.g., John Lyon, *"The Merchant of Venice," Twayne's New Critical Introductions to Shakespeare* (Boston: Twayne Publishers, 1988), 59.

As my student Kathryn Robinson Kross has pointed out to me, the poem in the silver casket could be read in a less contradictory way: even if you were to wed, you would still be a fool (and therefore are not worthy of a wife). In addition, if this textual detail is indeed contradictory, it may have been planned that way to characterize Portia's father.

3. Norman Rabkin, *Shakespeare and the Problem of Meaning,* 30–31.

Cf., e.g., Walter Cohen: "Some of the merit of *The Merchant of Venice* ironically lies in the failure of its central design to provide a completely satisfying resolution to the dilemmas raised in the course of the action" ("*The Merchant of Venice* and the Possibilities of Historical Criticism," *ELH* 49 [1982]: 775); and Lyon:

> Here Shakespeare's vision is multifaceted, protean, magnanimous and fecund, but not free of the discrepancies to which its creative excesses give rise. Such creativity proves resistant to selection . . . . The play of mind evinced in *The Merchant of Venice* never quite succeeds in converging its discrepant materials into complex coherence. Hence unified readings of the play . . . are unsatisfactory, not because they misinterpret the text, but because in the interests of that coherence they necessarily suppress some elements . . . which we find not merely discrepant but rich in intelligence and insight. (*"Merchant,"* 96)

Although the basis of Rabkin's likening the play's world to our own is epistemological, as is mine, *Merchant* has convinced a sizable number of critics that its particulars derive from historical—real—sources. I am not sure, in fact, that any Shakespearean play except the chronicle histories (and perhaps *The Tempest*) has elicited so much commentary on very precise ways in which the play reflects turn-of-the-century Europe. Examples would include discussions of parallels between Shakespeare's trial and actual court cases, especially one in which ownership of the Theatre was being determined (Herbert

Berry, "Shylock, Robert Miles, and Events at the Theatre," *Shakespeare Quarterly* 44 [1993]: 183–97), and those between Shylock and a real Jewish merchant in London (Richard H. Popkin, "A Jewish Merchant of Venice," *Shakespeare Quarterly* 40 [1989]: 329–31); between Antonio and Don Antonio, against whose life the Portuguese physician Roderigo Lopez was accused of conspiring (John Gross, *Shylock: A Legend and Its Legacy* [New York: Simon & Schuster, 1992], 32–33; Steven Mullaney, "Brothers and Others, or the Art of Alienation," in *Cannibals, Witches, and Divorce: Estranging the Renaissance*, ed. Marjorie Garber [Baltimore: Johns Hopkins University Press, 1987], 76); between Bassanio and the Bassano family, erstwhile Italian Jews relocated in London as musicians (Gross, *Shylock*, 34); between Antonio and Shakespeare's father, who lent money (ibid., 59) and who went to Chancery in a two-year court battle over property that he had mortgaged and, ultimately, lost (ibid., 78–79); between gendered power structures in the play and in England and Italy (Leventen, "Patrimony and Patriarchy"; Karen Newman, "Portia's Ring: Unruly Women and Structures of Exchange in *The Merchant of Venice*," *Shakespeare Quarterly* 38 [1987]: 19–33); and, most applicable to my discussion, between Antonio's and Shylock's social alienation and the sociopolitical alienation arising from colonialism and implicit in monarchy (Mullaney, "Brothers and Others"). In addition, most analyses of the play include information on actual lending practices, views of usury, and so forth, in relation to how those issues are handled in the play.

4. Rabkin, *Shakespeare and the Problem of Meaning*, 28.

5. The locus classicus of this idea is John Russell Brown's work on the play, especially that in *Shakespeare and His Comedies* (2nd ed. [London: Methuen, 1962], chap. 3). Many echoes of Brown have followed—e.g., Keith Geary's remark that "Antonio, finally, applies the diction of finance to love more completely than any other character. He will literally pay Bassanio's debt with all his heart" ("The Nature of Portia's Victory: Turning to Men in *The Merchant of Venice*," *Shakespeare Survey* 37 [1984]: 65). Ronald A. Sharp has written an engaging study of gift exchange in *Merchant* ("Gift Exchange and the Economics of Spirit in *The Merchant of Venice*," *Modern Philology* 83 [1985–86]: 250–65).

6. Moreover, as John Doebler points out, the "melancholy man without cause" was a Renaissance "stock character" (*Shakespeare's Speaking Pictures: Studies in Iconic Imagery* [Albuquerque: University of New Mexico Press, 1974], 41).

Since John Russell Brown attributed Antonio's melancholy to Bassanio's departure for Belmont (*The Merchant of Venice*, by William Shakespeare, New Arden ed. [Cambridge: Harvard University Press, 1955], xlvi on 1.1.119), many critics have followed, thereby raising the inevitable question about the nature of Antonio's and Bassanio's feelings for each other. Are those feelings friendly or erotic, at least on Antonio's part, if not on Bassanio's? Here is likely an instance where labels are more self-defeating than helpful, as Marjorie Garber has recently argued about the futility of efforts to categorize sexual identity (*Vice Versa: Bisexuality and the Eroticism of Everyday Life* [New York: Simon & Schuster, 1995]). Even so, I must agree with Joseph Pequigney about the absence of any recognizably erotic language in Antonio's and Bassanio's speeches to and about each other ("The Two Antonios and Same Sex Love in *Twelfth Night* and *The Merchant of Venice*," *English Literary Renaissance* 22 [1992], see especially 210–21). Their relationship seems a friendship. In any case, I am relying on the assumption that the emotional bond between the two men as it conflicts with Bassanio and Portia's marriage bond is of central concern, whatever the specific nature of the male bonding at hand. Shakespeare is perennially interested in how male-female relationships are negotiatated with same-sex relationships to form a workable (if neither completely harmonious nor absolutely fixed) social structure—as in, for example, *A Midsummer Night's Dream, Much Ado about Nothing*, and other works, including two more in this study, *Twelfth Night* and *Antony and Cleopatra*. In my opinion this negotiation is both troublesome and troubling in *Merchant*; I disagree with Pequigney's assertion that the resolution brought about in the love relationships here is relatively trouble-free (see "The Two Antonios," especially 218–21). On these relationships see also the essays of Alice N. Benston ("Portia, the Law, and the Tripartite Structure of *The Merchant of Venice*," *Shakespeare Quarterly* 30 [1979]: 367–85), Geary ("The Nature of Portia's Victory"), and Newman ("Portia's Ring").

7. *The Oxford English Dictionary* (1989).

8. Christopher Spencer shows that the Christians refer to Shylock as "Jew" sixty-one times in *Merchant* and only fifteen times call him by his proper name (*The Genesis of Shakespeare's "Merchant of Venice,"* in *Studies in British Literature*, vol. 3. [Lewiston, N.Y.: Edwin Mellen, 1988], 95).

9. For a reading of Bassanio's motives similar to mine, see Terry Eagleton: "Having improvidently thrown his money around, Bassanio has come to Belmont to buy up the well-heeled Portia with the aid of Antonio's loan, rashly jeopardizing his friend's life in the process" (*William Shakespeare* [Oxford: Basil Blackwell, 1986], 45).

10. David Beauregard has recently read Antonio as an Aristotelian-Thomistic embodiment of the very virtue of liberality. Beauregard adds to the list of Antonio's sacrifices his patient endurance in 4.1 in the face of injustice (*Virtue's Own Feature: Shakespeare and the Virtue Ethics Tradition* [Newark, Del.: University of Delaware Press, 1995], 88, 99).

11. So much has been written about Shylock's appropriation of Jacob and Laban's story that some acknowledgment of the variety in critical opinion is in order. In brief, critics tend to disagree over whether Shylock's apology for usury is in any sense defensible or is, rather, specious; the latter view is adopted more often, most notably by Joan Ozark Holmer in a brief article ("'When Jacob Graz'd His Uncle Laban's Sheep': A New Source for *The Merchant of Venice*," *Shakespeare Quarterly* 36 [1985]: 64–65). My own sense of Shakespeare's purpose is informed by other parallels in *Merchant* between Shylock and Jacob. In particular, that Shylock's wife was named Leah does not reflect ironically on Shylock but positively (see Gross, *Shylock*, 68–69). All told, neither the association between the two men nor Shylock's narration of the story in 1.3 seems to me to be charged with a particular tone, but, rather, both seem mixed in tone, capable of evoking irony *and* sympathy. Hence my use of the word *trickster* for Jacob and Shylock both: it incorporates several overtones and looks forward to Shylock's defeat by Portia, another trickster.

12. Evidence that Jews were regarded in Elizabethan England as the devil's kin continues to arise, as in Ruth Samson Luborsky's recent note "The Pictorial Image of the Jew in Elizabethan Secular Books" (*Shakespeare Quarterly* 46 [1995]: 449–53).

13. One recent director of the play has observed that it "can be seen as a warning, as a picture of how we allow our religious beliefs to mask our God-given humanity" (quoted in Felicia Hardison Londré, "Confronting Shakespeare's 'Political Incorrectness' in Production: Contemporary American Audiences and the New 'Problem Plays,'" in *Staging Difference: Cultural Pluralism in American Theatre and Drama*, ed. Marc. Maufort, American University Studies, series 26, vol. 25 [New York: Peter Lang Publishing, 1995], 90).

14. Many critics remark on Shylock's role in alienating himself, perhaps most interestingly Mullaney, "Brothers and Others," 82. Other critics have also noticed, as I do, Antonio and Shylock's deeper resemblance beneath their enmity—for example, Jan Lawson Hinely: "Antonio, looking at Shylock, sees himself, distorted but still recognizable" ("Bond Priorities in *The Merchant of Venice*," *Studies in English Literature* 20 [1980]: 223).

15. See Brown, *Merchant*, note to 3.3.27. Brown also notes the difficulty of Antonio's language here in notes to 3.3.19, 30–31.

16. Stephen J. Greenblatt, "Marlowe, Marx, and Anti-Semitism" in *Learning to Curse: Essays in Early Modern Culture* (New York: Routledge, 1990), 43. In fairness to Greenblatt, I must admit that I have lifted his words from a context antithetical to mine, where he is arguing that "the Jew seems to embody the abstract principle of *difference* itself" (43).

17. Sinead Cusack, "Portia in *The Merchant of Venice*," in *"The Merchant of Venice": Critical Essays*, ed. Thomas Wheeler (New York: Garland Publishing, 1991), 342–43.

18. W. Moelwyn Merchant, ed., *The Merchant of Venice*, by William Shakespeare (Middlesex: Penguin, 1967), note to 1.2.108.

19. John Julius Norwich, *A History of Venice* (New York: Knopf, 1982), 129–31.

Most critics who have taken up the matter of Portia's racism have apologized for it, but I think it is pronounced in 1.2 by being repeated through hints in 2.1.1–3 and more overtly in 2.3.79. Furthermore, why would all the suitors except Bassanio be foreigners to Italy unless to present a perceptual problem to Portia comparable to that posed by the casket test (of which she is herself skeptical)? Surely the lesson that appearances can deceive is not confined to young men.

20. *As You Like It*, 2.7.139–66. As Anne Barton has stated so well: "[Jaques's] words are no sooner spoken than Orlando enters bearing old Adam: a man enfeebled by his years, dependent now upon a younger life, but also the living image of all that Jaques has left out of his type picture: loyal, honest, and discriminating" (introduction to *The Merchant of Venice*, by William Shakespeare, in *The Riverside Shakespeare*, ed. G. Blakemore Evans [Boston: Houghton Mifflin, 1974], 367).

21. The dramatic irony of Portia's comparison of Bassanio to the "young Alcides" is subtle but true (3.2.54–57): as the note in *The Riverside Shakespeare* (Boston: Houghton Mifflin, 1974) points out, "Hercules' motive in rescuing the Trojan princess Hesione [the "virgin tribute" of l. 56] . . . was not love for her but a desire to possess the horses which Laomedon, her father, had promised him as a reward." Here again is the familiar strain of Bassanio's mixed motives (unless, of course, Shakespeare did not know or remember the story faithfully, which is a distinct possibility).

22. Many critics have read Bassanio's casket choice as a complete theatrical performance, contending that Portia drops pregnant hints to her love throughout 3.2, which include her reference to Bassanio's choice as a "hazard," echoing the inscription on the lead casket (2); her admonition to "[b]eshrow your eyes" (14); the rhyme of "lead" with "bred" and "head" in the round sung during Bassanio's apparently sincere deliberations (63–107); and Portia's line, "I stand for sacrifice" (57). Yet I must agree with other critics who believe that Bassanio's decision is relatively free of assistance and that Portia does her best to uphold the letter and spirit of her father's will. For me, the most convincing evidence lies in her having used the word *hazard* in describing the same lottery to both Morocco (2.1.45) and Arragon (2.9.18). Surely she does not intend to coach either one of them.

23. For much of the material in this paragraph, I am indebted to the fine work of Mullaney and Eagleton. Throughout "Brothers and Others, or the Art of Alienation," Mullaney remains intrigued by the confluence of fictions in the *Merchant*, especially that in the staged trial scene and that in the regime of Elizabeth I. He also notices the benighted Shylock's impotence in the face of an opponent, Portia, who only appears impartial (82–84). Eagleton stresses the notion that systems such as language and law are, in *Merchant* as well as in life, always subject to interpretation (*William Shakespeare*).

The idea that the play's systems are as mutable as are its concepts about issues like individual identity and human existence is refracted in the feminist criticism of Catherine Belsey and Newman. The latter wonders whether certain aspects of the "Elizabethan sex/gender system" are in fact questioned by this play's peculiar version of transvestism (Newman, "Portia's Ring," 32). Belsey speculates that all examples of transvestitism in Shakespearean comedy "can be read as disrupting sexual difference, calling in question that set of relations between terms which proposes as inevitable an antithesis between masculine and feminine, men and women" ("Disrupting Sexual Difference: Meaning and Gender in the Comedies," in *Alternative Shakespeares*, ed. John Drakakis [New York: Methuen, 1985], 167).

24. See, e.g., Joan Ozark Holmer, "The Education of *The Merchant of Venice*" (*Studies in English Literature* 25 [1985]), 312, and Walter Cohen, "*The Merchant of Venice*," 768. Holmer also calls Antonio's love for Bassanio a kind of "surfeit" (307).

25. Thomas Wilson, *A Discourse Upon Usury*, ed. R. H. Tawney (New York: A. M. Kelley, 1963), 292. Although I have gone straight to Wilson for my reference, I should acknowledge Holmer for the information; Holmer herself is actually discussing the views of Hinely (Holmer, "Education," 326–27; Hinely, "Bond Priorities," 229), but expands on her own ideas in *"The Merchant of Venice": Choice, Hazard, and Consequence* (New York: Methuen, 1995), 249–50.

26. Geary, "The Nature of Portia's Victory," 63.

27. Lyon, *"Merchant,"* 48.

28. Evidence of Lucio's uncanny insight into the duke's identity and machinations is scattered throughout the play but concentrated in 3.2.86–184. I have argued elsewhere that Lucio reflects the duke's aloofness from his subjects and his corresponding need to become more directly involved with his subjects; Lucio's lies about the duke, in a profound sense, tell the truth about the duke's weaknesses as governor (see Cynthia Lewis, "'Dark Deeds Darkly Answered': Duke Vincentio and Judgment in *Measure for Measure*," *Shakespeare Quarterly* 34 [1983]: 271–89).

29. Interestingly, in this aspect too Gratiano parallels Lucio, whose apparent split in personality from the beginning of *Measure* to the end makes his characterization seem incoherent. In the first two acts, he is Claudio's friend and Isabella's advocate; later, his character turns much darker as he slanders the duke and is revealed to have fathered a child for whom he intends to take no responsibility.

30. More, *Utopia*, 27–28.

31. Richard Horwich has observed that "*The Merchant of Venice* is filled with difficult choices" ("Riddle and Dilemma in *The Merchant of Venice*," *Studies in English Literature* 17 [1977]: 191), although he builds differently on this point than I do, citing that, "where Belmont is full of riddles, Venice is the natural habitat of dilemmas" (197). He also maintains that, in the case of dilemmas, "the alternatives are equally desirable or . . . undesirable," availing themselves of no solutions (196), while "riddles have single and wholly correct answers, . . . however hard those answers may be to come by" (198). As

useful as I find this distinction, I still think that Belmont is not devoid of dilemmas, as I believe my examples testify. Hinely offers yet a different approach to the play's interest in the "problem" of "evaluating the claims of contradictory demands" ("Bond Priorities," 218–19)—that of how this problem influences the presentation of bonds in *Merchant*. Both Horwich and Hinely notice that Launcelot Gobbo's initial speech in 2.2 mimics lightly the difficult decisions, as that between "fiend" and "conscience," forced upon all the characters (Horwich, "Riddle and Dilemma," 197; Hinely, "Bond Priorities," 219).

32. Cusack, "Portia," 349.

33. Holmer, "Education," 328.

34. I do not mean to glide over the implications of the father's lottery as if they were exclusively advantageous to Portia. As Leventen, Newman, and others have shown, the will is an especially enticing metaphor for patriarchy, including the most stifling, repressive confinements thereof. I do believe, however, that the negative and positive connotations of the will are inseparably entangled. For example, perhaps Portia cannot take control of a trial otherwise dominated by patriarchs without having first been immersed in and irritated by a patriarchal structure like the will.

35. Lawrence Normand, in his provocative essay on the body as scripture in *Merchant*, phrases this idea thus: "Were [Antonio] to realize the scenario he projects, his love for Bassanio would be inscribed in his living body, and its truth proved by incisions which would be neither deletable nor reversible. . . . [This] exchange . . . would turn his physical death into social discourse aimed at recording and validating a certain meaning for it" ("Reading the Body in *The Merchant of Venice*," *Textual Practice* 5 [1991]: 67–68). In other words, Antonio is attempting to freeze emotion in a fluid world; the act of preservation, ironically, perverts the feeling.

36. Exactly how to understand this passage dramatically is a bit baffling, since, in its entirety, it suggests that Portia's question—"Which is the merchant here? and which the Jew?" (174)—is offhand and posed before she has taken opportunity to look about the room. Hence, probably, the duke's follow-up order: "Antonio and old Shylock, both stand forth" (175). By the same token, however, she has too much to lose by not speaking deliberately to begin with; her question is no doubt partly calculated to produce one effect or another. Finally, no matter how harmless may be Portia's intent, her question cannot avoid all dramatic irony, since to the audience (at whom Shakespeare aims the joke) Shylock is so very prominent in appearance.

37. Lyon, *"Merchant,"* 110.

38. Holmer, "Education," 316–17.

39. My remarks about Antonio in act 4 are meant in part to address the sanguine conviction of Holmer and others that, when Antonio judges Shylock, "We observe none of Antonio's former vindictiveness" (Holmer, "Education," 317). Cf. Beauregard, who envisions Antonio's "division of [Shylock's] wealth," which jeopardizes Shylock's very "life" (4.1.376), as a just recompense for Shylock's having sought to take Antonio's life (*Virtue's Own Feature*, 100–101).

40. While I see Walter Cohen's point that the "romantic comedy" of act 5 acts to "obliterate the memory of what has preceded" it (*"The Merchant of Venice*," 777), I also agree with the many critics who see act 5 as integrated thematically and through its action into the whole play. In particular, Lyon senses that the ties between act 5 and the body of the play are even more intricately knit than is often thought—for instance, by the recapitulation between Bassanio's wedding ring and the ring that Leah once gave Shylock (*"Merchant,"* 117).

41. I hesitate to overread this detail, lest I commit the same sort of indiscretion that I have taken to task at the beginning of this chapter. One does wonder, however, whether Shakespeare was conscious of the delicious parallel between this numerical detail and all manner of references to relativism throughout act 5. Why three out of six, only half?

The name of the rocks on which Antonio's ships wreck is also an intriguing detail in view of any personal growth that may be seen to result for Antonio from his ordeal: the name "Goodwins"—or Goodwin Sands—literally means "good friends" (*The Concise Oxford Dictionary of Place Names* [Oxford: Clarenden Press, 1960]).

42. Lyon, *"Merchant,"* 112.

3: "Willing love": Antonio, Viola, and Epiphany in *Twelfth Night*

1. Samuel Pepys, *Diary*, ed. Ernest Rhys, vol. 1 (New York: E. P. Dutton, 1906), 6 January 1663.

2. Anne Barton, introduction to *Twelfth Night*, by William Shakespeare, ed. G. Blakemore Evans (Boston: Houghton Mifflin, 1974), 404.

3. Lewalski, "Thematic Patterns in *Twelfth Night*," 169.

4. John Hollander, "*Twelfth Night* and the Morality of Indulgence" (1959; rprt., in *Twentieth Century Interpretations of "Twelfth Night": A Collection of Critical Essays*, ed. Walter N. King, Englewood Cliffs, N.J.: Prentice-Hall, 1968), 85–86.

5. *The Oxford English Dictionary.*

6. Other critical works of interest here would include Richard Henze, "*Twelfth Night*: Free Disposition on the Sea of Love" (*The Sewanee Review* 83 [1975]), which explores the juxtaposition (and seeming irreconcilability) of secular and festive elements of *Twelfth Night* and the play's Christian allusions. See also R. Chris Hassel, *Renaissance Drama and the English Church Year* (Lincoln: University of Nebraska Press, 1979) and *Faith and Folly in Shakespeare's Romantic Comedies* (Athens: University of Georgia Press, 1980), and the more recent work detailing the play's specific doctrinal concerns by Maurice Hunt, "Malvolio, Viola, and the Question of Instrumentality: Defining Providence in *Twelfth Night*" (*Studies in Philology* 90 [1993]) and "The Religion of *Twelfth Night*" (*C.L.A. Journal* 37 [1993–94]). John Astington, in "Malvolio and the Eunuchs: Texts and Revels in *Twelfth Night*" (*Shakespeare Survey* 46 [1994]), discusses how biblical allusions and carnivalesque elements interpenetrate in the play.

7. Hassel, *Renaissance Drama*, 84–85, 95–101.

8. Cf. Lewalski's statements that some of the most metaphorically rich passages "[resist] simplistic allegorical equations" ("Thematic Patterns in *Twelfth Night*," 177). A useful analogy here may be psychologically-based readings of literature, which do not profess to treat fictional characters as living subjects, but in which a set of paradigms can illuminate a literary text.

9. Geoffrey Bullough, ed., *Narrative and Dramatic Sources of Shakespeare* (New York: Columbia University Press, 1958), 2:348–50.

10. Jane Brown mentions the two sea captains as one of several doublings in *Twelfth Night* but does not finally work the captains into her theory about "high" and "low" plot-

ting within the play's "two worlds" ("Double Plotting in Shakespeare's Comedies: The Case of *Twelfth Night*," in *Aesthetic Illusion: Theoretical and Historical Approaches*, ed. Frederick Burwick [Berlin: W. de Gruyter, 1990], 313).

11. Recent attention to what most critics call the "homoerotic" attraction between Antonio and Sebastian raises numerous questions. Not the least of these is whether the relationship is most accurately referred to as "homosexual," "homoerotic," or "homosocial." (This is Joseph Pequigney's question about the Antonios in *Merchant* and *Twelfth Night* ["The Two Antonios," 201 and passim].) Valerie Traub actually makes the case for erotic desire in Antonio's language that most critics who call the relationship either "homosexual" or "homoerotic" only assume (*Desire and Anxiety: Circulations of Sexuality in Shakespearean Drama* [New York: Routledge, 1992], 133–34; cf. Pequigney, "The Two Antonios," 204–10). Still other critics would subscribe to Hunt's term for the relationship, a "same-sex friendship" ("Love, Disguise, and Knowledge in *Twelfth Night*," 490).

Another question arises as to the tone of the play toward this love between male characters, especially when, in 5.1, Sebastian has elected to marry Olivia and Antonio remains bound and excluded. This question also involves the overtones of same-sex attraction in Viola/Cesario's appeal to Olivia. Most critics take Sebastian's line to Olivia at face value—"So comes it, lady, you have been mistook; / But Nature to her bias drew in that" (5.1.259–60)—believing that, at the last, heterosexuality is defined as "natural" and, by implication, homosexuality is "unnatural." For some critics, this perceived distinction resolves, rather than raises, problems. See, e.g., Hunt: "When Sebastian stands distinct from Cesario, Olivia can clearly know the slight but crucial differences between her two ideas of manliness, reject the one diluted by her own conceits, and credit her natural passion for her self-fulfilling opposite" ("Love, Disguise, and Knowledge in *Twelfth Night*," 491). Others find in Antonio's final isolation a troubling anxiety, reminiscent of our own society's confusion about the place of homosexuals in a predominantly heterosexual community. See, e.g., Laurie E. Osborne, discussing how Antonio's final pardon has been injected into the script and handled historically on stage: "The [ambiguity] of the pardon itself and the staging of the pardon's implications anticipate our ongoing conflict between understanding Antonio's love as acceptably passionate, even erotic male friendship and a love that must be isolated at the end of the play *because* of its homoeroticism" ("Antonio's Pardon," *Shakespeare Quarterly* 45 [1994]: 114). Cf. the views of Douglas E. Green ("Shakespeare's Violation: 'One face, one voice, one habit, and two persons,'" in *Reconsidering the Renaissance*, ed. Mario A. Di Cesare [Binghamton: Medieval and Renaissance Texts and Studies, 1992], 93:337 n. 34), Cristina Malcolmson ("'What You Will': Social Mobility and Gender in *Twelfth Night*," in *The Matter of Difference*, ed. Valerie Wayne [Ithaca: Cornell University Press, 1991], 56 n. 31), Smith (*Homosexual Desire*, 154), and Traub (*Desire and Anxiety*, 123). Traub goes so far as to suggest that the heterosexual pairings at the play's end are rendered unstable by Sebastian's lingering attraction to Antonio in 5.1.218–21.

While I do not want to argue that Shakespeare's portrayal of love simply transcends boundaries of gender and class, neither can I finally agree with critics who see those boundaries in *Twelfth Night* as ultimately rigid. Where the specific matter of Antonio's homoerotic attraction is concerned, I believe that a large part of the point is that perceived obstacles to love—whether fear, grief, gender, or otherwise—are false barriers. Nor is love in this context restricted to physical love but may embrace the physical as well as the emotional and spiritual. Much as Robert Kimbrough and Bruce Smith interpret Viola's cross-dressing as a form of "free[ing]" her "to act out the full range of her human personality" (Kimbrough, *Shakespeare and the Art of Humankindness*, 118)—as a means of illustrating "the liberating possibilities in playing about with gender roles" (Smith, *Homosexual Desire*, 183–84)—I view Antonio's love, which ultimately makes no distinction between male (Sebastian) and female (Viola/Cesario), as testing and defying conventional boundaries of many sorts.

12. As engaging as recent studies of social class in the play have been, none acknowledges a metaphorical layer to the concept and language of servanthood in the play. Karin S. Coddon focuses on the "instability of rank and order that persists outside the world of the play" ("'Slander in an Allowed Fool': *Twelfth Night*'s Crisis of the Aristocracy," *Studies in English Literature* 33 [1993]: 314–15); Lisa Jardine explores the "way in which, in the early modern period, erotic attention—an attention bound up with sexual availability and historically specific forms of economic dependency—is focused upon boys and upon women in the *same* way" ("Twins and travesties: Gender, dependency and sexual availability in *Twelfth Night*," in *Erotic Politics: Desire on the Renaissance Stage*, ed. Susan Zimmerman [New York: Routledge, 1992], 28). In her superbly and intricately argued essay, Malcolmson proposes that *Twelfth Night* "offers us women and servants who [freely] exchange their independence for a willing desire for another" without disrupting the social order ("What You Will," 47); in this context she describes Antonio as the "model for the new servant imagined by the play, since his service is based on desire rather than duty or reverence" (49). While I agree especially with Malcolmson's approach and conclusions, I finally find them, like so much of the criticism on sexuality in the play, too confining for the play's broadest terms, through which the meaning of "service" is extended beyond the material and into the spiritual realm.

13. Camille Wells Slights argues that this ideal is not altruism but reciprocated love ("The Principle of Recompense in *Twelfth Night*," *Modern Language Review* 77 [1982]: 537–46), while Marilyn French believes that Antonio's passion renders him, in the play's context, a "subversive," a "misfit," a "starving dispossessed" (*Shakespeare's Division of Experience* [New York: Summit Books, 1981], 118–20).

14. The contrast between Antonio and Feste as servants finds a later analogy in the pairing of Kent and Lear's fool. Recalling Antonio, Kent lands himself in the stocks for his plain-speaking, while the Fool "tarr[ies]," free to assist Lear with his artistry (2.4.82). He makes sure to ridicule the foolishly wise Kent for his impolitic behavior:

> *Kent*. Where learned you this, Fool?
>
> *Fool*. Not i' the stocks, fool.
>
> (2.4.86–87)

Robert Hillis Goldsmith attributes the motives of a Pauline wise fool—that is, a true servant—to Lear's fool (*Wise Fools in Shakespeare* [East Lansing: Michigan State University Press, 1955], chap. 4).

15. For a fuller discussion of More's treatment of pride and wise folly, see chap. 1.

16. Several critics have, over the years, described Feste's role in *Twelfth Night* partly as one of bridging two worlds, whether the main plot and the subplot (Goldsmith, *Wise Fools in Shakespeare*, chap. 4), the fictive world of the play and the real world of the audience (Coddon, "Slander," 316, 318, 323), or others; and of course Feste glides between Olivia's and Orsino's households. C. L. Barber's point about subplots in many of Shakespeare's comedies also aptly describes Feste's tendencies as an individual: "Shakespeare's imagination tends to dwell on situations and motives where the energies

of life lead to degradation or destruction" (*Shakespeare's Festive Comedy* [1959; rprt., Princeton: Princeton University Press, 1972], 259).

17. Astington deals with precisely this issue when he discusses the appropriateness of the revelers' violence in the context of the carnivalesque ("Malvolio and the Eunuchs," passim).

18. The source of this definition from the *Oxford English Dictionary* is John Florio, 1598.

19. See, e.g., Alexander S. Leggatt ("*Twelfth Night*," in *"Twelfth Night": Critical Essays*, ed. Stanley Wells [New York: Garland Publishing, 1986], 248–51) and Karen Greif ("Plays and Playing in *Twelfth Night*," in *"Twelfth Night": Critical Essays*, ed. Stanley Wells [New York: Garland Publishing, 1986], 275).

20. This reading of the fool as healer is buttressed, I think, by the characterization of the real priest in *Twelfth Night*. Although he has only one speech, which is often cut in performance, it is every bit as absurd in its mock high-seriousness as anything Feste says, as was discovered by my "Performing Shakespeare" class when they produced *Twelfth Night* in 1986 and heard the fellow who played the priest respond to Olivia:

Oli. Father, I charge thee by thy reverence
Here to unfold . . .
                    What thou dost know
Hath newly pass'd between this youth and me.

Priest. A contract of eternal bond of love,
Confirm'd by mutual joinder of your hands,
Attested by the holy close of lips,
Strength'ned by interchangement of your rings,
And all the ceremony of this compact
Seal'd in my function, by my testimony;
Since when, my watch hath told me, toward my grave
I have travell'd but two hours.

(5.1.151–63)

The unintentional silliness of this speech implicitly links up with Feste's silly mock-seriousness as Sir Topas, a connection that, in turn, implicitly links the priest's holiness to Feste. Moreover, Feste repeatedly speaks in the form of benediction (e.g., 1.5.97–98, 2.4.73–75, 3.1.44–45), associating his foolery with Christian wise folly.

If Feste appears in some respects to be Malvolio's "deliverer," however, I cannot agree with some critics that Malvolio actually responds to Feste's gibes in the prison scene by changing or becoming more enlightened. See, e.g., Hunt: "The candlelight that Malvolio begs—and that Feste supplies—figuratively signifies Malvolio's newly illumined mind" ("Malvolio," 291).

21. By far the majority of critics hold Malvolio ultimately responsible for his lack of generosity in 5.1, omitting reference to Feste's vengeful motive. See Hunt's remarks on this issue ("Malvolio," 291).

22. A student of mine recommended this idea to me years ago, and it has steadily come to make good sense to me. Of course, only more time would tell if Maria has made a good bargain for herself by marrying Sir Toby.

23. The case for a tragic Malvolio has been made, most recently perhaps by Donald Sinden, who played Malvolio for the Royal Shakespeare Company in 1970 (see Philip Brockbank, ed., *Players of Shakespeare* [New York: Cambridge University Press, 1985], 43).

24. Feste, as Hassel has shown, derives from Festus, "the presiding spirit of Christmastide festivity" (*Renaissance Drama*, 85). I question, though, Hassel's assertion that Feste "gives that title a dignity its Saturnalian wearers never possessed" (85). Perhaps Feste's name also glances at the second-century Roman grammarian named Sextus Pompeius Festus, who was especially interested in etymologies of words, as well as their meanings.

25. Harry Levin's essay is one notable exception to the general lack of critical interest in the subplot ("The Underplot of *Twelfth Night*," in *"Twelfth Night": Critical Essays*, ed. Stanley Wells [New York: Garland Publishing, 1986], 161–69). Yet, while Levin sees the subplot as orbiting around Malvolio, I hope to have shown that its moral interest centers on Feste and radiates out to the other revelers.

26. Does he draw it out further by extracting another coin from her in lines 49–53? Viola/Cesario's line "'tis well begg'd" suggests that he does.

27. Barber, *Shakespeare's Festive Comedy*, 254.

28. Since becoming popular in the 1970s, critical study of individual identity in *Twelfth Night* has focused on Viola's disguise as a destabilizing force. For critics in the 1970s, like Helene Moglen, the central issue is the main characters' psychosexual development. Moglen sees Viola's disguise as a cocoon within which she can experiment in a homoerotic relationship before she is ready to engage in a mature union with Orsino ("Disguise and Development: The Self and Society in *Twelfth Night*," *Literature and Psychology* 23 [1973]: 13–20). Such experimentation, of course, centers on Viola's wooing of Olivia in 1.5 and 3.1, and Viola's transitional androgyny, says Moglen, also permits both Orsino and Olivia to explore their sexuality. Recently, Pequigney has taken issue with Moglen's view of sexuality in the play ("The Two Antonios," 209 n. 9). In the vein of Moglen's work, see also the works by Dennis Huston ("'When I Came to Man's Estate': *Twelfth Night* and Problems of Identity," *Modern Language Quarterly* 33 [1972]: 274–88) and Nancy K. Hayles ("Sexual Disguise in *As You Like It* and *Twelfth Night*," *Shakespeare Survey* 32 [1979]: 63–72). Related criticism in the 1980s and 1990s has analyzed not so much psychosexual growth as the very concept of sexual identity—in particular, whether gendered identity is fixed. In this connection, see especially Catherine Belsey, who argues, in essence, that Viola is at points a "speaker who. . . occupies a place which is not precisely masculine or feminine, where the notion of identity itself is disrupted to display a difference within subjectivity, and the singularity which resides in *this* difference" ("Disrupting Sexual Difference," 187). See also the works of Green ("Shakespeare's Violation"), Jardine ("Twins and transvestites"), and Malcolmson ("What You Will").

29. Elizabeth M. Yearling ("Language, Theme, and Character in *Twelfth Night*," *Shakespeare Survey* 35 [1982]) vividly describes Viola's method of refusing Antonio in 3.4.341–47:

> Viola's [offer of money to Antonio] is a carefully thought-out *loan* to a helpful but puzzling stranger. She moves slowly towards the offer. "I'll lend" is preceded by a series of subordinate clauses and phrases outlining her reasons and stressing her poverty. "My having is not much" repeats the content of the line before, and adds to

our impression that Viola feels an uncomfortable need to justify herself. (82; emphasis added)

Yearling's context here is entirely different from mine, yet she aptly makes my point about Viola's extreme caution in giving, as contrasted with Antonio's unstinting charity.

30. To my knowledge, Viola has not failed to persuade any other critic; perhaps because she is in many ways endearing and because her lot is pitiable, she is, without exception, taken at her word. Many scholars view her lines to time, in fact, as speaking for the whole play's vision of a humanity with limited free will, subject to the tides of time and fortune or, in some cases, to the universal control of Providence. See, e.g., Leggatt: "When we compare [Viola] with Rosalind we see how much she is the creature rather than the creator of the plot" ("*Twelfth Night*," 252); see also Hunt's "Malvolio." While acknowledging that, for the characters, time, together with human patience and fortitude, plays a major role in determining events, I cannot ignore the abundant references in *Twelfth Night* to the efficacy of human will and the autonomy of human action. In one such instance, Olivia hopes that her own "act" of secretly marrying Sebastian will also please the "heavens" (4.3.34–35). This example, with its theatrical pun on *act*, returns full circle to the matter of disguise, which, although it appears passive, nevertheless *enacts* a free choice, thus belying Viola's repeated claim that to remain incognito is to "commit" her future to "time" (1.2.60; 2.2.40–41). Cf. the similar theatrical pun in Sebastian's lines about his father: "He finished indeed his mortal act / That day that made my sister thirteen years" (5.1.247–48).

31. We know at least that it is not a "light air" (15), but I also wonder if the song itself can be performed in any way but mock-seriously, so pronounced is its melodrama.

32. As one of my most inquisitive Shakespeare students recently concluded, the only way the outcome of the romantic plot makes sense is if read, paradoxically, as such divine nonsense. The same principle applies, I think, to Orsino's sudden, largely inexplicable satisfaction at marrying Viola rather than Olivia; although the play yields evidence of Orsino's growing emotional attachment to Viola/Cesario, whereby the audience is prepared for his easy exchange of wives (e.g., 2.4), the switch is nonetheless so hasty as to appear yet another lunatic occurrence. On the other hand, who could resist falling instantaneously in love with a woman who would risk her life as Viola does? Perhaps not even Orsino, who may well be thinking to himself, "Is not *this* love indeed?"

33. That Olivia repeats the word, referring to both herself and Viola, is, I think, notable. The concept at work would seem to be the dissolution of a variety of barriers to love. See n. 11, above.

34. The wording is that of the Geneva Bible; the wording of the Bishops' Bible is virtually identical. The original Latin is "Noli me tangere."

35. For a fuller discussion of the biblical background to this passage, see my "Viola's 'Do not embrace me' as Icon" (*Notes and Queries* 233 [1988], 473–74).

36. Where Antonio's continued imprisonment is concerned, recent critics are prone to sense homophobia or at least subconscious discomfort within the play toward unleashing Antonio's homoeroticism on the heterosexuality through which the romantic ending is being resolved. See, e.g., Green, "Shakespeare's Violation," 337; Osborne, "Antonio's Pardon," 114; Traub, *Desire and Anxiety*, 143. Pequigney thoroughly disagrees, holding that the ending poses no such difficulty for either the Antonio of *Twelfth Night* or the Antonio of *The Merchant of Venice*: "Why the nearly universal assent to the mistaken critical view that both Antonios at the finish are excluded and unhappy? Since the Shakespearean text does not lend support to the view—quite the reverse—it must be imported

and imposed by readers" ("The Two Antonios," 218). Not to belabor the obvious, but Antonio's bondage in the last scene of *Twelfth Night*, which no one on stage clearly addresses or seeks to undo, probably accounts for the widespread view that he is less than content.

4: "The world's great snare": Antony, Cleopatra, and Game

1. Jonathan Dollimore, "*Virtus* under Erasure," in *Radical Tragedy: Religion, Ideology, and Power in the Drama of Shakespeare and His Contemporaries* (Chicago: University of Chicago Press, 1984), 211.

2. I am indebted for some items on this list to the 1993 production of *Antony and Cleopatra* by the Shenandoah Shakespeare Express, which was especially sensitive to the humor implicit at the end of act 4. The director of that production, Ralph A. Cohen, later published an essay in which he lists his own set of jokes aimed at Antony ("Staging Comic Divinity: The Collision of High and Low in *Antony and Cleopatra*," *Shakespeare Bulletin* 13.3 [Summer 1995], 5–8). Not surprisingly, our lists overlap somewhat. Cohen's perceptions of the humor and the uses to which it is put, however, differ widely from mine. For instance, to his mind the tone of the joking is lighter than I am describing it. For elaboration on the contrast between his interpretation and mine, see n. 64, below.

3. W. B. Worthen, "The Weight of Antony: Staging 'Character' in *Antony and Cleopatra*," *Studies in English Literature* 26 (1986): 295–96. Citations for the rest of the paragraph follow: Brian Cheadle, "'His legs bestrid the ocean' as a 'form of life,'" in *Drama and Philosophy*, ed. James Redmond, Themes in Drama Series, 12 (Cambridge: Cambridge University Press, 1990), 88. Robert Ornstein, "The Ethic of the Imagination: Love and Art in *Antony and Cleopatra*," in *Twentieth Century Interpretations of "Antony and Cleopatra*," ed. Mark Rose (Englewood Cliffs, N.J.: Prentice-Hall, 1977), 82. Martha Tuck Rozett, "The Comic Structures of Tragic Endings: The Suicide Scenes in *Romeo and Juliet* and *Antony and Cleopatra*," *Shakespeare Quarterly* 36 (1985): 160. Barbara C. Vincent, "Shakespeare's *Antony and Cleopatra* and the Rise of Comedy," *English Literary Renaissance* 12 (1982): 53–86. Leslie Thomson, "*Antony and Cleopatra*, Act 4 scene 16: 'A Heavy Sight,'" *Shakespeare Survey* 41 (1988): 83.

4. Margaret Lamb's appendix on staging the monument scene in her history of *Antony and Cleopatra* on the English stage mentions no humor at all (*"Antony and Cleopatra" on the English Stage* [Rutherford, N.J.: Fairleigh Dickinson University Press, 1980]). In a different key, Lucy Hughes-Hallett sees the double suicide as utterly somber, lending "significance and purpose to [the characters'] lives" but also "condemn[ing]" them to death brought on by a "sterile" passion (*Cleopatra: Histories, Dreams, and Distortions* [New York: Harper & Row, 1990], 149). In her view, then, Antony is not so much derided as rejected for his immorality.

5. Rosalie Colie, "The Significance of Style," in *Modern Critical Interpretations: "Antony and Cleopatra*," ed. Harold Bloom (New Haven: Yale University Press, 1988), 83.

Most critics who sense the distancing humor at the play's end hasten to deny its persistence. Examples would include Ornstein, who believes that the play finally upholds the "honesty of the imagination" over the "facts of imperial conquest" working against

Antony and Cleopatra ("Ethic of the Imagination," 84), and Bernard Beckerman, who, entertaining the opportunities for awkwardness about Antony's being lifted to Cleopatra's monument, concludes: "Despite the obstacles, . . . Antony was raised in a manner which, we must suppose, was not ludicrous" (*Shakespeare at the Globe, 1599–1609* [New York: Macmillan Publishing, 1962], 231).

6. Examples here would include Janet Adelman, for whom Antony becomes the embodiment of the play's most positive valuation of love (*The Common Liar: An Essay on "Antony and Cleopatra"* [New Haven: Yale University Press, 1973], 139) and Evelyn Gajowski, who believes Antony gradually matures in his ability to love (*The Art of Loving: Female Subjectivity and Male Discursive Traditions in Shakespeare's Tragedies* [Newark: University of Delaware Press, 1992], chap. 4). Anne Barton sees not Antony's suicide, but Cleopatra's, as the act that "redeems" Antony's "bungl[ing]" and that settles the conflict in the play's tone between "the sublime and the ridiculous, the tragic and comic" ("'Nature's Piece 'Gainst Fancy': The Divided Catastrophe in *Antony and Cleopatra*," in *Modern Critical Interpretations: "Antony and Cleopatra*," ed. Harold Bloom [New York: Chelsea House, 1988], 53, 51). Significant exceptions to the critical trend of overapologizing for Antony present themselves in such authors as Thomson, for whom Antony's love, though great, remains ever flawed ("Act 4 scene 16," 90); J. Leeds Barroll, who locates Antony's tragedy in the final failure of his love to endure the ravages of Caesar's world (*Shakespearean Tragedy: Genre, Tradition, and Change in "Antony and Cleopatra"* [Washington: Folger Books, 1984], 269, 272); and Jonathan Dollimore, who views the play without a shred of romanticism and Antony as a true fool, because his self-centered infatuation for Cleopatra leads him to "kiss away kingdoms" and thus "also the lives of thousands" ("*Virtus* under Erasure," 215).

7. Two critics in particular who have discussed the role of Christian references in *Antony and Cleopatra* are Andrew Fichter ("*Antony and Cleopatra*: 'The Time of Universal Peace,'" *Shakespeare Survey* 33 [1980]: 99–111) and C. W. R. D. Moseley ("Cleopatra's Prudence: Three Notes on the Use of Emblems in *Antony and Cleopatra*," *Jahrbuch der Deutschen Shakespeare Gesellschaft West* 1986: 119–37), both of whose work I shall address in more detail below. See also the brief comments of Northrop Frye (*Northrop Frye on Shakespeare*, ed. Robert Sandler [New Haven: Yale University Press, 1986], 138–39).

8. Several critics have lately challenged the apparent binaries in the play. Jonathan Gil Harris takes a political-sexual approach, arguing that the alleged differences between things Roman and Egyptian are really just a false front for Roman narcissism ("'Narcissus in thy face': Roman Desire and the Difference it Fakes in *Antony and Cleopatra*," *Shakespeare Quarterly* 45 [1994]: 408–25, passim). Linda Charnes finds the superficial distinction between public politics and private love a mere mask for Antony's entrapment by both: "Although the play encourages us to misrecognize Antony's love for Cleopatra as an alternative to the identity and project he bears for Rome, we see that in his role as *Cleopatra's* Antony he is put to similar use" (*Notorious Identity: Materializing the Subject in Shakespeare* [Cambridge: Harvard University Press, 1993], 141–42, passim).

9. Other critics who have, in different contexts, treated the dichotomy between the worldly and the spiritual include Adelman (*Common Liar*), Peter Berek ("Doing and Undoing: The Value of Action in *Antony and Cleopatra*," *Shakespeare Quarterly* 32 [1981]: 295–304), Fichter ("Time of Universal Peace"), William D. Wolf ("'New Heaven, New Earth': The Escape from Mutability in *Antony and Cleopatra*," *Shakespeare Quarterly* 33 [1982]: 328–35), and A. S. Weber ("New Physic for the Nonce: A

Stoic and Hermetic Reading of Shakespeare's *Antony and Cleopatra*," *Renaissance Papers* 1995: 93–107).

10. Although M. R. Ridley, editor of the New Arden *Antony and Cleopatra* (New York: Methuen, 1981), believes that this line is meant for Menas, his reasoning seems stretched. The printing of the folio makes somewhat unclear Enobarbus's addressee, but the sequence and sense of the speeches makes Antony the logical choice.

11. Several readers have examined the world of *Antony and Cleopatra* as one marked by "flux," as Maynard Mack calls it ("*Antony and Cleopatra*: The Stillness and the Dance," in *Shakespeare's Art: Seven Essays*, ed. Milton Crane [Chicago: University of Chicago Press, 1973], 89), and thus as one that defies the characters' vision much as the play resists our neat explanations. See especially Mack, Adelman (*Common Liar*), Margot Heinemann ("'Let Rome in Tiber Melt': Order and Disorder in *Antony and Cleopatra*," in "*Antony and Cleopatra*," ed. John Drakakis, New Casebooks [New York: St. Martin's Press, 1994], 167–73), and, on multiple perspectives in the play, Sidney R. Homan ("Divided Response and the Imagination in *Antony and Cleopatra*," *Philological Quarterly* 49 [1970]: 460–68). The paradigm of unyielding choice that I am discussing here is, I believe, a feature of this ever-changing world, which keeps propagating new and yet unsatisfying alternatives.

12. In a psychoanalytic study of Antony's melancholy and audiences' responses to it, Cynthia Marshall writes of how Antony is affected by a virtual crisis of identity: "He feels himself to be coming apart" ("Man of Steel Done Got the Blues: Melancholic Subversion of Presence in *Antony and Cleopatra*," *Shakespeare Quarterly* 44 [1993]: 392). In Marshall's analysis, as in Charnes's, Antony's identity is the "terrain" on which the "real battle" of the play—"that between Caesar and Cleopatra"—is waged (Charnes, *Notorious Identity*, 112).

13. Susan Snyder expresses the same idea thus: "Antony can bring together incompatible modes of life only when he has no more life to live" ("Patterns of Motion in *Antony and Cleopatra*," *Shakespeare Survey* 33 [1980]: 120).

14. This, of course, is a difficult statement to support in few words. Suffice it to say that English Renaissance society generally thought of Roman moral values in a way that reflects the ancient Romans' conceptions of themselves: that is, as founders of government whose individual talents and energies were to be directed toward that public good. Indeed, according to Charles Wells: "[In the Roman tradition], softer feelings had no place in public affairs of any kind" (*The Wide Arch: Roman Values in Shakespeare* [New York: St. Martin's Press, 1992], 159). John Ferguson points out that, although these Roman "public" virtues "were not easily compatible with the gentler virtues of humility and compassion," eventually peace within the empire "[saw] other qualities thrusting themselves to the fore, generosity, and forethought, and clemency" (*Moral Values in the Ancient World* [London: Methuen, 1958], 178). In addition, some writers whom Shakespeare knew, principally Virgil, sought to reconcile imperial "single-mindedness" with "compassionate feeling" (178). That the problem in the *Aeneid* of reconciling public duty with private desire is on Shakespeare's mind in *Antony and Cleopatra* appears clear from Antony's reference to Aeneas and Dido in 4.14.51–54. But the point about the issue at hand—Antony's motivation for suicide—is that, even judged against imperial Roman values, it may appear somehow craven. See also Beverly Taylor on the medieval view of Antony's suicide as motivated by selfish desires, not real martyrdom ("The Medieval Cleopatra: The Classical and Medieval Tradition of Chaucer's *Legend of Cleopatra*," *Journal of Medieval and Renaissance Studies* 7 [1977]: 261, 263).

15. For a fuller discussion of Erasmus's identification of Mark Antony with wise Christian folly, see chap. 1. Although Christopher Wortham argues that, since Antony is an antitype of Hercules and Hercules is a type for Christ, Antony is, by extension, a virtual antitype of Christ, Wortham has not considered Antony's associations with Christ through the figure of Saint Anthony ("Temperance and the End of Time: Emblematic *Antony and Cleopatra*," *Comparative Drama* 29 [1995]: 20).

16. The notion is partly that, because Christian tenets are natural, they predated Christianity in pagan form. This belief was popular among Christian humanists like Thomas More and Erasmus. See, for example, Raphael Hythloday's description of "Religions" in book 2 of More's *Utopia*. The Utopians received Christianity so quickly because they had already arrived at its tenets independently (i.e., naturally) (124).

While I agree with Fichter that Antony and Cleopatra are unaware of the religious significance of the many Christian references and allusions surrounding them, I think that the relationship between the two perspectives he identifies—that of pagan-secular/Christian-religious—implies more than that the pagan is about to give way to the Christian in thirty years or so; it also shows that the characters' worldliest acts can appear holier than their apparently saintlier behavior ("Time of Universal Peace," 99–101, passim).

See also Phyllis Rackin's superb discussion of two worlds and two perspectives in *Antony and Cleopatra* grown out of Cleopatra's skill as an artist ("Shakespeare's Boy Cleopatra, the Decorum of Nature, and the Golden World of Poetry," *PMLA* 87 [1972]: 201–11).

17. As Heinemann points out, this view of Antony (as well as of Octavius and Lepidus) as "self-seeking heirs of Julius Caesar" with an "insatiable ambition for power" derives ultimately from the republican view of Roman history that characterized Plutarch ("Order and Disorder," 175).

18. Plutarch, *The Life of Marcus Antonius*, T. J. B. Spencer, *Shakespeare's Plutarch* (London: Penguin, 1968), 178, etc.

19. Fichter, "Time of Universal Peace," 105. Fichter actually cites J. Middleton Murry as the source of the observation (*Shakespeare*, 1965 ed. [London: John Cope, 1936], 303), but himself dilates upon it.

20. Enobarbus is often viewed as the voice of temperance against Antony's intemperance. See, e.g., Adelman: "Enobarbus is a figure of moderation who attempts to live in a world of excess" (*Common Liar*, 131). I believe he has his own excesses, which reflect Antony's. Allyson Newton approaches such excesses in an intriguing way by observing that Enobarbus's "emphatic denials almost always wind up making powerful claims for belief . . . that strain against the resolve of his seemingly pragmatic skepticism" ("'At the Very Heart of Loss': Shakespeare's Enobarbus and the Rhetoric of Remembering," *Renaissance Papers* 1995: 89).

21. Gajowski shares this view, albeit in a different context, when, having remarked on Enobarbus's fear of losing his manhood (*Art of Loving*, 99), she comments on his change: "In the end, Enobarbus embodies the value of honor in love, not war. . . . He epitomizes Roman control of emotions, yet he dies out of love for Antony . . . . Enobarbus dies heartbroken, speaking with the same density of feeling as the lovers" (110). I cannot agree with Ornstein that Enobarbus's desertion is itself an "act of love" (because he cannot endure watching Antony's fall "[Ethic of the Imagination," 93–94]); rather, it is a part of a process toward love.

22. Fichter refers to Enobarbus's betrayal of Antony as "Judas-like" but does not elaborate ("Time of Universal Peace," 105). See especially the Bishops' Bible, Acts 1:18 and the Bishops' and Geneva Bibles, Matthew 27:3–8.

23. Caesar's "tears" here (41), suggesting genuine sympathy, are problematic in light of an earlier reference to his expression of sorrow in 3.2.50–59. Enobarbus and Agrippa imply between themselves that both Caesar's and Antony's public displays of grief are mere self-conscious extensions of their political personae. Enobarbus's word *rheum* to describe Antony's weeping over Julius Caesar and Brutus mockingly suggests crocodile tears (for similar uses of the word, see, e.g., *Much Ado about Nothing* 5.2.83, *King John* 4.3.108, *Richard II* 1.4.8, *Coriolanus* 5.6.45, and *Othello* 3.4.51).

24. Doubling is necessitated in this company's productions by its historically accurate size of twelve players. This particular example contradicts Stephen Booth's alluring theory that, originally, Antony was doubled with Dolabella ("Speculations on Doubling in Shakespeare's Plays," in *Shakespeare: The Theatrical Dimension*, ed. Philip C. McGuire and David A. Samuelson [New York: AMS Press, 1979]). Even if Antony and Dolabella were doubled, that fact would not entirely eliminate the possibility that the same actor also played the Clown. I do think, however, that Dolabella's appearance at the opening of 5.1, a split second after Antony's corpse has been borne off stage, raises serious suspicion about the possible doubling of Antony and Dolabella.

25. Seneca, as quoted in William D. Nietzmann, "Seneca on Death: The Courage to Be or Not to Be," *International Philosophical Quarterly* 6 (1966): 89.

26. Moseley, "Cleopatra's Prudence," 124–25.

27. Although Moseley uses the words *prudence* and *wisdom* interchangeably, I wonder if, even in his own examples, they are always the same. The one seems to connote practical ability ("careful management," *The American Heritage Dictionary of the English Language*, 3rd ed. [Boston: Houghton Mifflin, 1992]); the other, often, "understanding" (*American Heritage*). Obviously, I think Shakespeare sometimes distinguishes between the two ideas.

28. Moseley ("Cleopatra's Prudence," 122–23) discusses the two emblems of the Colossus that I am including here from George Wither's *A Collection of Emblemes, Ancient and Moderne* (London: Printed by A. M. for Robert Allot, 1635; rprt., Brookfield, Vt.: Gower Publishing, 1989). The poem for the one in book 1 (xxxi) reads noticeably like the Pauline theology at hand:

> The Soule of Man is nobler then the Spheres;
> And, if it gaine the Place which may be had,
> Not here alone on Earth, the Rule it beares,
> But, is the Lord, of all that God hath made.
>   Be wise in him; and, if just cause there bee,
>   The Sunne and Moone, shall stand and wayt on thee.

See also Barbara J. Bono on the ambiguity of the Hercules/Antony analogy (*Literary Transvaluation: From Vergilian Epic to Shakespearean Tragicomedy* [Berkeley: University of California Press, 1984], 154).

29. Historically, Caesar renamed himself Augustus because his triumph over Cleopatra occurred in August, so important to him was that conquest (Hughes-Hallett, *Cleopatra*, 32). Furthermore, the historical Caesar may have deliberately manipulated Cleopatra into committing suicide through making her believe that he would treat her badly if she

remained alive; he could thus easily eliminate the difficult problem of what to do with her (Hughes-Hallett, *Cleopatra*, 31–32). Although I am not suggesting that Shakespeare knew or made use of this precise theory, its mere existence speaks to the intensity with which Caesar pursued Cleopatra, on which Shakespeare capitalizes.

30. Charnes, *Notorious Identity*, 145.

31. Of all the criticism I have perused, only Gajowski's seems to me to acknowledge the irony with which "[n]early every character on stage . . . accentuates Cleopatra's victory and Octavius's defeat in this final battle of wills and wits" (*Art of Loving*, 116–17). Barroll, however, does comment on the "absurd post-mortem" and the irony of Caesar's continued trust in Dolabella (*Shakespearean Tragedy*, 222). Also of interest here may be the information that, according to Taylor, in medieval lore Octavius was seen as both "perfect earthly ruler" and as "partial prefiguration of Christ," not as foolish fool ("Medieval Cleopatra," 267).

32. Laura Quinney, "Enter a Messenger," in *Modern Critical Interpretations: "Antony and Cleopatra,"* ed. Harold Bloom (New Haven: Yale University Press, 1988), 158.

33. Barroll offers a rich discussion of Caesar's obsession with control, down to his abstinence from drink (2.7) and his icy exploitation of Octavia's feelings to trap Antony (3.6) (*Shakespearean Tragedy*, chap. 5).

34. Thomson sees Cleopatra's ability to draw Antony and others to her as a "key organizing principle" of the play ("Act 4 scene 16," 78).

35. Although Plutarch assigns purely selfish motives to Cleopatra for encouraging Antony to fight by sea (*Marcus Antonius*, 250–54), I can only agree with those critics who point out that Shakespeare handles the matter differently, neither giving Cleopatra any clear motivation to indulge Antony's choice, nor showing Cleopatra to push Antony in that direction. See, e.g., Ornstein ("Ethic of the Imagination," 94–95) and Ronald Macdonald ("Playing Till Doomsday: Interpreting *Antony and Cleopatra*," *English Literary Renaissance* 15 [1985]: 89).

36. Apologists for Cleopatra are prone to this ironic reading of Cleopatra's tone in 3.13. See, e.g., Gajowski's certainty that Cleopatra's lines to Thidias are "rich" in "sarcasm" and that Enobarbus "readily misinterprets the exchange" (*Art of Loving*, 104). But such is the rule, not the exception, among all critics who write about this scene; nearly all make assumptions about Cleopatra's tone that would be extremely difficult to prove.

37. Ornstein argues that Enobarbus uses this occasion to exact his "jealous revenge" on Cleopatra, but does not explain how Enobarbus has suddenly become so gullible as to mistake Cleopatra's irony ("Ethic of the Imagination," 94–95). She could, of course, be insincere without adopting a clearly ironic tone, but in that case the audience would be unable to follow what was happening.

38. Ibid., 94.

39. Harry Levin, "Two Monumental Death Scenes in *Antony and Cleopatra*, 4.15, 5.2," in *Shakespeare, Text, Language, and Criticism: Essays in Honor of Marvin Spevack*, ed. Bernhard Fabian and Kurt Tetzeli von Rosador (New York: Olms-Weidmann, 1987), 157.

40. See, e.g., 3.6.30–37.

41. Levin aptly refers to Dolabella's "naive vanity" ("Monumental Death Scenes," 158).

42. The debate over Cleopatra's motives for suicide has been approached from many angles besides the obvious contrast between Shakespeare's ambiguity and Plutarch's relative clarity. For example, Mary Ann Bushman argues that Cleopatra's inscrutability, especially in her speeches, "invite[s] the audience to complete" her unfinished characterization ("Representing Cleopatra," in *In Another Country: Feminist Perspectives on Renaissance Drama*, ed. Dorothea Kehler and Susan Baker [Metuchen, N.J.: Scarecrow Press, 1991], 40). Jyotsna Singh sees Cleopatra as a natural improviser, changing her mind as she progresses (and thus threatening male audience members) ("Renaissance Antitheatricality, Antifeminism, and Shakespeare's *Antony and Cleopatra*," *Renaissance Drama* 20 [1989]: 99–121). Wolf, among others, simply acknowledges that her motives are mixed ("Escape from Mutability," 334). I particularly favor Charnes's emphasis on the provisionality of Cleopatra's motives: "The play posits two versions of love: . . . love that is 'to die for' and love that is to die for if nothing else can be worked out" (*Notorious Identity*, 144).

43. Adelman elaborates on negative correspondences between the serpent and women (see especially *Common Liar*, 64). Rozett notices that, as the asp "sucks the nurse asleep" in 5.2.310, it "is metamorphosed from an instrument of death to a symbol of new life" ("Comic Structures," 162).

44. Moseley, "Cleopatra's Prudence," 127.

45. Here again, that association may be somewhat obscured by Moseley's easy interchange of the terms *wisdom* and *prudence*, which, though synonymous in the early seventeenth century (as per the *Oxford English Dictionary*), no longer share quite the identical meaning.

46. Moseley, "Cleopatra's Prudence," 129.

47. To show the striking resemblance between the last stage picture of Cleopatra and these icons, I have reproduced but a few of the many pertinent images. Not all of them picture Mary flanked, crowned, and enthroned; a subcategory of the nursing Mary image is, in fact, the so-called "Madonna of humility," who is humble by virtue of sitting on the ground rather than on a throne. Yet not all the elements of flanking, crown, and throne need be present for Cleopatra, asp applied to her breast, to mirror *Maria lactans*.

Also important to note is the post-Reformation plainness of Willem Basse's etching in particular (1628–48). Although the prevalence of the nursing Mary image declined in the North after the early sixteenth century, it continued to thrive on the Continent in the seventeenth and eighteenth centuries. Northern examples include Peter Paul Rubens's *Holy Family with Saints Elizabeth and John the Baptist* (c. 1615), and a later Italian instance is Francesco de Mura's *Charity* (1743–44) (both in the Art Institute of Chicago). Like so many icons in Protestants' hands, the nursing Mary was sometimes refashioned by Northern artists to appear nearly secular, thus furthering the viewer's identification with, not idolatry of, the portrait's subject. In fact, Basse's portraits of the nursing Virgin tend to be indistinguishable from his portraits where the subjects are common nursing mothers. See n. 59, below, for more discussion of the image's post-Reformation history, and see chap. 1 (sec. 2) for an outline of the similar history that images of Saint Anthony underwent.

48. Gertrud Schiller, *The Iconography of Christian Art*, trans. Janet Seligman (Greenwich: New York Graphic Society, 1966–), 1:122n. 186.

Hughes-Hallett discusses the assimilation of Egyptian and early Christian theology into Roman culture as one in which the overlapping of deities, a common phenomenon, included the identification of Isis with the Virgin Mary. So, by extension, did Cleopatra, who often appeared publicly as Isis the mother, historically come to be associated with Mary (*Cleopatra*, 80–84). Hughes-Hallett elaborates:

> The idea that Cleopatra, known to us, as she was to her Roman contemporaries, as the profligate libertine, could have any link with the Virgin Mary seems almost laughable. . . . Yet to her subjects she must have embodied just those qualities of self-denying love, fidelity and compassion which the Virgin Mary shares with Isis. Isis the Great Mother was her favourite role model. (83)

Laura Severt King has also written about the correspondence between the Cleopatra of act 5 and the Virgin Mary, yet in a context and with a thrust very different from mine. King sees Cleopatra, in the end, "trading the iconography of Isis for that of the Virgin Mary" ("Blessed when they were riggish: Shakespeare's Cleopatra and Christianity's Penitent Prostitutes," *Journal of Medieval and Renaissance Studies* 22 [1992]: 429). The exchange, she reasons, results from a split in Cleopatra's two natures—the profane and the holy—and results in Cleopatra's tragic fall, such that the last "tableau" of her with the asp "simultaneously travesties the Madonna and child and acknowledges their ascendancy as models" (449). I also perceive this ascendancy, but not at odds with or at the cost of Cleopatra's worldliness. In addition, the reference specifically to the *nursing* Mary, as will become clear in my text, is of most crucial importance to my reading.

49. Gertrud Schiller, *Ikonographic der Christlichen Kunst* (Gütersloh: Mohn, 1980), 4:2:22.

50. Ibid., 4.2:180.

51. Gail McMurray Gibson, *The Theater of Devotion: East Anglian Drama and Society in the Late Middle Ages* (Chicago: University of Chicago Press, 1989), 137.

52. Millard Meiss, *Painting in Florence and Siena after the Black Death: The Arts, Religion and Society in the Mid-Fourteenth Century*, Harper Torchbook ed. (New York: Harper & Row, 1964), 151.

53. Theresa Coletti, "Devotional Iconography in the N-Town Marian Plays," *Comparative Drama* 11 (1977): 37. The association between Mary's milk and saving grace, as Coletti states, seems to derive from another association between Christ's open wound, out of which pours redemptive blood, and Mary's freely offered breast. The two images are often paired in medieval and Renaissance art. For a fascinating discussion of the parallels between Christ's wound and Mary's breast, see Caroline Walker Bynum (*Fragmentation and Redemption: Essays on Gender and the Human Body in Medieval Religion* [New York: Zone Books, 1991], 93–211).

54. Further evidence of the lack of contradiction between Cleopatra's worldly and spiritual aspects lies in an emblem by Cesare Ripa, from *Iconologia* (1611), that I discovered in Jeanne Addison Roberts's *The Shakespearean Wild: Geography, Genus, and Gender* ([Lincoln: University of Nebraska Press, 1991], 11). Entitled *Natura*, the emblem represents Nature herself as a lactating mother, thereby illustrating that the image applies to physical, as well as spiritual, nurturance. Indeed, Cleopatra's reference to nursing the snake does not ally her with virginity but with the Virgin's maternal sustenance.

55. The doubleness I am describing here comes very close to Adelman's perception of Cleopatra as the "potential site of both generation and regeneration"—of the mortal and the redemptive (*Suffocating Mothers*, 183). Furthermore, Cleopatra's transformative power over Antony (and, as I have argued, over Dolabella) is, in Adelman's psychoanalytic analysis, related to the female act of "remembering" the "dismembered" male (as when Cleopatra reinfuses the figuratively emasculated Antony with new masculinity in the dream she recounts to Dolabella) (183–85). Through this power, Adelman contends,

the capacity for spiritual/psychological healing is "transferred from the divine to the human plane in Cleopatra" (185).

56. Gibson, *Theater of Devotion*, 138.

57. C. W. R. D. Moseley, *A Century of Emblems* (Brookfield, Vt.: Gower Publishing, 1989), 111.

58. Ibid., 111.

59. The importation of religious images of lactation into secular and quasi-secular contexts was common in the English Renaissance. Willett's own case may have been influenced (at least subconsciously) by the image of his Cantabrigian Alma Mater lactating knowledge, as pictured in the device of the Cambridge University Press, which came into use at the turn of the seventeenth century. (Although the earliest known example of the device dates to 1600 and thus postdates Willett's emblem book in question, another of Willett's books, published in 1605, bears the lactating Alma Mater Cantabrigia. Moreover, the image may have existed at Cambridge long before it was adopted by the press. For the image itself, see Ronald McKerrow, *Printers' and Publishers' Devices in England and Scotland, 1485–1640* [London: Cheswick (Bibliographical Society), 1913], nos. 325–27, 329.) Spenser and others (some, much earlier) also appropriated the icon to the figure of Charity (*Faerie Queene*, bk. 1), an association that comes, I think, especially close to Shakespeare's application of it to Cleopatra.

60. For a recent discussion of the first association, see Hackett (*Virgin Maiden*), and for studies of the second parallel, see, e.g., Helen Morris ("Queen Elizabeth I 'Shadowed' in Cleopatra," *Huntington Library Quarterly* 32 [1969]: 271–78), Keith Rinehart ("Shakespeare's Cleopatra and England's Elizabeth," *Shakespeare Quarterly* 23 [1972]: 81–86), and, more recently, Theodora A. Jankowski, "'As I am Egypt's Queen': Cleopatra, Elizabeth I, and the Female Body Politic" (*Assays* V [1989]: 91–110).

61. In criticism to date, I can find only one acknowledgment—Gajowski's—that the icon at play here is the pietà. She writes: "The emblem of Cleopatra embracing the dying Antony conflates the grief of the pietà and the nurturance of the Madonna" (*Art of Loving*, 112). As Fichter has shown, Charmian's reference to Cleopatra as "eastern star" also involves her in the notion of holy nativity ("Time of Universal Peace," 109). From a psychoanalytic perspective, Cleopatra's identity easily "elides," in Marshall's words, "with that of the mother" ("Man of Steel," 395). See also Adelman, *Suffocating Mothers* (passim).

62. These crowns appearing later in the play stand separate from ones mentioned earlier in 2.5.40 and 2.7.116.

63. Meiss, *Painting in Florence*, 152–54.

64. In discussion, Ralph A. Cohen has used this biblical verse to describe the action of *Antony and Cleopatra*, but differently from me (Discussion at Workshop, "From Critic to Director: Teachers Staging Shakespeare," Folger Shakespeare Library, 19–20 March 1993). While he sees Antony and Cleopatra jointly surrendering the things of this world to achieve spiritual union together, I see just one of them, Cleopatra, as fulfilling herself spiritually through behaving most humanly. Commentators in Renaissance Bibles, especially the Geneva version, take pains not so much to oppose the political and the heavenly kingdoms that are mentioned in this verse as to stress their interdependency. And although those commentators' context is far afield of Shakespeare's (in that they envision the magistrate as God's appointed servant on earth who must, therefore, be obeyed), the spirit in which they interpret Christ's words to the Pharisees approaches the play's

acknowledgment, as I see it, of the place of humanity on earth (see, e.g., gloss of Geneva Bible to 1 Peter 2:17–20).

65. Several critics of late have stressed the inclusiveness of the play's values by the end, the openness of the work to multiple viewpoints, and the lack of friction among Cleopatra's many aspects. See, e.g., Adelman, *Suffocating Mothers*, 191–92; Marshall, "Man of Steel," 408 ("Cleopatra models an exuberant, indeed almost comic, delight in plural subjectivity."); and, in another key, Heinemann, "Order and Disorder," 177–79. Of an entirely different mind is Peggy Muñoz Simonds, whose rich study of emblems in the play is brought to the narrow conclusion that Antony and Cleopatra are exclusively of this world and, in failing to transcend it, must be purged from it before the Christian era (and any true spirituality) can begin ("'To the Very Heart of Loss': Renaissance Iconography in *Antony and Cleopatra*," *Shakespeare Studies* 22 [1994]: 220–76, passim).

5: Prospero's "false brother": Shakespeare's Final Antonio

1. John Milton, *Areopagitica*, in *John Milton: Complete Poems and Major Prose*, ed. Merritt Y. Hughes (New York: Bobbs-Merrill, 1957), 728.

In an essay on Prospero as both wise man and hero, Paul Cantor concludes that "*The Tempest* . . . stresses the difference between knowledge and lack of it" ("Shakespeare's *The Tempest*: The Wise Man as Hero," *Shakespeare Quarterly* 31 [1980]: 75). By contrast, I think *The Tempest* stresses the difference between the virtuous use and the abuse of knowledge.

2. Recent scholarship that pays particular attention to either classical or Christian influences (or both) on *The Tempest* includes that of David Beauregard, *Virtue's Own Feature*; Lynette Cook Black, "Suppertime at Six: Prospero's New Creation," *Publications of the Arkansas Philological Association* 15 (1989): 59–72; Cantor, "Wise Man as Hero"; E. J. Devereux, "Sacramental Imagery in *The Tempest*," *The Humanities Association Bulletin* (Canada) 19 (1968): 50–62; R. A. D. Grant, "Providence, Authority, and the Moral Life in *The Tempest*," *Shakespeare Studies* 16 (1983): 235–63; Mary Ellen Rickey, "Prospero's Living Drolleries," *Renaissance Papers* 1964: 35–42; James Walter, "From Tempest to Epilogue: Augustine's Allegory in Shakespeare's Drama," *PMLA* 98 (1983): 60–76; and Rosemary Wright, "Prospero's Lime Tree and the Pursuit of 'Vanitas,'" *Shakespeare Survey* 37 (1984): 133–40.

The idea that the effects of virtue are properly realized in the world is not, in itself, necessarily non-Christian, as attested by the Catholic doctrine of good works and the Protestant notion that good works naturally follow from saving faith. Yet Shakespeare is clearly referring in *The Tempest* to the classical notion that *gnosis* should result in *praxis*, the notion that Sidney uses in *The Apology for Poetry* to defend the capacity of imaginative literature to instill practical virtue. Narrowly speaking, that notion conflicts with Paul's that "the wisdom of this world is foolishness with God." Nonetheless, part of the wisdom that proliferated around Saint Anthony himself took a temperate approach toward shunning participation in this world, as discussed in chap. 1.

3. Probably Harry Berger should be credited with the most influential stand toward what he calls the "sentimental" reading of Prospero and the play ("Miraculous Harp: A Reading of Shakespeare's *Tempest*," *Shakespeare Studies* 5 [1969]: 254), against which

he proposed a "hard-nosed" interpretation (279 n. 3). Meredith Anne Skura's parallel terms—"idealist" versus "revisionist" ("Discourse and the Individual: The Case of Colonialism in *The Tempest*," *Shakespeare Quarterly* 40 [1989]: 42–43)—may not fully capture the degree to which the two camps often differ in their understanding of Prospero and *The Tempest*. The "revisionists" include mainly new historicists, interested in the play's colonialist content, and psychological critics, two groups whose interests Skura seeks to correlate. For a challenging essay on the matter of approaching *The Tempest* from a new historicist/cultural materialist perspective, see Russ McDonald ("Reading *The Tempest*," *Shakespeare Survey* 44 [1991]: 15–28), and for an intriguing discussion of continuities between modernist and new historicist approaches to Shakespeare, see Richard Halpern's "Shakespeare in the Tropics: From High Modernism to New Historicism" (*Representations* 45 [1994]: 1–25).

4. Berger, "Miraculous Harp," 254.

5. One of the bleakest views of the play's conclusion must be Jan Kott's: "The ending of *The Tempest* is more disturbing than that of any other Shakespearean drama" (*Shakespeare Our Contemporary* [Garden City, N.Y.: Doubleday, 1964], 164).

6. Grant, "Providence," 254.

7. Walter, "Tempest to Epilogue," 71.

8. As early as 1937, D. G. James attributed much the same phenomenon to *The Tempest* (*Scepticism and Poetry: An Essay on the Poetic Imagination* [London: George Allen, 1937]). Yet to him any disjunction between symbol and meaning grew out of Shakespeare's restlessness with conventional myths and symbols, which proved "inadequate to embody all that was present in [his] imagination" (220). "Driven to be unfaithful" to convention (220), he minted less fixed, sometimes ambiguous symbols. James cites Caliban's "sense of glory" about the island's enchantment as just such a "complication of symbolism" (227).

See also Anne Barton on this same defiance of *The Tempest* to be reduced (introduction to *The Tempest*, by William Shakespeare, New Penguin ed. [Harmondsworth: Penguin, 1968], e.g., 17, 21–22).

9. Thomas More, *Utopia*, 67.

10. Critics have long been fascinated by Prospero's suggestions, however conscious they may or may not be, of his shared guilt in Antonio's temptation. See, for example, Berger ("Miraculous Harp," 254); James Black ("The Latter End of Prospero's Commonwealth," *Shakespeare Survey* 44 [1991]: 31); Devereux ("Sacramental Imagery," 53); and Stephen Orgel ("Prospero's Wife," in *Modern Critical Interpretations: William Shakespeare's "The Tempest,"* ed. Harold Bloom [New York: Chelsea House, 1988], 110).

11. Michel de Montaigne, "Of Cannibals," in *Essays*, trans. John Florio, ed. J. I. M. Stewart (New York: Modern Library, 1933).

12. Walter, "Tempest to Epilogue," 65.

Cf., e.g., Frank Kermode's comments on the relationship between "Of Cannibals" and *The Tempest*, which are related to his widely influential view that "Caliban is the core of the play" (*The Tempest*, by William Shakespeare, New Arden, 6th ed. [New York: Methuen, 1958], xxxiv–xxxviii). As my argument will continue to show, I would contend that Prospero is at the play's heart.

13. Several critics have cited similar evidence—for example, Walter ("Tempest to Epilogue," 67) and William G. Masden, who notes, "Lilies that fester smell far worse than weeds" ("The Destiny of Man in *The Tempest*," *Emory University Quarterly* 20

[1964]: 176). Alden T. and Virginia Mason Vaughan include an especially clear paragraph, in their book about Caliban, proposing that Montaigne purveys "cultural relativism": "Brazilian cannibals, Montaigne asserted with acerbic irony, are more virtuous than their French contemporaries" (*Shakespeare's Caliban: A Cultural History* [New York: Cambridge University Press, 1991], 47).

14. Montaigne, "Of Cannibals," 163, 166, 167.

15. Stephen Greenblatt and Karen Flagstad see reason in this parallel to wonder whether Prospero is actually responsible for Caliban's cursing, symbolic of his barbarity and hatred (Greenblatt, "Learning to Curse": Aspects of Linguistic Colonialism in the Sixteenth Century," in *Learning to Curse: Essays in Early Modern Culture* [New York: Routledge, 1990], passim; Flagstad, "'Making this Place Paradise': Prospero and the Problem of Caliban in *The Tempest*," *Shakespeare Studies* 18 [1986]: 206). I think that such an argument goes too far, although, as will become clear, I would agree with both writers that Caliban represents to Prospero the barbarism in himself that he would just as soon ignore.

16. Christopher Marlowe, *Dr. Faustus*, in *The Complete Works of Christopher Marlowe*, ed. Roma Gill (Oxford: Clarendon Press, 1990), 2:13.15.

17. I can only agree with the now shrinking number of editors who reassign the most despairing speech in 1.2 from Miranda (as in the Folio) to Prospero:

Abhorred slave,
Which any print of goodness wilt not take,
Being capable of all ill! . . .
thy vild race
(Though thou didst learn) had that in't which good natures
Could not abide to be with.

(351–62)

I suppose that the trauma of being attacked might account for this single instance in the whole play where Miranda sounds like her father: in her emotional turmoil, she may have absorbed Prospero's cynical view of Caliban, as well as the harsh language in which he typically condemns Caliban. But common sense seems to me to dictate otherwise. This speech has nothing in common with Miranda's outlook or language elsewhere in the play, although it does echo many of Prospero's sentiments about Caliban's inability to grow morally, including some expressed in this very scene, as in lines 345–48.

"Human care" is "humane care" in the Folio (1.2.346).

18. The tendency of new historicist and psychological criticism has been to sentimentalize Caliban so much as to make Prospero's suppression of him seem thoroughly unfair. A good example would be Bernard J. Paris, for whom Caliban's illicit behavior appears virtually insignificant: "Prospero's rationalization of his treatment of Caliban works so well that the majority of critics have accepted his point of view and have felt that Caliban deserves what he gets, although some have been sympathetic toward Caliban's suffering and uneasy about Prospero's behavior" ("*The Tempest*: Shakespeare's Ideal Solution," in *Shakespeare's Personality*, ed. Norman N. Holland (and introd.), Sidney Homan, and Bernard J. Paris [Berkeley: University of California Press, 1988], 216). While I am not denying that Prospero's extreme harshness toward Caliban is linked to a problem in Prospero's character, I would argue vigorously that "Caliban's suffering" naturally results in large part from suffering he has caused.

19. Several critics have taken approaches similar to mine in portraying Prospero as a character defined by struggle. See particularly Flagstad ("'Making this Place Paradise,'" 218–28) and Skura ("Discourse," esp. 57–69) on the tension in Prospero's psyche between what he desires and what he can actually have, and Paris's discussion of the Horneyan paradigm in relation to both Prospero and Shakespeare ("Ideal Solution," passim). See also Peggy Muñoz Simonds on Prospero as an Orpheus, who must "master his own baser passions" in exercising art and statecraft ("'Sweet Power of Music': The Political Magic of 'the Miraculous Harp' in Shakespeare's *The Tempest*," *Comparative Drama* 29 [1995]: 64).

20. For example, Flagstad believes that Prospero intends vengeance ("'Making this Place Paradise,'" 206, passim), as does Alvin B. Kernan (*The Playwright as Magician: Shakespeare's Image of the Poet in the English Public Theater* [New Haven: Yale University Press, 1979], 140); Paris argues that Prospero's magic enables him to relieve his vengeful feelings without actually enacting revenge ("Ideal Solution," 212, passim); but most critical studies clearly state or assume that Prospero never means to take revenge from the very beginning. Barton stresses the audience's ignorance as to what Prospero intends through the first four acts (introduction to *The Tempest*, 9, 12, 16).

21. Skura, "Discourse," 63. Skura's context is somewhat different from mine in that she is discussing Caliban as an embodiment of traits that Prospero is loath to accept about himself, but, ultimately, we are both addressing Prospero's limited understanding.

22. I wish for clearer words here because Shakespeare's use of them, although frequent, does not always preserve the distinctions that I am according them. Take, for instance, Ferdinand's lines to Miranda in 3.1:

> The very instant that I saw you, did
> My heart fly to your service, there resides,
> To make me slave to it, and for your sake
> Am I this patient log-man.
>
> (64–67)

Here, *slave* has about it a flavor of courtly love, which, although it does not obscure Ferdinand's willing love ("service"), muddles the semantics a bit.

Ariel is the obvious exception to my two categories, since he craves absolute freedom after Prospero releases him from the cloven pine. I shall discuss his example more fully below.

23. Walter describes mercy in *The Tempest* as that virtue which, especially as formulated in the Epilogue, gives "all human words, deeds, and creation . . . their final meaning" ("Tempest to Epilogue," 73).

24. Cf. Grant's definition of Providence as "not God himself . . ., but God's purpose *in the world*" ("Providence," 239). See also Grant on Prospero as "minister of Providence" (241–42) and on the relationship of freedom and self-restraint (255).

Although Grant sees Gonzalo as "in his limited way a direct human representative of the Providential power that lies behind the play" (249), I think that Gonzalo's portrait is finally more perplexing and, alas, less satisfying than Grant asserts. In addition to the allegorical value Grant assigns him, Gonzalo extends Shakespeare's study of loyal service that pervades *The Winter's Tale*, especially in the figures of Camillo and Antigonus. Much like Antigonus, Gonzalo good-naturedly, but uncritically, carries out whatever orders his superiors issue. If he has supplied Prospero with staples and books (1.2.160–

68), he has also refrained from objecting to the exile in the first place. For this problematic loyalty to the regime at any cost, Prospero and others pay dear. Moreover, although Prospero does not resent Gonzalo's role in his banishment, his liberality seems to stem less from Gonzalo's past behavior itself than from Prospero's willingness to interpret that behavior exclusively in terms of its liberality.

25. This connection with Providence, I think, accounts for why, as Kermode notes, Art is capitalized throughout the Folio (*The Tempest*, xli).

Cf. to Ariel's "not forgetting" in line 73 his "remember" in line 68.

26. In this regard, if in no other, Prospero resembles Cleopatra: she fulfills both private and political goals through her suicide, while his art is capable of reconciling the private with both the political and the providential. See chap. 4.

27. Such struggle also characterizes Prospero's predecessor, the artist Paulina in *The Winter's Tale*. For, even as she upholds the oracle of Apollo in her treatment of Leontes (3.2.134–36), she must also be tempted to take personal vengeance on Leontes for having killed her husband Antigonus and, presumably, her lady Hermione. Caught between duty and self-interest, she treads a fine line between faith in Leontes' ability to repent and despair that he ever can (3.2.207–24). Though she has no right to doubt that Leontes can be forgiven, she has reason.

28. Harriet Hawkins, *Classics and Trash: Traditions and Taboos in High Literature and Popular Modern Culture* (Toronto: University of Toronto Press, 1990), 179. See also Maurice Hunt, who discusses "shared passion," including compassion, as the basis of "personal and general salvation in *The Tempest*" (*Shakespeare's Labored Art: Stir, Work, and the Late Plays* [New York: Peter Lang, 1995], 189–90).

29. See especially Ariel's song—"Full fadom five thy father lies" (1.2.397–405)—and Alonso's description of Ferdinand as "mudded in that oozy bed" (5.1.151).

30. James Black observes that, as Miranda gains independence from Prospero, she behaves increasingly like Antonio ("Latter End," 30–31), a point that underscores the inevitable and marked transition from innocence to experience.

31. Beauregard points out that "according to Aristotle and Thomas, wonder (*admiratio*: thus Miranda's name) begins in ignorance" (*Virtue's Own Feature*, 174).

32. Masden's discussion of Gonzalo balances well the advantages of his supremely kind disposition against its disadvantages ("Destiny of Man," 181–82). Gonzalo, by the way, may appear awfully gullible, yet he also reveals in 2.1 that he understands more of Antonio and Sebastian's gibes against him than he earlier lets on (2.1.176–84). He implies, in other words, that his good will is not thoroughly unthinking, but possibly somewhat deliberate.

33. For Peter Holland, the love of Ferdinand and Miranda is the "triumph" at the play's core and the basis for all other human compassion therein ("The Shapeliness of *The Tempest*," *Essays in Criticism* 45 [1995]: 226–27).

34. For further discussion of this point, see James Black's essay ("Latter End"), which analyzes Prospero's manipulations as centered on marrying Miranda responsibly.

35. As Shakespeare and much of his audience well knew, Sir Philip Sidney grounds his defense of the creative imagination in a twofold premise concerning the relationship of art to nature. First, he asserts, art repairs that branch of nature that fell along with Adam and Eve by presenting a "golden" world (*An Apology for Poetry*, in *Criticism: The Major Texts*, ed. Walter Jackson Bate [New York: Harcourt Brace Jovanovich, 1970], 85). To do so, however, it must spring from a source other than the human soul, which is itself fallen. Here follows the second prong of Sidney's premise, that the source of art is

unfallen Nature, the eternal and immutable ordering principle of the universe (see, e.g., 85). Hence, Sidney concludes, art is licensed by unfallen Nature even if it alters fallen nature, since the alteration is, morally, for the better—that is, intent on teaching us to follow "our erected wit" (86). This natural basis of art, together with the poet's stature as divinely inspired *vates* (84), protects art, in Sidney's scheme, from human corruption. This issue of art's purity is of course debated by Polixenes and Perdita in 4.3 of *The Winter's Tale*.

36. Wright, "Prospero's Lime Tree," 134.

37. Sidney, *Apology*, 86.

38. See, e.g., *Areopagitica* (passim; e.g., "the knowledge and survey of vice is in this world . . . necessary to the constituting of human virtue, and the scanning of error to the confirmation of truth," 729). This idea, a form of the more general notion of *felix culpa*, finds further reflection in 1.2.148–51 and 5.1.205–13.

39. Nor do I consider mine ideal. Berger includes many helpful observations about Ariel as both character and metaphor, especially those relating the spirit to Prospero ("Miraculous Harp," 255–59).

40. This example of Prospero's response to the masque—conveying the modesty to identify with his audience and to be affected as they are, rather than lose himself in admiration of his artifice—directly opposes a statement like Berger's about Prospero's failings: "Prospero delight[s] in art which . . . continually distracts him from his ethical purpose" ("Miraculous Harp," 257). True enough, Prospero was first exiled for being so distracted. In *The Tempest*, however, he is continuing to learn not to repeat his mistake. Wright takes another approach to argue, similarly, that Prospero is oblivious to the reality of danger around him when she compares him to the sleeping peddler in the emblem of the peddler and the apes, an "idle dreamer" who loses his goods because he is too dull to notice that his apes are pilfering them ("Prospero's Lime Tree," 137–40). But both Wright and Berger neglect the difference between the former Prospero and the present one, who is struggling to overcome his desire to dream instead of act.

41. Orgel, "Prospero's Wife," 110–11.

42. Ibid., 111.

43. As Barton writes: "What [Ariel] significantly declines to tell his audience is whether his master instructed him to exempt Antonio and Sebastian from the charmed sleep" (introduction to *The Tempest*, 17).

44. Stephen J. Greenblatt, *Shakespearean Negotiations: The Circulation of Social Energy in Renaissance England* (Berkeley: University of California Press, 1988), 137. Greenblatt elaborates: "William Tyndale suggested that St. Paul had written the Epistle to the Romans precisely to generate a suffering that could be joyously relieved" (137). One might especially think in this connection of Duke Vincentio's stated reason for deluding Isabella about Claudio's execution (*Measure for Measure*, 4.3.109–11) and also of the anxiety he produces, then relieves, in Angelo. Yet, here again (and as I have argued elsewhere), such anxiety is merely a portion of a complex mission on Vincentio's part to excite sympathetic imagination in his subjects (see Lewis, "'Dark Deeds Darkly Answered,'" 271–89).

45. Kermode, *The Tempest*, n. heading 3.3.

46. Rickey also sees Prospero's aims in the banquet scene as largely "penitential, not punitive," although she does not elaborate greatly from there ("Prospero's Living Drolleries," 38).

47. Detecting sarcasm in Sebastian's line ("A most high miracle!") is currently fashionable (see, e.g., Barton, introduction to *The Tempest*, 17, 37; Flagstad, "Making this Place Paradise," 228; Kernan, *Playwright as Magician*, 138). But I see no textual evidence for a cynical reading of the line. In fact, Sebastian's earlier practice, when conveying doubt in this same scene about Prospero's magic, is to speak without irony (i.e., l. 129; the Folio, as is typical, does not designate this line as an aside). The context of line 177 is, to quote Kermode, "language [that] assumes a hieratic quality" (*The Tempest*, n. to l. 177). If Sebastian's line cut across this grain, surely another character would notice and respond.

48. That same "self-negation," Rickey points out, characterizes Ferdinand and Miranda's attitude toward each other in the chess game (5.1.172–75; Rickey, "Prospero's Living Drolleries," 37). On Caliban's similarities to the innocent Miranda, see the Vaughans (*Shakespeare's Caliban*, 17–18).

49. The particular view I mention is Greenblatt's, in "Learning to Curse" (26). See also, e.g., Skura, whose reading of the line attempts to reconcile a colonialist approach with a psychological methodology: "Prospero acknowledges the child-like Caliban as his own, and although he does not thus undo hierarchy, he moves for the first time towards accepting the child in himself rather than trying to dominate and erase that child . . . in order to establish his adult authority" ("Discourse," 66).

50. To return briefly to the comparison with Marlowe's hero-magician, Faustus is finally dragged into hell by demons that he cannot admit lurk within him. He remains his own victim, while Prospero dredges up just enough self-recognition to salvage what is left of his days on earth.

51. Several other critics' interpretations of Prospero's extreme tactics converge with, while others' diverge from, mine. For examples of the former, see Walter's assessment of *The Tempest* as "Shakespeare's profound look . . . at the poet's ability to redeem a world degenerated in the imaginations of the degenerate" ("Tempest to Epilogue," 64) and Grant's "guarded optimism" toward inferring from *The Tempest* that the "corruption of human nature . . . is . . . largely curable" ("Providence," 257). Contrasting ideas are epitomized in the work of Paris, who, echoing Orgel, finds Prospero's artistry self-serving (in that it "enables him to resolve his psychological conflicts," "Ideal Solution," 212) and who describes Prospero's forgiveness as "compulsive and indiscriminate" (224), as well as a form of passive vengeance: "The worse Antonio is, the more charitable Prospero is to forgive him" (219).

52. Barton reads such details of the last scene with greater skepticism. For example, she emphasizes the streak of "contempt" in Prospero's mercy toward Antonio, which she would probably call only technically unconditional (introduction to *The Tempest*, 38). She also underlines what she sees as Antonio's (and Sebastian's) "refus[al] to be absorbed into any final harmony" and implies that Prospero's ongoing challenge, even after the play closes, is such characters' (as well as Caliban's) "unalterable will to evil" (39, 30).

53. In both his concluding silence and his earlier verbal seduction of Sebastian, of course, Antonio resembles Iago, who raises similar questions about the origins of and motives for evil.

54. Walter, "Tempest to Epilogue," 70.

55. Michel de Montaigne, "Of Experience," in *The Complete Essays of Montaigne*, trans. Donald M. Frame (Stanford: Stanford University Press, 1958), 855.

56. I would not belabor the sentiment of the Epilogue, which seems so clear, if I did not find so many recent readings of it dishearteningly cynical, as well as overread for purposes of driving home points that seem alien to the play. Berger's account of it is intriguing but surely distorting: "The end is a final attempt [on Prospero's part] to reestablish mastery. The closing couplet has too much bite and sweep to it to be characterized as expressing weariness alone. It points the finger . . . . He has shifted his role slightly but significantly in the final couplet, from that of fellow sinner to that of homilist, the voice of conscience" ("Miraculous Harp," 279). Greenblatt's notion, that the Epilogue savors of "subversive politics" by way of a prince's reliance on a forgiving public, seems to me similarly wide of the mark (*Shakespearean Negotiations*, 157).

Conclusion: "No way out but through": Shakespeare's Antonios and the Wisdom of This World

1. Seneca, quoted in Montaigne, "Of Experience," 853.

2. Ibid., 857.

Bibliography

Adelman, Janet. *The Common Liar: An Essay on "Antony and Cleopatra."* New Haven: Yale University Press, 1973.

———. *Suffocating Mothers: Fantasies of Maternal Origin in Shakespeare's Plays, "Hamlet" to "The Tempest."* New York: Routledge, 1992.

The American Heritage Dictionary of the English Language. 3rd ed. Boston: Houghton Mifflin, 1992.

Astington, John. "Malvolio and the Eunuchs: Texts and Revels in *Twelfth Night*." *Shakespeare Survey* 46 (1994): 23–34.

St. Augustine. *The Confessions*. Translated by Sir Tobie Matthew. Revised by Roger Hudleston. London: Burns & Oates, 1954.

Barber, C. L. *Shakespeare's Festive Comedy*. 1959. Reprint, Princeton: Princeton University Press, 1972.

Barroll, J. Leeds. *Shakespearean Tragedy: Genre, Tradition, and Change in "Antony and Cleopatra."* Washington: Folger Books, 1984.

Barton, Anne. Introduction to *As You Like It*, by William Shakespeare. In *The Riverside Shakespeare*, edited by G. Blakemore Evans, 365–68. Boston: Houghton Mifflin, 1974.

———. Introduction to *The Merchant of Venice*, by William Shakespeare. In *The Riverside Shakespeare*, edited by G. Blakemore Evans, 250–53. Boston: Houghton Mifflin, 1974.

———. Introduction to *Twelfth Night*, by William Shakespeare. In *The Riverside Shakespeare*, edited by G. Blakemore Evans, 403–7. Boston: Houghton Mifflin, 1974.

———. "'Nature's Piece 'Gainst Fancy': The Divided Catastrophe in *Antony and Cleopatra*." In *Modern Critical Interpretations: "Antony and Cleopatra*," edited by Harold Bloom. New York: Chelsea House, 1988. First published as *An Inaugural Lecture*, 1972.

———, ed. Introduction to *The Tempest*, by William Shakespeare. New Penguin ed. Harmondsworth: Penguin, 1968.

Battisti, Carlo, and Giovanni Alessio. *Dizionario etimologico italiano*. Florence: G. Barbèra, 1950–57.

Beauregard, David N. *Virtue's Own Feature: Shakespeare and the Virtue Ethics Tradition*. Newark: University of Delaware Press, 1995.

Beckerman, Bernard. *Shakespeare at the Globe, 1599–1609.* New York: Macmillan Publishing, 1962.

Belsey, Catherine. "Disrupting Sexual Difference: Meaning and Gender in the Comedies." In *Alternative Shakespeares*, edited by John Drakakis, 166–90. New York: Methuen, 1985.

Benston, Alice N. "Portia, the Law, and the Tripartite Structure of *The Merchant of Venice*." *Shakespeare Quarterly* 30 (1979): 367–85.

Berek, Peter. "Doing and Undoing: The Value of Action in *Antony and Cleopatra*." *Shakespeare Quarterly* 32 (1981): 295–304.

Berger, Harry, Jr. "Miraculous Harp: A Reading of Shakespeare's *Tempest*." *Shakespeare Studies* 5 (1969): 253–83.

Berry, Herbert. "Shylock, Robert Miles, and Events at the Theatre." *Shakespeare Quarterly* 44 (1993): 183–97.

Bible. Bishops' version. London: Christopher Barker, Printer, 1585.

Bible. Geneva version. Facsimile of the 1560 ed. Madison: University of Wisconsin Press, 1969.

Bible. Revised Standard Version.

Black, James. "The Latter End of Prospero's Commonwealth." *Shakespeare Survey* 44 (1991): 29–41.

Black, Lynette Cook. "Suppertime at Six: Prospero's New Creation." *Publications of the Arkansas Philological Association* 15 (1989): 59–72.

Bono, Barbara J. *Literary Transvaluation: From Vergilian Epic to Shakespearean Tragicomedy.* Berkeley: University of California Press, 1984.

Booth, Stephen. "Speculations on Doubling in Shakespeare's Plays." In *Shakespeare: The Theatrical Dimension*, edited by Philip C. McGuire and David A. Samuelson. New York: AMS Press, 1979.

Boswell, Jackson Campbell. *Sir Thomas More in the English Renaissance: An Annotated Catalogue*. Vol. 83. Binghamton: Medieval and Renaissance Texts and Studies, 1994.

Brockbank, Philip, ed. *Players of Shakespeare*. New York: Cambridge University Press, 1985.

Brown, Jane K. "Double Plotting in Shakespeare's Comedies: The Case of *Twelfth Night*." In *Aesthetic Illusion: Theoretical and Historical Approaches*, edited by Frederick Burwick, 313–23. Berlin: W. de Gruyter, 1990.

Brown, John Russell, ed. *The Merchant of Venice*, by William Shakespeare. New Arden ed. Cambridge: Harvard University Press, 1955.

———. *Shakespeare and His Comedies*. 2nd ed. London: Methuen, 1962.

Bullough, Geoffrey, ed. *Narrative and Dramatic Sources of Shakespeare*. 8 vols. New York: Columbia University Press, 1958.

Bushman, Mary Ann. "Representing Cleopatra." In *In Another Country: Feminist Perspectives on Renaissance Drama*, edited by Dorothea Kehler and Susan Baker, 36–49. Metuchen, N.J.: Scarecrow Press, 1991.

Bynum, Caroline Walker. *Fragmentation and Redemption: Essays on Gender and the Human Body in Medieval Religion*. New York: Zone Books, 1991.

Cantor, Paul. "Shakespeare's *The Tempest*: The Wise Man as Hero." *Shakespeare Quarterly* 31 (1980): 64–75.

Caxton, William, trans. *The Golden Legend*, by Jacobus de Voragine. Facsimile ed. by William Morris. Vol 1. Hammersmith: Kelmscott, 1892.

Chapman, Alison. "The Fool and Hythloday: Unliked and Unlikeable." Unpublished essay, 1986.

Charnes, Linda. *Notorious Identity: Materializing the Subject in Shakespeare*. Cambridge: Harvard University Press, 1993.

Cheadle, Brian. "'His legs bestrid the ocean' as a 'form of life.'" In *Drama and Philosophy*, edited by James Redmond, 87–106. Themes in Drama Series, 12. Cambridge: Cambridge University Press, 1990.

Coddon, Karen S. "'Slander in an Allowed Fool': *Twelfth Night*'s Crisis of the Aristocracy." *Studies in English Literature* 33 (1993): 309–25.

Cohen, Ralph A. Discussion at Workshop, "From Critic to Director: Teachers Staging Shakespeare." Folger Shakespeare Library, 19–20 March 1993.

———. "Staging Comic Divinity: The Collision of High and Low in *Antony and Cleopatra*." *Shakespeare Bulletin* 13.3 (Summer 1995): 5–8.

Cohen, Walter. "*The Merchant of Venice* and the Possibilities of Historical Criticism." *ELH* 49 (1982): 765–85.

Coletti, Theresa. "Devotional Iconography in the N-Town Marian Plays." *Comparative Drama* 11 (1977): 22–44.

Colie, Rosalie. "The Significance of Style." In *Modern Critical Interpretations: "Antony and Cleopatra*," edited by Harold Bloom, 57–85. New Haven: Yale University Press, 1988. First published as chap. 4 of *Shakespeare's Living Art* (Princeton: Princeton University Press, 1974).

The Concise Oxford Dictionary of Place-Names. Oxford: Clarendon Press, 1960.

Corballis, R. P. "The Name Antonio in English Renaissance Drama." *Cahiers Elisabéthains: Etudes sur la Pré-Renaissance et la Renaissance Anglaises* 25 (1984): 61–72.

Cusack, Sinead. "Portia in *The Merchant of Venice*." In *"The Merchant of Venice": Critical Essays*, edited by Thomas Wheeler, 339–50. New York: Garland Publishing, 1991.

Davidson, Clifford. "The Middle English Saint Play and Its Iconography." In *The Saint Play in Medieval Europe*, edited by Clifford Davidson, 31–122. Early Drama, Art, and Music Monograph Series, 8. Kalamazoo: Medieval Institute Publications, Western Michigan University, 1986.

Delehaye, Hippolyte. *The Legends of the Saints*. Translated by Donald Attwater. New York: Fordham University Press, 1962.

Dessen, Alan C. *Elizabethan Stage Conventions and Modern Interpreters*. New York: Cambridge University Press, 1984.

———. *Recovering Shakespeare's Theatrical Vocabulary*. New York: Cambridge University Press, 1995.

Devereux, E. J. "Sacramental Imagery in *The Tempest*." *The Humanities Association Bulletin* (Canada) 19 (1968): 50–62.

Diehl, Huston. "Graven Images: Protestant Emblem Books in England." *Renaissance Quarterly* 39 (1986): 49–66.

Dixon, Laurinda S. "Bosch's 'St. Anthony Triptych'—An Apothecary's Apotheosis." *Art Journal* 44 (1984): 119–31.

Doebler, John. *Shakespeare's Speaking Pictures: Studies in Iconic Imagery*. Albuquerque: University of New Mexico Press, 1974.

Dollimore, Jonathan. "*Virtus* under Erasure." In *Radical Tragedy: Religion, Ideology, and Power in the Drama of Shakespeare and his Contemporaries*. Chicago: University of Chicago Press, 1984.

Eagleton, Terry. *William Shakespeare*. Oxford: Basil Blackwell, 1986.

Erasmus, Desiderius. *De Contemptu Mundi*. Translated by Thomas Paynell. Gainesville, Fla.: Scholars' Facsimiles and Reprints, 1967.

———. *In Praise of Folly*. London: Reeves & Turner, 1876.

Evans, G. Blakemore, gen. ed. *The Riverside Shakespeare*. Boston: Houghton Mifflin, 1974.

Falvey, Kathleen C. "The Italian Saint Play: The Example of Perugia." In *The Saint Play in Medieval Europe*, edited by Clifford Davidson, 181–204. Early Drama, Art, and Music Monograph Series, 8. Kalamazoo: Medieval Institute Publications, Western Michigan University, 1986.

Farmer, David Hugh. *The Oxford Dictionary of Saints*. Oxford: Clarendon Press, 1978.

Ferguson, John. *Moral Values in the Ancient World*. London: Methuen, 1958.

Fichter, Andrew. "*Antony and Cleopatra*: 'The Time of Universal Peace.'" *Shakespeare Survey* 33 (1980): 99–111.

Flagstad, Karen. "'Making this Place Paradise': Prospero and the Problem of Caliban in *The Tempest*." *Shakespeare Studies* 18 (1986): 205–33.

Flesch, William. *Generosity and the Limits of Authority: Shakespeare, Herbert, Milton*. Ithaca: Cornell University Press, 1992.

French, Marilyn. *Shakespeare's Division of Experience*. New York: Summit Books, 1981.

Frye, Northrop. *Northrop Frye on Shakespeare*. Edited by Robert Sandler. New Haven: Yale University Press, 1986.

Gajowski, Evelyn. *The Art of Loving: Female Subjectivity and Male Discursive Traditions in Shakespeare's Tragedies*. Newark: University of Delaware Press, 1992.

Garber, Marjorie. *Vice Versa: Bisexuality and the Eroticism of Everyday Life*. New York: Simon & Schuster, 1995.

Gardiner, Harold C. *Mysteries' End: An Investigation of the Last Days of the Medieval Stage*. 1946. Reprint, New Haven: Yale University Press, 1967.

Geary, Keith. "The Nature of Portia's Victory: Turning to Men in *The Merchant of Venice*." *Shakespeare Survey* 37 (1984): 55–68.

Gibson, Gail McMurray. *The Theater of Devotion: East Anglian Drama and Society in the Late Middle Ages*. Chicago: University of Chicago Press, 1989.

Goldsmith, Robert Hillis. *Wise Fools in Shakespeare*. East Lansing: Michigan State University Press, 1955.

Graham, Rose. "The Order of St. Antoine de Viennois and Its English Commandery, St. Anthony's, Threadneedle Street." *Archaeological Journal* 34 (1927): 341–406.

———, ed. *A Picture Book of the Life of St. Anthony the Abbot*, by Jean Macellard. Oxford: Roxburghe Club, 1937.

Grant, R. A. D. "Providence, Authority, and the Moral Life in *The Tempest*." *Shakespeare Studies* 16 (1983): 235–63.

Green, Douglas E. "Shakespeare's Violation: 'One face, one voice, one habit, and two persons.'" In *Reconsidering the Renaissance*, edited by Mario A. Di Cesare, 93:327–38. Binghamton: Medieval and Renaissance Texts and Studies, 1992.

Greenblatt, Stephen J. "Learning to Curse: Aspects of Linguistic Colonialism in the Sixteenth Century." In *Learning to Curse: Essays in Early Modern Culture*, 16–39. New York: Routledge, 1990.

———. "Marlowe, Marx, and Anti-Semitism." In *Learning to Curse: Essays in Early Modern Culture*, 40–58. New York: Routledge, 1990.

———. *Shakespearean Negotiations: The Circulation of Social Energy in Renaissance England*. Berkeley: University of California Press, 1988.

Greg, W. W., ed. *The Book of Sir Thomas More*. Malone Soc. Reprints. 1911. Oxford: Oxford University Press, 1961.

Gregg, Robert C., trans. and ed. *The Life of Antony*, by Athanasius. Classics of Western Spirituality. New York: Paulist Press, 1980.

Greif, Karen. "Plays and Playing in *Twelfth Night*." In *"Twelfth Night": Critical Essays*, edited by Stanley Wells, 261–77. New York: Garland Publishing, 1986.

Grimm, Jacob and Wilhelm. *Deutsches Wörterbuch*. Leipzig: Hirzel, 1935.

Gross, John. *Shylock: A Legend and Its Legacy*. New York: Simon & Schuster, 1992.

Hackett, Helen. *Virgin Maiden, Maiden Queen: Elizabeth I and the Cult of the Virgin Mary*. New York: St. Martin's Press, 1995.

Halpern, Richard. "Shakespeare in the Tropics: From High Modernism to New Historicism." *Representations* 45 (1994): 1–25.

Happé, Peter. "The Protestant Adaptation of the Saint Play." In *The Saint Play in Medieval Europe*, edited by Clifford Davidson, 205–40. Early Drama, Art, and Music Monograph Series, 8. Kalamazoo: Medieval Institute Publications, Western Michigan University, 1986.

Harcourt, C. G. V. *Legends of St. Augustine, St. Anthony, and St. Cuthbert, Painted on the Back of the Stalls in Carlisle Cathedral*. Carlisle: C. Thurnam, 1868.

Harper's Latin Dictionary. New York: American Book, 1879.

Harpham, Geoffrey Galt. *The Ascetic Imperative in Culture and Criticism*. Chicago: University of Chicago Press, 1987.

Harris, Jonathan Gil. "'Narcissus in thy face': Roman Desire and the Difference it Fakes in *Antony and Cleopatra*." *Shakespeare Quarterly* 45 (1994): 408–25.

Hassel, R. Chris. *Faith and Folly in Shakespeare's Romantic Comedies*. Athens: University of Georgia Press, 1980.

———. *Renaissance Drama and the English Church Year*. Lincoln: University of Nebraska Press, 1979.

Hawkins, Harriet. *Classics and Trash: Traditions and Taboos in High Literature and Popular Modern Culture*. Toronto: University of Toronto Press, 1990.

Hayles, Nancy K. "Sexual Disguise in *As You Like It* and *Twelfth Night*." *Shakespeare Survey* 32 (1979): 63–72.

Heffernan, Thomas J. *Sacred Biography: Saints and Their Biographers in the Middle Ages*. New York: Oxford University Press, 1989.

Heinemann, Margot. "'Let Rome in Tiber Melt': Order and Disorder in *Antony and Cleopatra*." In "*Antony and Cleopatra*," edited by John Drakakis. New Casebooks. New York: St. Martin's Press, 1994.

Henze, Richard. "*Twelfth Night*: Free Disposition on the Sea of Love." *The Sewanee Review* 83 (1975): 267–83.

Hinely, Jan Lawson. "Bond Priorities in *The Merchant of Venice*." *Studies in English Literature* 20 (1980): 217–39.

Holland, Peter. "The Shapeliness of *The Tempest*." *Essays in Criticism* 45 (1995): 208–29.

Hollander, John. "*Twelfth Night* and the Morality of Indulgence." 1959. Reprint, in *Twentieth Century Interpretations of "Twelfth Night": A Collection of Critical Essays*, edited by Walter N. King, 75–89. Englewood Cliffs, N.J.: Prentice-Hall, 1968.

Holmer, Joan Ozark. "The Education of *The Merchant of Venice*." *Studies in English Literature* 25 (1985): 307–35.

———. *"The Merchant of Venice": Choice, Hazard, and Consequence*. New York: Methuen, 1995.

———. "'When Jacob Graz'd His Uncle Laban's Sheep': A New Source for *The Merchant of Venice*." *Shakespeare Quarterly* 36 (1985): 64–65.

Homan, Sidney R. "Divided Response and the Imagination in *Antony and Cleopatra*." *Philological Quarterly* 49 (1970): 460–68.

Horwich, Richard. "Riddle and Dilemma in *The Merchant of Venice*." *Studies in English Literature* 17 (1977): 191–200.

Hughes-Hallett, Lucy. *Cleopatra: Histories, Dreams, and Distortions*. New York: Harper & Row, 1990.

Hunt, Maurice. "Love, Disguise, and Knowledge in *Twelfth Night*." *C.L.A. Journal* 32 (1988–89): 484–93.

———. "Malvolio, Viola, and the Question of Instrumentality: Defining Providence in *Twelfth Night*." *Studies in Philology* 90 (1993): 277–97.

———. "The Religion of *Twelfth Night*." *C.L.A. Journal* 37 (1993–94): 189–203.

———. *Shakespeare's Labored Art: Stir, Work, and the Late Plays*. New York: Peter Lang Publishing, 1995.

Hunter, G. K. "Flatcaps and Bluecoats: Visual Signals on the Elizabethan Stage." *Essays and Studies* 33 (1980): 16–47.

Huston, J. Dennis. "'When I Came to Man's Estate': *Twelfth Night* and Problems of Identity." *Modern Language Quarterly* 33 (1972): 274–88.

James, D. G. *Scepticism and Poetry: An Essay on the Poetic Imagination*. London: George Allen, 1937.

Jankowski, Theodora A. "'As I am Egypt's Queen': Cleopatra, Elizabeth I, and the Female Body Politic." *Assays* V (1989): 91–110.

Jardine, Lisa. "Twins and travesties: Gender, dependency and sexual availability in *Twelfth Night*." In *Erotic Politics: Desire on the Renaissance Stage*, edited by Susan Zimmerman, 27–38. New York: Routledge, 1992.

Jeffrey, David L. "English Saints' Plays." In *Medieval Drama*, edited by Malcolm Bradbury and David Palmer, 69–90. Stratford-upon-Avon Studies 16. London: Edward Arnold, 1973.

Kermode, Frank, ed. *The Tempest*, by William Shakespeare. New Arden, 6th ed. New York: Methuen, 1958.

Kernan, Alvin B. *The Playwright as Magician: Shakespeare's Image of the Poet in the English Public Theater*. New Haven: Yale University Press, 1979.

Kimbrough, Robert. *Shakespeare and the Art of Humankindness: the essay toward androgyny*. Atlantic Highlands, N.J.: Humanities Press International, 1990.

King, Laura Severt. "Blessed when they were riggish: Shakespeare's Cleopatra and Christianity's Penitent Prostitutes." *Journal of Medieval and Renaissance Studies* 22 (1992): 429–49.

Kipling, Gordon. *The Triumph of Honour: Burgundian Origins of the Elizabethan Renaissance*. The Hague: Leiden University Press, 1977.

Kott, Jan. *Shakespeare Our Contemporary*. Garden City, N.Y.: Doubleday, 1964.

Lamb, Margaret. *"Antony and Cleopatra" on the English Stage*. Rutherford, N.J.: Fairleigh Dickinson University Press, 1980.

Leggatt, A. S. "*Twelfth Night*." In *"Twelfth Night": Critical Essays*, edited by Stanley Wells, 227–59. New York: Garland Publishing, 1986.

Leventen, Carol. "Patrimony and Patriarchy in *The Merchant of Venice*." In *The Matter of Difference*, edited by Valerie Wayne, 59–79. Ithaca: Cornell University Press, 1991.

Levin, Harry. "Two Monumental Death Scenes in *Antony and Cleopatra*, 4.15, 5.2." In *Shakespeare, Text, Language, and Criticism: Essays in Honor of Marvin Spevack*, edited by Bernhard Fabian and Kurt Tetzeli von Rosador, 147–63. New York: Olms-Weidmann, 1987.

———. "The Underplot of *Twelfth Night*." In *"Twelfth Night": Critical Essays*, edited by Stanley Wells, 161–69. New York: Garland Publishing, 1986.

Lewalski, Barbara K. "Thematic Patterns in *Twelfth Night*." *Shakespeare Studies* 1 (1965): 168–81.

Lewis, Cynthia. "'Dark Deeds Darkly Answered': Duke Vincentio and Judgment in *Measure for Measure*." *Shakespeare Quarterly* 34 (1983): 271–89.

———. "Viola's 'Do not embrace me' as Icon." *Notes and Queries* 233 (1988): 473–74.

Londré, Felicia Hardison. "Confronting Shakespeare's 'Political Incorrectness' in Production: Contemporary American Audiences and the New 'Problem Plays.'" In *Staging Difference: Cultural Pluralism in American Theatre and Drama*, edited by Marc Maufort, 85–95. American University Studies, series 26, vol. 25. New York: Peter Lang Publishing, 1995.

Luborsky, Ruth Samson. "The Pictorial Image of the Jew in Elizabethan Secular Books." *Shakespeare Quarterly* 46 (1995): 449–53.

Lyon, John. *"The Merchant of Venice." Twayne's New Critical Introductions to Shakespeare*. Boston: Twayne Publishers, 1988.

Macdonald, Ronald R. "Playing Till Doomsday: Interpreting *Antony and Cleopatra*." *English Literary Renaissance* 15 (1985): 78–99.

Mack, Maynard. "*Antony and Cleopatra*: The Stillness and the Dance." In *Shakespeare's Art: Seven Essays*, edited by Milton Crane, 79–113. Chicago: University of Chicago Press, 1973.

Malcolmson, Cristina. "'What You Will': Social Mobility and Gender in *Twelfth Night*." In *The Matter of Difference*, edited by Valerie Wayne, 29–57. Ithaca: Cornell University Press, 1991.

Marius, Richard. *Thomas More: A Biography*. New York: Knopf, 1984.

Marlowe, Christopher. *Dr. Faustus*. In *The Complete Works of Christopher Marlowe*, edited by Roma Gill. Vol. 2. Oxford: Clarendon Press, 1990.

Marshall, Cynthia. "Man of Steel Done Got the Blues: Melancholic Subversion of Presence in *Antony and Cleopatra*." *Shakespeare Quarterly* 44 (1993): 385–408.

Marston, John. *Antonio's Revenge*. Edited by G. K. Hunter. Regents Renaissance Drama Series. Lincoln: University of Nebraska Press, 1965.

Masden, William G. "The Destiny of Man in *The Tempest*." *Emory University Quarterly* 20 (1964): 175–82.

McDonald, Russ. "Reading *The Tempest*." *Shakespeare Survey* 44 (1991): 15–28.

McKerrow, Ronald B. *Printers' and Publishers' Devices in England and Scotland, 1485–1640*. London: Cheswick (Bibliographical Society), 1913.

Meiss, Millard. *Painting in Florence and Siena after the Black Death: The Arts, Religion and Society in the Mid-Fourteenth Century*. Harper Torchbook ed. New York: Harper & Row, 1964.

Mellinkoff, Ruth. *The Devil at Isenheim: Reflections of Popular Belief in Grünewald's Altarpiece*. California Studies in the History of Art, Discovery Series 1. Berkeley: University of California Press, 1988.

Merchant, W. Moelwyn, ed. *The Merchant of Venice*, by William Shakespeare. Middlesex: Penguin, 1967.

Middleton, Thomas. *Women Beware Women*. Edited by J. R. Mulryne. London: Methuen, 1975.

———, and William Rowley. *The Changeling*. In *Drama of the English Renaissance*, edited by Russell A. Fraser and Norman Rabkin, 2:399–429. New York: Macmillan, 1976.

Miles, Leland, ed. *A Dialogue of Comfort against Tribulation*, by Thomas More. Bloomington: Indiana University Press, 1965.

Milton, John. *Areopagitica*. In *John Milton: Complete Poems and Major Prose*, edited by Merritt Y. Hughes. New York: Bobbs-Merrill, 1957.

Moglen, Helene. "Disguise and Development: The Self and Society in *Twelfth Night*." *Literature and Psychology* 23 (1973): 13–20.

Montaigne, Michel de. "Of Cannibals." In *Essays*, translated by John Florio, edited by J. I. M. Stewart, 160–74. New York: Modern Library, 1933.

———. "Of Experience." In *The Complete Essays of Montaigne*, translated by Donald M. Frame, 815–57. Stanford: Stanford University Press, 1958.

More, Thomas. *A Dialogue of Comfort against Tribulation*. Edited by Leland Miles. Bloomington: Indiana University Press, 1965.

———. *Utopia*. Edited by J. Churton Collins. Translated by Ralph Robynson. Oxford: Clarendon Press, 1904.

Morris, Helen. "Queen Elizabeth I 'Shadowed' in Cleopatra." *Huntington Library Quarterly* 32 (1969): 271–78.

Moseley, C. W. R. D. *A Century of Emblems*. Brookfield, Vt.: Gower Publishing, 1989.

———. "Cleopatra's Prudence: Three Notes on the Use of Emblems in *Antony and Cleopatra*." *Jahrbuch der Deutschen Shakespeare Gesellschaft West* 1986: 119–37.

Muir, Lynette R. "The Saint Play in Medieval France." In *The Saint Play in Medieval Europe*, edited by Clifford Davidson, 123–80. Early Drama, Art, and Music Monograph Series, 8. Kalamazoo: Medieval Institute Publications, Western Michigan University, 1986.

Mullaney, Steven. "Brothers and Others, or the Art of Alienation." In *Cannibals, Witches, and Divorce: Estranging the Renaissance*, edited by Marjorie Garber, 67–89. Baltimore: Johns Hopkins University Press, 1987.

Murry, J. Middleton. *Shakespeare*. 1965 ed. London: John Cope, 1936.

Newman, Karen. "Portia's Ring: Unruly Women and Structures of Exchange in *The Merchant of Venice*." *Shakespeare Quarterly* 38 (1987): 19–33.

Newton, Allyson P. "At 'the Very Heart of Loss': Shakespeare's Enobarbus and the Rhetoric of Remembering." *Renaissance Papers* 1995: 81–91.

Nietzmann, William D. "Seneca on Death: The Courage to Be or Not to Be." *International Philosophical Quarterly* 6 (1966): 81–89.

Normand, Lawrence. "Reading the Body in *The Merchant of Venice*." *Textual Practice* 5 (1991): 55–73.

Norwich, John Julius. *A History of Venice*. New York: Knopf, 1982.

Orgel, Stephen. "Prospero's Wife." In *Modern Critical Interpretations: William Shakespeare's "The Tempest,"* edited by Harold Bloom, 99–112. New York: Chelsea House, 1988.

Ornstein, Robert. "The Ethic of the Imagination: Love and Art in *Antony and Cleopatra*." In *Twentieth Century Interpretations of "Antony and Cleopatra,"* edited by Mark Rose, 82–98. Englewood Cliffs, N.J.: Prentice-Hall, 1977. First published in *Later Shakespeare, Stratford-upon-Avon Studies 8*, edited by John Russell Brown and Bernard Harris, 1966, 31–46.

Osborne, Laurie E. "Antonio's Pardon." *Shakespeare Quarterly* 45 (1994): 108–14.

The Oxford English Dictionary. Oxford: Clarendon Press, 1989.

Panofsky, Erwin. "Comments on Art and Reformation." In *Symbols in Transformation: Iconographic Themes at the Time of the Reformation*. Princeton: The Art Museum, Princeton University, 1969.

Paris, Bernard J. "*The Tempest*: Shakespeare's Ideal Solution." In *Shakespeare's Personality*, edited by Norman N. Holland (and introd.), Sidney Homan, and Bernard J. Paris, 206–25. Berkeley: University of California Press, 1988.

Peacham, Henry. *Minerva Britanna, or A Garden Heroical*. London, 1612.

Pepys, Samuel. *Diary*. Edited by Ernest Rhys. Vol. 1. New York: E. P. Dutton, 1906.

Pequigney, Joseph. "The Two Antonios and Same Sex Love in *Twelfth Night* and *The Merchant of Venice*." *English Literary Renaissance* 22 (1992): 201–21.

Phillips, John Ransome. *The Reformation of Images: Destruction of Art in England, 1535–1660*. Berkeley: University of California Press, 1973.

Plutarch. *The Life of Marcus Antonius*. In *Shakespeare's Plutarch*, by T. J. B. Spencer. London: Penguin, 1968.

Popkin, Richard H. "A Jewish Merchant of Venice." *Shakespeare Quarterly* 40 (1989): 329–31.

Quinney, Laura. "Enter a Messenger." In *Modern Critical Interpretations: "Antony and Cleopatra,"* edited by Harold Bloom, 151–67. New Haven: Yale University Press, 1988.

Rabkin, Norman. *Shakespeare and the Problem of Meaning*. Chicago: University of Chicago Press, 1981.

Rackin, Phyllis. "Shakespeare's Boy Cleopatra, the Decorum of Nature, and the Golden World of Poetry." *PMLA* 87 (1972): 201–11.

Réau, Louis. *Iconographie de l'art chrétien.* Vol. 3. Paris: Presses Universitaires de France, 1959.

Rickey, Mary Ellen. "Prospero's Living Drolleries." *Renaissance Papers* 1964: 35–42.

Ridley, M. R., ed. *Antony and Cleopatra*, by William Shakespeare. New Arden ed. New York: Methuen, 1981.

Rinehart, Keith. "Shakespeare's Cleopatra and England's Elizabeth." *Shakespeare Quarterly* 23 (1972): 81–86.

Roberts, Jeanne Addison. *The Shakespearean Wild: Geography, Genus, and Gender.* Lincoln: University of Nebraska Press, 1991.

Rozett, Martha Tuck. "The Comic Structures of Tragic Endings: The Suicide Scenes in *Romeo and Juliet* and *Antony and Cleopatra*." *Shakespeare Quarterly* 36 (1985): 152–64.

Schiller, Gertrud. *The Iconography of Christian Art*. Translated by Janet Seligman. Vol. 1. Greenwich: New York Graphic Society, 1966–.

———. *Ikonographic der Christlichen Kunst.* Vol. 4.2. Gütersloh: Mohn, 1980.

Shakespeare, William. *The Riverside Shakespeare*, edited by G. Blakemore Evans. Boston: Houghton Mifflin, 1974.

Sharp, Ronald A. "Gift Exchange and the Economics of Spirit in *The Merchant of Venice*." *Modern Philology* 83 (1985–86): 250–65.

Sidney, Sir Philip. *An Apology for Poetry*. In *Criticism: The Major Texts*, edited by Walter Jackson Bate, 77–106. New York: Harcourt Brace Jovanovich, 1970.

Simonds, Peggy Muñoz. "'Sweet Power of Music': The Political Magic of 'the Miraculous Harp' in Shakespeare's *The Tempest*." *Comparative Drama* 29 (1995): 61–90.

———. "'To the Very Heart of Loss': Renaissance Iconography in *Antony and Cleopatra*." *Shakespeare Studies* 22 (1994): 220–76.

Singh, Jyotsna. "Renaissance Antitheatricality, Antifeminism, and Shakespeare's *Antony and Cleopatra*." *Renaissance Drama* 20 (1989): 99–121.

Skura, Meredith Anne. "Discourse and the Individual: The Case of Colonialism in *The Tempest*." *Shakespeare Quarterly* 40 (1989): 42–69.

Slights, Camille Wells. "The Principle of Recompense in *Twelfth Night*." *Modern Language Review* 77 (1982): 537–46.

Smith, Bruce R. *Homosexual Desire in Shakespeare's England*. Chicago: University of Chicago Press, 1991.

Snyder, Susan. "Patterns of Motion in *Antony and Cleopatra*." *Shakespeare Survey* 33 (1980): 113–22.

Sozomen. *The Ecclesiastical History of Sozomen*. In *Nicene and Post-Nicene Fathers of the Christian Church*, edited by Philip Schaff and Henry Wace, 179–427. 2nd ser. Vol. 2. Grand Rapids, Mich.: Eerdmans, 1952.

Spencer, Christopher. *The Genesis of Shakespeare's "Merchant of Venice*." In *Studies in British Literature*. Vol. 3. Lewiston, N.Y.: Edwin Mellen Press, 1988.

Tanzer, Helen, ed. *Praise of Folly*, by Desiderius Erasmus. Facsimile ed. with the marginal drawings of Hans Holbein. 1515. Basle: H. Oppermann, 1931.

Taylor, Beverly. "The Medieval Cleopatra: The Classical and Medieval Tradition of Chaucer's *Legend of Cleopatra*." *Journal of Medieval and Renaissance Studies* 7 (1977): 249–69.

Thompson, E. Margaret. *The Carthusian Order in England*. New York: Macmillan, 1930.

Thomson, Leslie. "*Antony and Cleopatra*, Act 4 scene 16: 'A Heavy Sight.'" *Shakespeare Survey* 41 (1988): 77–90.

Todd, Margo. "Humanists, Puritans and the Spiritualized Household." *Church History* 49 (1980): 18–34.

Traub, Valerie. *Desire and Anxiety: Circulations of Sexuality in Shakespearean Drama*. New York: Routledge, 1992.

Vaughan, Alden T., and Virginia Mason Vaughan. *Shakespeare's Caliban: A Cultural History*. New York: Cambridge University Press, 1991.

Vincent, Barbara C. "Shakespeare's *Antony and Cleopatra* and the Rise of Comedy." *English Literary Renaissance* 12 (1982): 53–86.

Walter, James. "From Tempest to Epilogue: Augustine's Allegory in Shakespeare's Drama." *PMLA* 98 (1983): 60–76.

Wasson, John. "The Secular Saint Plays of the Elizabethan Era." In *The Saint Play in Medieval Europe*, edited by Clifford Davidson, 241–60. Early Drama, Art, and Music Monograph Series, 8. Kalamazoo: Medieval Institute Publications, Western Michigan University, 1986.

Weber, A. S. "New Physics for the Nonce: A Stoic and Hermetic Reading of Shakespeare's *Antony and Cleopatra*." *Renaissance Papers* 1995: 93–107.

Webster, John. *The Duchess of Malfi*. In *Drama of the English Renaissance*, edited by Russell A. Fraser and Norman Rabkin, 2:475–515. New York: Macmillan, 1976.

Wells, Charles. *The Wide Arch: Roman Values in Shakespeare*. New York: St. Martin's Press, 1992.

Wilson, Thomas. *A Discourse Upon Usury*. Edited by R. H. Tawney. New York: A. M. Kelley, 1963.

Wither, George. *A Collection of Emblemes, Ancient and Moderne*. London: Printed by A. M. for Robert Allot, 1635. Reprint, Brookfield, Vt.: Gower Publishing, 1989.

Wolf, William D. "'New Heaven, New Earth': The Escape from Mutability in *Antony and Cleopatra*." *Shakespeare Quarterly* 33 (1982): 328–35.

Wortham, Christopher. "Temperance and the End of Time: Emblematic *Antony and Cleopatra*." *Comparative Drama* 29 (1995): 1–37.

Worthen, W. B. "The Weight of Antony: Staging 'Character' in *Antony and Cleopatra*." *Studies in English Literature* 26 (1986): 295–308.

Wright, Rosemary. "Prospero's Lime Tree and the Pursuit of 'Vanitas.'" *Shakespeare Survey* 37 (1984): 133–40.

Yearling, Elizabeth M. "Language, Theme, and Character in *Twelfth Night*." *Shakespeare Survey* 35 (1982): 79–86.

Index